Praise for *Learning Domain-Driven Design*

"Vladik Khononov is a unique thinker who has been applying DDD to solve real business problems for years. His ideas constantly move the whole DDD community forward, and this book will inspire beginning DDD practitioners."

—*Nick Tune, Technology Consultant*

"Reflecting on my readings of drafts of this book, the thing that comes to mind, with a great deal of joy at the thought, is that it delivers on its title! It is an inviting and informative practice guide, covering the scope of DDD from strategy to technical design. I've gained new insight and understanding in areas where I have experience and filled in concepts and practices I'd had less exposure to. Vlad is a wonderful teacher!"

—*Ruth Malan, Architecture Consultant*
at Bredemeyer Consulting

"Vlad has a lot of hard-won experience as a DDD practitioner working on some deeply complex projects and has been generous in sharing that knowledge. In this book, he tells the story of DDD in a unique way providing a great perspective for learning. This book is aimed at newcomers, yet as a longtime DDD practitioner who also writes and speaks about DDD, I found that I learned so much from his perspective."

—*Julie Lerman, Software Coach, O'Reilly Author,*
and Serial DDD Advocate

Learning Domain-Driven Design

Aligning Software Architecture
and Business Strategy

Vlad Khononov

Beijing · Boston · Farnham · Sebastopol · Tokyo

Learning Domain-Driven Design

by Vlad Khononov

Copyright © 2022 Vladislav Khononov. All rights reserved.

Published by O'Reilly Media, Inc., 1005 Gravenstein Highway North, Sebastopol, CA 95472.

O'Reilly books may be purchased for educational, business, or sales promotional use. Online editions are also available for most titles (*http://oreilly.com*). For more information, contact our corporate/institutional sales department: 800-998-9938 or *corporate@oreilly.com*.

Acquisitions Editor: Melissa Duffield
Development Editor: Jill Leonard
Production Editor: Katherine Tozer
Copyeditor: Audrey Doyle
Proofreader: James Fraleigh

Indexer: Sue Klefstad
Interior Designer: David Futato
Cover Designer: Karen Montgomery
Illustrator: Kate Dullea

October 2021:   First Edition

Revision History for the First Edition
2021-10-08:   First Release

See *http://oreilly.com/catalog/errata.csp?isbn=9781098100131* for release details.

The O'Reilly logo is a registered trademark of O'Reilly Media, Inc. *Learning Domain-Driven Design*, the cover image, and related trade dress are trademarks of O'Reilly Media, Inc.

The views expressed in this work are those of the author, and do not represent the publisher's views. While the publisher and the author have used good faith efforts to ensure that the information and instructions contained in this work are accurate, the publisher and the author disclaim all responsibility for errors or omissions, including without limitation responsibility for damages resulting from the use of or reliance on this work. Use of the information and instructions contained in this work is at your own risk. If any code samples or other technology this work contains or describes is subject to open source licenses or the intellectual property rights of others, it is your responsibility to ensure that your use thereof complies with such licenses and/or rights.

978-1-098-10013-1

[LSI]

Table of Contents

Part II.   Tactical Design

Part III.   Applying Domain-Driven Design in Practice

Foreword

Domain-driven design provides a set of practices for a collaborative approach to building software from the perspective of the business—that is, the domain, and its problems that you are targeting. It was originally coined by Eric Evans in 2003 with the publication of what is fondly known in the DDD community as "The Blue Book." The book's title is *Domain-Driven Design: Tackling Complexity in the Heart of Software*.

While tackling complexity and providing a path to clarity is the goal of domain-driven design, there are so many great ideas that can be applied to even less complicated software projects. DDD reminds us that software developers are not the only people involved in building software. The domain experts, for whom the software is being built, bring critical understanding of the problems being solved. We create a partnership throughout the stages of creation as we first apply "strategic design" to understand the business problem, a.k.a. the domain, and break the problem down into smaller, solvable, interconnected problems. The partnership with the domain experts also drives us to communicate in the language of the domain, rather than forcing those on the business side to learn the technical language of software.

The second stage of a DDD-based project is "tactical design," where we transform the discoveries of strategic design into software architecture and implementation. Again, DDD provides guidance and patterns for organizing these domains and avoiding further complexity. Tactical design continues the partnership with the domain experts who will recognize their domain language even as they look at the code built by the software teams.

Over the years since the publication of "The Blue Book," not only have many organizations benefited from the ideas, but a community of experienced DDD practitioners has evolved. And the collaborative nature of DDD has resulted in this community sharing their experiences and perspective and creating tools to help teams embrace and benefit from these ideas. In a keynote at Explore DDD in 2019, Eric Evans encouraged the community to continue to evolve DDD—not only its practices but in finding ways to more effectively share its ideas.

And this brings me to why I am such a fan of *Learning Domain-Driven Design*. I was already a fan of Vlad through his conference speaking and other writings. He has a lot of hard-won experience as a DDD practitioner working on some deeply complex projects and has been generous in sharing that knowledge. In this book, he tells the "story" of DDD (not its history, but its concepts) in a unique way, providing a great perspective for learning. This book is aimed at newcomers, yet as a longtime DDD practitioner who also writes and speaks about DDD, I found that I learned so much from his perspective. I was eager to reference his book in my DDD Fundamentals course on Pluralsight before the book was even published and have already been sharing some of this perspective in conversations with clients.

Getting started with DDD can be confusing. Just as we use DDD to reduce the complexity of projects, Vlad presents DDD in a way that reduces the complexity of the topic itself. And he does more than explain the principles of DDD. The latter portion of the book shares some important practices that have evolved from DDD, such as EventStorming, addresses the problem of evolving the business focus or organization and how this might affect the software, and discusses how DDD aligns with microservices and how you can integrate it with a slew of well-known software patterns. I think *Learning Domain-Driven Design* will be an excellent introduction to DDD for newcomers, and a very worthy read for experienced practitioners as well.

— *Julie Lerman*
Software Coach, O'Reilly Author,
and Serial DDD Advocate

Preface

I vividly remember the day I started my first real software engineering job. I was both ecstatic and terrified. After hacking software for local businesses during my high school years, I was eager to become a "real programmer" and write some code for one of the country's largest outsourcing companies.

In my first days there, my new colleagues were showing me the ropes. After setting up the corporate email and going through the time-tracking system, we finally moved on to the interesting stuff: the company's coding style and standards. I was told that "here, we always write well-designed code and use the layered architecture." We went through the definition of each of the three layers—the data access, business logic, and presentation layers—and then discussed the technologies and frameworks for addressing the layers' needs. Back then, the accepted solution for storing data was Microsoft SQL Server 2000, and it was integrated using ADO.NET in the data access layer. The presentation layer rocked either WinForms for desktop applications or ASP.NET WebForms for the web. We spent quite some time on these two layers, so I was puzzled when the business logic layer didn't get any attention:

> "But what about the business logic layer?"
>
> "That one is straightforward. Here is where you implement the business logic."
>
> "But what is business logic?"
>
> "Oh, business logic is all the loops and 'if-else' statements you need in order to implement the requirements."

That day I began my journey to find out what exactly business logic is and how on earth it should be implemented in well-designed code. It took me more than three years to finally find the answer.

The answer was in Eric Evans's seminal book, *Domain-Driven Design: Tackling Complexity in the Heart of Software*. It turned out that I wasn't wrong. Business logic is indeed important: it is the heart of software! Unfortunately, however, it took me another three years to understand the wisdom Eric shared. The book is very advanced, and the fact that English is my third language didn't help.

Eventually, though, everything fell into place, and I made peace with the domain-driven design (DDD) methodology. I learned the principles and patterns of DDD, the intricacies of modeling and implementing the business logic, and how to tackle the complexity in the heart of the software that I was building. Despite the obstacles, it definitely was worth it. Getting into domain-driven design was a career-changing experience for me.

Why I Wrote This Book

Over the past 10 years, I have introduced domain-driven design to my colleagues at different companies, conducted in-person classes, and taught online courses. The teaching perspective not only helped me deepen my knowledge, but also allowed me to optimize the way I explain the principles and patterns of domain-driven design.

As often happens, teaching is even more challenging than learning. I'm a huge fan of Eliyahu M. Goldratt's (*https://oreil.ly/ZZdXf*) work and teachings. Eliyahu used to say that even the most complex systems are inherently simple when viewed from the right angle. During my years of teaching DDD, I was looking for a model of the methodology that would uncover the inherent simplicity of domain-driven design.

This book is the result of my efforts. Its goal is to democratize domain-driven design; make it easier to understand and more accessible to employ. I believe that the DDD methodology is absolutely invaluable, especially when designing modern software systems. This book will give you just enough tools to start applying domain-driven design in your day-to-day work.

Who Should Read This Book

I believe that knowledge of domain-driven design principles and patterns will be useful for software engineers at all levels: junior, senior, staff, and principal. Not only does DDD provide tools and techniques for modeling and effectively implementing software, it also illuminates an often-overlooked aspect of software engineering: the context. Equipped with the knowledge of the system's business problem, you will be much more effective at choosing the appropriate solution. A solution that is not under- or over-engineered, but addresses business needs and goals.

Domain-driven design is even more important for software architects, and even more so for aspiring software architects. Its strategic design decision tools will help you decompose a large system into components—services, microservices, or subsystems—and design how the components are integrated with one another to form a system.

Ultimately, in this book we will discuss not only how to design software, but also how to co-evolve the design with changes in its business context. That crucial aspect of software engineering will help you keep the system's design "in shape" over time and prevent its degradation into a big ball of mud.

Navigating the Book

This book is divided into four parts: strategic design, tactical design, DDD in practice, and DDD's relationships to other methodologies and patterns. In Part I, we cover tools and techniques for making large-scale software design decisions. In Part II, we focus on the code: the different ways to implement a system's business logic. Part III discusses techniques and strategies for applying DDD in real-life projects. Part IV continues the discussion of domain-driven design, but this time in the context of other methodologies and patterns.

Here is a short summary of what you will find in each chapter:

- Chapter 1 establishes the context of a software engineering project: the business domain, its goals, and how the software is intended to support them.
- Chapter 2 introduces the notion of a "ubiquitous language": domain-driven design's practice for effective communication and knowledge sharing.
- Chapter 3 discusses how to tackle the complexity of business domains and design the system's high-level architectural components: bounded contexts.
- Chapter 4 explores the different patterns of organizing the communication and integration between the bounded contexts.
- Chapter 5 starts the discussion of business logic implementation patterns with two patterns addressing the cases of simple business logic.
- Chapter 6 advances from simple to complex business logic and introduces the domain model pattern for tackling its complexity.
- Chapter 7 adds the perspective of time and introduces an even more advanced way to model and implement business logic: the event-sourced domain model.
- Chapter 8 shifts the focus to a higher level and describes three architectural patterns for structuring components.
- Chapter 9 provides the patterns needed to orchestrate the work of the system's components.
- Chapter 10 ties together the patterns discussed in the earlier chapters into a number of simple rules of thumb that streamline the process of making design decisions.
- Chapter 11 explores software design from the perspective of time and how it is supposed to change and evolve through its lifespan.

- Chapter 12 introduces EventStorming: a low-tech workshop for effectively sharing knowledge, building shared understanding, and designing software.

- Chapter 13 addresses the difficulties you may face when introducing domain-driven design to brownfield projects.

- Chapter 14 discusses the relationship between the microservices architectural style and domain-driven design: where they differ and where they complement each other.

- Chapter 15 explores domain-driven design patterns and tools in the context of the event-driven architecture.

- Chapter 16 shifts the discussion from operational systems to analytical data management systems and discusses the interplay between domain-driven design and the data mesh architecture.

All of these chapters end with a number of exercise questions to reinforce the learning. Some of the questions use the fictional company "WolfDesk" to demonstrate the various aspects of domain-driven design. Please read the following description of WolfDesk, and return to it when you answer relevant exercise questions.

Example Domain: WolfDesk

WolfDesk provides a help desk tickets management system as a service. If your start-up company needs to provide support to your customers, with WolfDesk's solution you can get up and running in no time.

WolfDesk uses a different payment model than its competitors. Instead of charging a fee per user, it allows the tenants to set up as many users as needed, and the tenants are charged for the number of support tickets opened per charging period. There is no minimum fee, and there are automatic volume discounts for certain thresholds of monthly tickets: 10% for opening more than 500 tickets, 20% for opening more than 750 tickets, and 30% for opening more than 1,000 tickets per month.

To prevent tenants from abusing the business model, WolfDesk's ticket lifecycle algorithm ensures that inactive tickets are closed automatically, encouraging customers to open new tickets when further support is needed. Moreover, WolfDesk implements a fraud detection system that analyzes messages and detects cases of unrelated topics being discussed in the same ticket.

To help its tenants streamline the support-related work, WolfDesk has implemented a "support autopilot" feature. The autopilot analyzes new tickets and tries to automatically find a matching solution from the tenant's ticket history. The functionality allows for further reducing the tickets' lifespans, encouraging customers to open new tickets for further questions.

WolfDesk incorporates all the security standards and measures to authenticate and authorize its tenants' users and also allows tenants to configure a single sign-on (SSO) with their existing user management systems.

The administration interface allows tenants to configure the possible values for the tickets' categories, as well as a list of the tenant's products that it supports.

To be able to route new tickets to the tenant's support agents only during their working hours, WolfDesk allows the entry of each agent's shift schedule.

Since WolfDesk provides its service with no minimal fee, it has to optimize its infrastructure in a way that minimizes the costs of onboarding a new tenant. To do that, WolfDesk leverages serverless computing, which allows it to elastically scale its compute resources based on the operations on active tickets.

Conventions Used in This Book

The following typographical conventions are used in this book:

Italic
> Indicates new terms, URLs, email addresses, filenames, and file extensions.

`Constant width`
> Used for program listings, as well as within paragraphs to refer to program elements such as variable or function names, databases, data types, environment variables, statements, and keywords.

 This element signifies a general note.

Using Code Examples

Supplemental material (code examples, exercises, etc.) is available for download at *https://learning-ddd.com*.

All the code samples presented in the book are implemented in the C# language. Generally, the code samples you see in the chapters are excerpts demonstrating the discussed concepts.

Of course, the concepts and techniques discussed in the book are not limited to the C# language or to the object-oriented programming approach. Everything is relevant for other languages and other programming paradigms. As a result, feel free to implement the book's samples in your favorite language and share them with me. I'll be happy to add them to the book's website.

If you have a technical question or a problem using the code examples, please email *bookquestions@oreilly.com*.

This book is here to help you get your job done. In general, if example code is offered with this book, you may use it in your programs and documentation. You do not need to contact us for permission unless you're reproducing a significant portion of the code. For example, writing a program that uses several chunks of code from this book does not require permission. Selling or distributing examples from O'Reilly books does require permission. Answering a question by citing this book and quoting example code does not require permission. Incorporating a significant amount of example code from this book into your product's documentation does require permission.

We appreciate, but generally do not require, attribution. An attribution usually includes the title, author, publisher, and ISBN. For example: "*Learning Domain-Driven Design* by Vlad Khononov (O'Reilly). Copyright 2022 Vladislav Khononov, 978-1-098-10013-1."

If you feel your use of code examples falls outside fair use or the permission given above, feel free to contact us at *permissions@oreilly.com*.

O'Reilly Online Learning

 For more than 40 years, *O'Reilly Media* has provided technology and business training, knowledge, and insight to help companies succeed.

Our unique network of experts and innovators share their knowledge and expertise through books, articles, and our online learning platform. O'Reilly's online learning platform gives you on-demand access to live training courses, in-depth learning paths, interactive coding environments, and a vast collection of text and video from O'Reilly and 200+ other publishers. For more information, visit *http://oreilly.com*.

How to Contact Us

Please address comments and questions concerning this book to the publisher:

O'Reilly Media, Inc.
1005 Gravenstein Highway North
Sebastopol, CA 95472
800-998-9938 (in the United States or Canada)
707-829-0515 (international or local)
707-829-0104 (fax)

We have a web page for this book, where we list errata, examples, and any additional information. You can access this page at *https://oreil.ly/lddd*.

Email *bookquestions@oreilly.com* to comment or ask technical questions about this book.

For news and information about our books and courses, visit *http://oreilly.com*.

Find us on Facebook: *http://facebook.com/oreilly*

Follow us on Twitter: *http://twitter.com/oreillymedia*

Watch us on YouTube: *http://youtube.com/oreillymedia*

Acknowledgments

Originally, this book was titled "What Is Domain-Driven Design?" and was published as a report in 2019. *Learning Domain-Driven Design* would not have seen the light of day without the report, and I'm obliged to thank those who made "What Is Domain-Driven Design?" possible: Chris Guzikowski, Ryan Shaw, and Alicia Young.[1]

This book also wouldn't have been possible without O'Reilly's Content Director and Diversity Talent Lead, Melissa Duffield, who championed the project and made it happen. Thank you, Melissa, for all your help!

Jill Leonard was the book's development editor, project manager, and head coach. Jill's role in this work cannot be overstated. Jill, thank you so much for all your hard work and help! Extra thanks for keeping me motivated, even when I considered changing my name and hiding in a foreign country.

---

1 Whenever I mention a group of people, the list is in alphabetical order by last name.

A huge thanks to the production team for making the book not only writable but readable: Kristen Brown, Audrey Doyle, Kate Dullea, Robert Romano, and Katherine Tozer. For that matter, I want to thank the whole O'Reilly team for the great work you do. It's a dream come true to be working with you!

Thanks to all the people I interviewed and consulted with: Zsofia Herendi, Scott Hirleman, Trond Hjorteland, Mark Lisker, Chris Richardson, Vaughn Vernon, and Ivan Zakrevsky. Thank you for your wisdom and for being there when I needed help!

Special thanks to the team of reviewers who read through the early drafts and helped me shape the final book: Julie Lerman, Ruth Malan, Diana Montalion, Andrew Padilla, Rodion Promyshlennikov, Viktor Pshenitsyn, Alexei Torunov, Nick Tune, Vasiliy Vasilyuk, and Rebecca Wirfs-Brock. Your support, feedback, and critique helped immensely. Thank you!

I also want to thank Kenny Baas-Schwegler, Alberto Brandolini, Eric Evans, Marco Heimeshoff, Paul Rayner, Mathias Verraes, and the rest of the amazing domain-driven design community. You know who you are. You are my teachers and mentors. Thank you for sharing your knowledge on social media, blogs, and conferences!

I'm most indebted to my dear wife, Vera, for always supporting me in my crazy projects and trying to guard me from things that could distract me from writing. I promise to finally declutter the basement. It is going to happen soon!

Finally, I want to dedicate this book to our beloved Galina Ivanovna Tyumentseva, who supported me so much in this project and whom we sadly lost during the writing of this book. We will always remember you.

#AdoptDontShop

Introduction

Software engineering is hard. To be successful at it, we have to learn continuously, whether it's trying new languages, exploring new technologies, or keeping up with new popular frameworks. However, learning a new JavaScript framework every week is not the hardest aspect of our job. Making sense of new business domains can be far more challenging.

Throughout our careers, it's not uncommon for us to have to develop software for a diverse range of business domains: financial systems, medical software, online retailers, marketing, and many others. In a sense, that is what differentiates our job from most other professions. People working in other fields are often surprised when they find out how much learning is involved in software engineering, especially when changing workplaces.

Failure to grasp the business domain results in suboptimal implementation of the business software. Unfortunately, that's quite common. According to studies, approximately 70% of software projects are not delivered on time, on budget, or according to the client's requirements. In other words, the vast majority of software projects fail. This issue is so deep and widespread that we even have a term for it: software crisis.

The term *software crisis* was introduced all the way back in 1968.[1] One would assume that things would have improved in the intervening 50 years. During those years, numerous approaches, methodologies, and disciplines were introduced to make software engineering more effective: Agile Manifesto, extreme programming, test-driven development, high-level languages, DevOps, and others. Unfortunately, things didn't change much. Projects are still failing quite often and the software crisis is still here.

---

1 "Software Engineering." Report on a conference sponsored by the NATO Science Committee, Garmisch, Germany, October 7–11, 1968.

Many studies have been conducted to investigate the reasons for the common project failures.[2] Although researchers have not been able to pinpoint a single cause, most of their findings share a common theme: communication. Communication issues thwarting projects can manifest themselves in different ways; for example, unclear requirements, uncertain project goals, or ineffective coordination of effort between teams. Yet again, over the years, we have tried to improve inter- and intrateam communication by introducing new communication opportunities, processes, and mediums. Unfortunately, the success rates of our projects still didn't change much.

Domain-driven design (DDD) proposes to attack the root cause for failed software projects from a different angle. Effective communication is the central theme of the domain-driven design tools and practices you are about to learn in this book. DDD can be divided into two parts: strategic and tactical.

The strategic tools of DDD are used to analyze business domains and strategy, and to foster a shared understanding of the business between the different stakeholders. We will also use this knowledge of the business domain to drive high-level design decisions: decomposing systems into components and defining their integration patterns.

Domain-driven design's tactical tools address a different aspect of communication issues. DDD's tactical patterns allow us to write code in a way that reflects the business domain, addresses its goals, and speaks the language of the business.

Both the strategic and tactical patterns and practices of DDD align software design with its business domain. That's where the name comes from: (business) domain-driven (software) design.

Domain-driven design won't make it possible to install the knowledge of new JavaScript libraries directly into your brain, like in *The Matrix*. However, it will make you a more effective software engineer by alleviating the process of making sense of business domains and guiding the design decisions according to the business strategy. As you will learn in the book's later chapters, the tighter the connection between the software design and its business strategy is, the easier it will be to maintain and evolve the system to meet the future needs of the business, ultimately leading to more successful software projects.

Let's start our DDD journey by exploring the strategic patterns and practices.

---

2 See, for example, Kaur, Rupinder, and Dr. Jyotsna Sengupta (2013), "Software Process Models and Analysis on Failure of Software Development Projects," *https://arxiv.org/ftp/arxiv/papers/1306/1306.1068.pdf*. See also Sudhakar, Goparaju Purna (2012), "A Model of Critical Success Factors for Software Projects." *Journal of Enterprise Information Management* 25(6), 537–558.

PART I

Strategic Design

There is no sense in talking about the solution before we agree on the problem, and no sense talking about the implementation steps before we agree on the solution.
   —Efrat Goldratt-Ashlag[1]

The domain-driven design (DDD) methodology can be divided into two main parts: strategic design and tactical design. The strategic aspect of DDD deals with answering the questions of "what?" and "why?"—what software we are building and why we are building it. The tactical part is all about the "how"—how each component is implemented.

We will begin our journey by exploring domain-driven design patterns and principles of strategic design:

- In Chapter 1, you will learn to analyze a company's business strategy: what value it provides to its consumers and how it competes with other companies in the industry. We will identify finer-grained business building blocks, evaluate their strategic value, and analyze how they affect different software design decisions.

- Chapter 2 introduces domain-driven design's essential practice for gaining an understanding of the business domain: the *ubiquitous language*. You will learn how to cultivate a ubiquitous language and use it to foster a shared understanding among all project-related stakeholders.

---

1 Goldratt-Ashlag, E. (2010). "The Layers of Resistance—The Buy-In Process According to TOC."

- Chapter 3 discusses another domain-driven design core tool: the *bounded context* pattern. You will learn why this tool is essential for cultivating a ubiquitous language and how to use it to transform discovered knowledge into a model of the business domain. Ultimately, we will leverage bounded contexts to design coarse-grained components of the software system.

- In Chapter 4, you will learn technical and social constraints that affect how system components can be integrated, and integration patterns that address different situations and limitations. We will discuss how each pattern influences collaboration among software development teams and the design of the components' APIs.

The chapter closes by introducing the *context map*: a graphical notation that plots communication between the system's bounded contexts and provides a bird's-eye view of the project's integration and collaboration landscapes.

CHAPTER 1

Analyzing Business Domains

If you are anything like me, you love writing code: solving complex problems, coming up with elegant solutions, and constructing whole new worlds by carefully crafting their rules, structures, and behavior. I believe that's what interested you in domain-driven design (DDD): you want to be better at your craft. This chapter, however, has nothing to do with writing code. In this chapter, you will learn how companies work: why they exist, what goals they are pursuing, and their strategies for achieving their goals.

When I teach this material in my domain-driven design classes, many students actually ask, "Do we need to know this material? We are writing software, not running businesses." The answer to their question is a resounding "yes." To design and build an effective solution, you have to understand the problem. The problem, in our context, is the software system we have to build. To understand the problem, you have to understand the context within which it exists—the organization's business strategy, and what value it seeks to gain by building the software.

In this chapter, you will learn domain-driven design tools for analyzing a company's business domain and its structure: its core, supporting, and generic subdomains. This material is the groundwork for designing software. In the remaining chapters, you will learn the different ways these concepts affect software design.

What Is a Business Domain?

A business domain defines a company's main area of activity. Generally speaking, it's the service the company provides to its clients. For example:

- FedEx provides courier delivery.
- Starbucks is best known for its coffee.

- Walmart is one of the most widely recognized retail establishments.

A company can operate in multiple business domains. For example, Amazon provides both retail and cloud computing services. Uber is a rideshare company that also provides food delivery and bicycle-sharing services.

It's important to note that companies may change their business domains often. A canonical example of this is Nokia, which over the years has operated in fields as diverse as wood processing, rubber manufacturing, telecommunications, and mobile communications.

What Is a Subdomain?

To achieve its business domain's goals and targets, a company has to operate in multiple *subdomains*. A subdomain is a fine-grained area of business activity. All of a company's subdomains form its business domain: the service it provides to its customers. Implementing a single subdomain is not enough for a company to succeed; it's just one building block in the overarching system. The subdomains have to interact with each other to achieve the company's goals in its business domain. For example, Starbucks may be most recognized for its coffee, but building a successful coffeehouse chain requires more than just knowing how to make great coffee. You also have to buy or rent real estate at effective locations, hire personnel, and manage finances, among other activities. None of these subdomains on its own will make a profitable company. All of them together are necessary for a company to be able to compete in its business domain(s).

Types of Subdomains

Just as a software system comprises various architectural components—databases, frontend applications, backend services, and others—subdomains bear different strategic/business values. Domain-driven design distinguishes between three types of subdomains: core, generic, and supporting. Let's see how they differ from a company strategy point of view.

Core subdomains

A *core subdomain* is what a company does differently from its competitors. This may involve inventing new products or services or reducing costs by optimizing existing processes.

Let's take Uber as an example. Initially, the company provided a novel form of transportation: ridesharing. As its competitors caught up, Uber found ways to optimize and evolve its core business: for example, reducing costs by matching riders heading in the same direction.

Uber's core subdomains affect its bottom line. This is how the company differentiates itself from its competitors. This is the company's strategy for providing better service to its customers and/or maximizing its profitability. To maintain a competitive advantage, core subdomains involve inventions, smart optimizations, business know-how, or other intellectual property.

Consider another example: Google Search's ranking algorithm. At the time of this writing, Google's advertising platform accounts for the majority of its profits. That said, Google Ads is not a subdomain, but rather a separate business domain with sub-domains comprising it, among its cloud computing service (Google Cloud Platform), productivity and collaboration tools (Google Workspaces), and other fields in which Alphabet, Google's parent company, operates. But what about Google Search and its ranking algorithm? Although the search engine is not a paid service, it serves as the largest display platform for Google Ads. Its ability to provide excellent search results is what drives traffic, and subsequently, it is an important component of the Ads plat-form. Serving suboptimal search results due to a bug in the algorithm or a competitor coming up with an even better search service will hurt the ad business's revenue. So, for Google, the ranking algorithm is a core subdomain.

Complexity. A core subdomain that is simple to implement can only provide a short-lived competitive advantage. Therefore, core subdomains are naturally complex. Continuing with the Uber example, the company not only created a new marketspace with ridesharing, it disrupted a decades-old monolithic architecture, the taxi indus-try, through targeted use of technology. By understanding its business domain, Uber was able to design a more reliable and transparent method of transportation. There should be high entry barriers for a company's core business; it should be hard for competitors to copy or imitate the company's solution.

Sources of competitive advantage. It's important to note that core subdomains are not necessarily technical. Not all business problems are solved through algorithms or other technical solutions. A company's competitive advantage can come from various sources.

Consider, for example, a jewelry maker selling its products online. The online shop is important, but it's not a core subdomain. The jewelry design is. The company can use an existing off-the-shelf online shop engine, but it cannot outsource the design of its jewelry. The design is the reason customers buy the jewelry maker's products and remember the brand.

As a more intricate example, imagine a company that specializes in *manual* fraud detection. The company trains its analysts to go over questionable documents and flag potential fraud cases. You are building the software system the analysts are work-ing with. Is it a core subdomain? No. The core subdomain is the work the analysts are doing. The system you are building has nothing to do with fraud analysis, it just displays the documents and tracks the analysts' comments.

Core Subdomain Versus Core Domain

Core subdomains are also called core domains. For example, in the original domain-driven design book, Eric Evans uses "core subdomain" and "core domain" interchangeably. Although the term "core domain" is used often, I prefer to use "core subdomain" for a number of reasons. First, it is a *subdomain,* and I prefer to avoid confusion with *business domains.* Second, as you will learn in Chapter 11, it's not uncommon for subdomains to evolve over time and change their types. For example, a core subdomain can turn into a generic subdomain. Hence, saying that "a *generic* subdomain has evolved into a *core* subdomain" is more straightforward than saying "a generic *subdomain* has evolved into a core *domain*."

Generic subdomains

Generic subdomains are business activities that all companies are performing in the same way. Like core subdomains, generic subdomains are generally complex and hard to implement. However, generic subdomains do not provide any competitive edge for the company. There is no need for innovation or optimization here: battle-tested implementations are widely available, and all companies use them.

For example, most systems need to authenticate and authorize their users. Instead of inventing a proprietary authentication mechanism, it makes more sense to use an existing solution. Such a solution is likely to be more reliable and secure since it has already been tested by many other companies that have the same needs.

Going back to the example of a jewelry maker selling its products online, jewelry design is a core subdomain, but the online shop is a generic subdomain. Using the same online retail platform—the same generic solution—as its competitors would not impact the jewelry maker's competitive advantage.

Supporting subdomains

As the name suggests, *supporting subdomains* support the company's business. However, contrary to core subdomains, supporting subdomains do not provide any competitive advantage.

For example, consider an online advertising company whose core subdomains include matching ads to visitors, optimizing the ads' effectiveness, and minimizing the cost of ad space. However, to achieve success in these areas, the company needs to catalog its creative materials. The way the company stores and indexes its physical creative materials, such as banners and landing pages, does not impact its profits. There is nothing to invent or optimize in that area. On the other hand, the creative catalog is essential for implementing the company's advertising management and serving systems. That makes the content cataloging solution one of the company's supporting subdomains.

The distinctive characteristic of supporting subdomains is the complexity of the solution's business logic. Supporting subdomains are simple. Their business logic resembles mostly data entry screens and ETL (extract, transform, load) operations; that is, the so-called CRUD (create, read, update, and delete) interfaces. These activity areas do not provide any competitive advantage for the company, and therefore do not require high entry barriers.

Comparing Subdomains

Now that we have a greater understanding of the three types of business subdomains, let's explore their differences from additional angles and see how they affect strategic software design decisions.

Competitive advantage

Only core subdomains provide a competitive advantage to a company. Core subdomains are the company's strategy for differentiating itself from its competitors.

Generic subdomains, by definition, cannot be a source for any competitive advantage. These are generic solutions—the same solutions used by the company and its competitors.

Supporting subdomains have low entry barriers and cannot provide a competitive advantage either. Usually, a company wouldn't mind its competitors copying its supporting subdomains—this won't affect its competitiveness in the industry. On the contrary, strategically the company would prefer its supporting subdomains to be generic, ready-made solutions, thus eliminating the need to design and build their implementation. You will learn in detail about such cases of supporting subdomains turning into generic subdomains, as well as other possible permutations, in Chapter 11. A real-life case study of such a scenario will be outlined in Appendix A.

The more complex the problems a company is able to tackle, the more business value it can provide. The complex problems are not limited to delivering services to consumers. A complex problem can be, for example, making the business more optimized and efficient. For example, providing the same level of service as competitors do, but at lower operational costs, is a competitive advantage as well.

Complexity

From a more technical perspective, it's important to identify the organization's subdomains, because the different types of subdomains have different levels of complexity. When designing software, we have to choose tools and techniques that accommodate the complexity of the business requirements. Therefore, identifying subdomains is essential for designing a sound software solution.

Supporting subdomains' business logic is simple. These are basic ETL operations and CRUD interfaces, and the business logic is obvious. Often, it doesn't go beyond validating inputs or converting data from one structure to another.

Generic subdomains are much more complicated. There should be a good reason why others have already invested time and effort in solving these problems. These solutions are neither simple nor trivial. Consider, for example, encryption algorithms or authentication mechanisms.

From a knowledge availability perspective, generic subdomains are "known unknowns." These are the things that you know you don't know. Furthermore, this knowledge is readily available. You can either use industry-accepted best practices or, if needed, hire a consultant specializing in the area to help design a custom solution.

Core subdomains are complex. They should be as hard for competitors to copy as possible—the company's profitability depends on it. That's why strategically, companies are looking to solve complex problems as their core subdomains.

At times it may be challenging to differentiate between core and supporting subdomains. Complexity is a useful guiding principle. Ask whether the subdomain in question can be turned into a side business. Would someone pay for it on its own? If so, this is a core subdomain. Similar reasoning applies for differentiating supporting and generic subdomains: would it be simpler and cheaper to hack your own implementation, rather than integrating an external one? If so, this is a supporting subdomain.

From a more technical perspective, it's important to identify the core subdomains whose complexity will affect software design. As we discussed earlier, a core subdomain is not necessarily related to software. Another useful guiding principle for identifying software-related core subdomains is to evaluate the complexity of the business logic that you will have to model and implement in code. Does the business logic resemble CRUD interfaces for data entry, or do you have to implement complex algorithms or business processes orchestrated by complex business rules and invariants? In the former case, it's a sign of a supporting subdomain, while the latter is a typical core subdomain.

The chart in Figure 1-1 represents the interplay between the three types of subdomains in terms of business differentiation and business logic complexity. The intersection between the supporting and generic subdomains is a gray area: it can go either way. If a generic solution exists for a supporting subdomain's functionality, the resultant subdomain type depends on whether it's simpler and/or cheaper to integrate the generic solution than it is to implement the functionality from scratch.

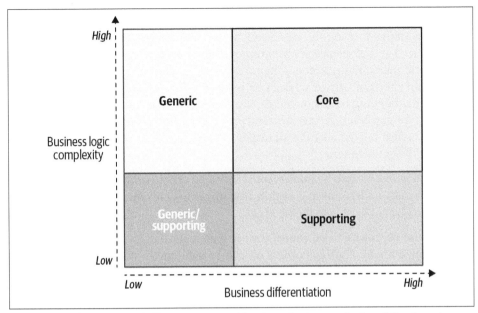

Figure 1-1. The business differentiation and business logic complexity of the three types of subdomains

Volatility

As mentioned previously, core subdomains can change often. If a problem can be solved on the first attempt, it's probably not a good competitive advantage—competitors will catch up fast. Consequently, solutions for core subdomains are emergent. Different implementations have to be tried out, refined, and optimized. Moreover, the work on core subdomains is never done. Companies continuously innovate and evolve core subdomains. The changes come in the form of adding new features or optimizing existing functionality. Either way, the constant evolution of its core subdomains is essential for a company to stay ahead of its competitors.

Contrary to the core subdomains, supporting subdomains do not change often. They do not provide any competitive advantage for the company, and therefore the evolution of a supporting subdomain provides a minuscule business value compared to the same effort invested in a core subdomain.

Despite having existing solutions, generic subdomains can change over time. The changes can come in the form of security patches, bug fixes, or entirely new solutions to the generic problems.

Solution strategy

Core subdomains provide the company its ability to compete with other players in the industry. That's a business-critical responsibility, but does it mean that supporting and generic subdomains are not important? Of course not. All subdomains are required for the company to work in its business domain. The subdomains are like foundational building blocks: take one away and the whole structure may fall down. That said, we can leverage the inherent properties of the different types of subdomains to choose implementation strategies to implement each type of subdomain in the most efficient manner.

Core subdomains have to be implemented in-house. They cannot be bought or adopted; that would undermine the notion of competitive advantage, as the company's competitors would be able to do the same.

It would also be unwise to outsource the implementation of a core subdomain. It is a strategic investment. Cutting corners on a core subdomain is not only risky in the short term but can have fatal consequences in the long run: for example, unmaintainable codebases that cannot support the company's goals and objectives. The organization's most skilled talent should be assigned to work on its core subdomains. Furthermore, implementing core subdomains in-house allows the company to make changes and evolve the solution more quickly, and therefore build the competitive advantage in less time.

Since core subdomains' requirements are expected to change often and continuously, the solution must be maintainable and easy to evolve. Thus, core subdomains require implementation of the most advanced engineering techniques.

Since generic subdomains are hard but already solved problems, it's more cost-effective to buy an off-the-shelf product or adopt an open source solution than invest time and effort into implementing a generic subdomain in-house.

Lack of competitive advantage makes it reasonable to avoid implementing supporting subdomains in-house. However, unlike generic subdomains, no ready-made solutions are available. So, a company has no choice but to implement supporting subdomains itself. That said, the simplicity of the business logic and infrequency of changes make it easy to cut corners.

Supporting subdomains do not require elaborate design patterns or other advanced engineering techniques. A rapid application development framework will suffice to implement the business logic without introducing accidental complexities.

From a staffing perspective, supporting subdomains do not require highly skilled technical aptitude and provide a great opportunity to train up-and-coming talent. Save the engineers on your team who are experienced in tackling complex challenges for the core subdomains. Finally, the simplicity of the business logic makes supporting subdomains a good candidate for outsourcing.

Table 1-1 summarizes the aspects in which the three types of subdomains differ.

Table 1-1. The differences between the three types of subdomains

Subdomain type	Competitive advantage	Complexity	Volatility	Implementation	Problem
Core	Yes	High	High	In-house	Interesting
Generic	No	High	Low	Buy/adopt	Solved
Supporting	No	Low	Low	In-house/outsource	Obvious

Identifying Subdomain Boundaries

As you can already see, identifying subdomains and their types can help considerably in making different design decisions when building software solutions. In later chapters, you will learn even more ways to leverage subdomains to streamline the software design process. But how do we actually identify the subdomains and their boundaries?

The subdomains and their types are defined by the company's business strategy: its business domains and how it differentiates itself to compete with other companies in the same field. In the vast majority of software projects, in one way or another the subdomains are "already there." That doesn't mean, however, that it is always easy and straightforward to identify their boundaries. If you ask a CEO for a list of their company's subdomains, you will probably receive a blank stare. They are not aware of this concept. Therefore, you'll have to do the domain analysis yourself to identify and categorize the subdomains at play.

A good starting point is the company's departments and other organizational units. For example, an online retail shop might include warehouse, customer service, picking, shipping, quality control, and channel management departments, among others. These, however, are relatively coarse-grained areas of activity. Take, for example, the customer service department. It's reasonable to assume that it would be a supporting, or even a generic subdomain, as this function is often outsourced to third-party vendors. But is this information enough for us to make sound software design decisions?

Distilling subdomains

Coarse-grained subdomains are a good starting point, but the devil is in the details. We have to make sure we are not missing important information hidden in the intricacies of the business function.

Let's go back to the example of the customer service department. If we investigate its inner workings, we will see that a typical customer service department is composed of finer-grained components, such as a help desk system, shift management and scheduling, telephone system, and so on. When viewed as individual subdomains, these activities can be of different types: while help desk and telephone systems are generic subdomains, shift management is a supporting one, while a company may develop its ingenious algorithm for routing incidents to agents having success with similar cases in the past. The routing algorithm requires analyzing incoming cases and identifying similarities in past experience—both of which are nontrivial tasks. Since the routing algorithm allows the company to provide a better customer experience than its competitors, the routing algorithm is a core subdomain. This example is demonstrated in Figure 1-2.

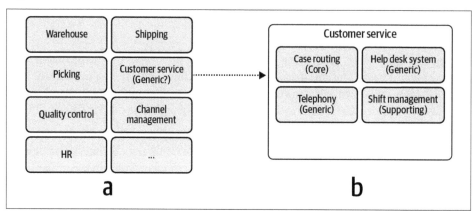

Figure 1-2. Analyzing the inner workings of a suspectedly generic subdomain to find the finer-grained core subdomain, supporting subdomain, and two generic subdomains

On the other hand, we cannot drill down indefinitely, looking for insights at lower and lower levels of granularity. When should you stop?

Subdomains as coherent use cases

From a technical perspective, subdomains resemble sets of interrelated, coherent use cases. Such sets of use cases usually involve the same actor, the business entities, and they all manipulate a closely related set of data.

Consider the use case diagram for a credit card payment gateway shown in Figure 1-3. The use cases are tightly bound by the data they are working with and the involved actors. Hence, all of the use cases form the credit card payment subdomain.

We can use the definition of "subdomains as a set of coherent use cases" as a guiding principle for when to stop looking for finer-grained subdomains. These are the most precise boundaries of the subdomains.

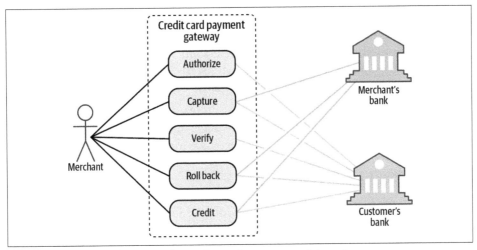

Figure 1-3. Use case diagram of a credit card payment subdomain

Should you always strive to identify such laser-focused subdomain boundaries? It is definitely necessary for core subdomains. Core subdomains are the most important, volatile, and complex. It's essential that we distill them as much as possible since that will allow us to extract all generic and supporting functionalities and invest the effort on a much more focused functionality.

The distillation can be somewhat relaxed for supporting and generic subdomains. If drilling down further doesn't unveil any new insights that can help you make software design decisions, it can be a good place to stop. This can happen, for example, when all of the finer-grained subdomains are of the same type as the original subdomain.

Consider the example in Figure 1-4. Further distillation of the help desk system subdomain is less useful, as it doesn't reveal any strategic information, and a coarse-grained, off-the-shelf tool will be used as the solution.

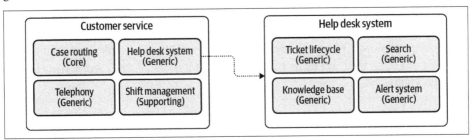

Figure 1-4. Distilling the help desk system subdomain, revealing generic inner components

Another important question to consider when identifying the subdomains is whether we need all of them.

Focus on the essentials

Subdomains are a tool that alleviates the process of making software design decisions. All organizations likely have quite a few business functionalities that drive their competitive advantage but have nothing to do with software. The jewelry maker we discussed earlier in this chapter is but one example.

When looking for subdomains, it's important to identify business functions that are not related to software, acknowledge them as such, and focus on aspects of the business that are relevant to the software system you are working on.

Domain Analysis Examples

Let's see how we can apply the notion of subdomains in practice and use it for making a number of strategic design decisions. I'm going to describe two fictitious companies: Gigmaster and BusVNext. As an exercise, while you are reading, analyze the companies' business domains. Try to identify the three types of subdomains for each company. Remember that, as in real life, some of the business requirements are implicit.

Disclaimer: of course, we cannot identify all the subdomains involved in each business domain by reading such a short description. That said, it is enough to train you to identify and categorize the available subdomains.

Gigmaster

Gigmaster is a ticket sales and distribution company. Its mobile app analyzes users' music libraries, streaming service accounts, and social media profiles to identify nearby shows that its users would be interested in attending.

Gigmaster's users are conscious of their privacy. Hence, all users' personal information is encrypted. Moreover, to ensure that users' guilty pleasures won't leak out under any circumstances, the company's recommendation algorithm works exclusively on anonymized data.

To improve the app's recommendations, a new module was implemented. It allows users to log gigs they attended in the past, even if the tickets weren't purchased through Gigmaster.

Business domain and subdomains

Gigmaster's business domain is ticket sales. That's the service it provides to its customers.

Core subdomains. Gigmaster's main competitive advantage is its recommendation engine. The company also takes its users' privacy seriously and works only on anonymized data. Finally, although not mentioned explicitly, we can infer that the mobile app's user experience is crucial as well. As such, Gigmaster's core subdomains are:

- Recommendation engine
- Data anonymization
- Mobile app

Generic subdomains. We can identify and infer the following generic subdomains:

- Encryption, for encrypting all data
- Accounting, since the company is in the sales business
- Clearing, for charging its customers
- Authentication and authorization, for identifying its users

Supporting subdomains. Finally, the following are the supporting subdomains. Here the business logic is simple and resembles ETL processes or CRUD interfaces:

- Integration with music streaming services
- Integration with social networks
- Attended-gigs module

Design decisions

Knowing the subdomains at play and the differences between their types, we can already make several strategic design decisions:

- The recommendation engine, data anonymization, and mobile app have to be implemented in-house using the most advanced engineering tools and techniques. These modules are going to change the most often.
- Off-the-shelf or open source solutions should be used for data encryption, accounting, clearing, and authentication.
- Integration with streaming services and social networks, as well as the module for attended gigs, can be outsourced.

BusVNext

BusVNext is a public transportation company. It aims to provide its customers with bus rides that are comfortable, like catching a cab. The company manages fleets of buses in major cities.

A BusVNext customer can order a ride through the mobile app. At the scheduled departure time, a nearby bus's route will be adjusted on the fly to pick up the customer at the specified departure time.

The company's major challenge was implementing the routing algorithm. Its requirements are a variant of the "travelling salesman problem" (*https://oreil.ly/LLHij*). The routing logic is continuously adjusted and optimized. For example, statistics show the primary reason for canceled rides is the long wait time for a bus to arrive. So, the company adjusted the routing algorithm to prioritize fast pickups, even if that means delayed drop-offs. To optimize the routing even more, BusVNext integrates with third-party providers for traffic conditions and real-time alerts.

From time to time, BusVNext issues special discounts, both to attract new customers and to level the demand for rides over peak and off-peak hours.

Business domain and subdomains

BusVNext provides optimized bus rides to its customers. The business domain is public transportation.

Core subdomains. BusVNext's primary competitive advantage is its routing algorithm that takes a stab at solving a complex problem ("travelling salesman") while prioritizing different business goals: for example, decreasing pickup times, even if it will increase overall ride lengths.

We also saw that the rides data is continuously analyzed for new insights into customers' behaviors. These insights allow the company to increase its profits by optimizing the routing algorithm. Finally, BusVNext's applications for its customers and its drivers have to be easy to use and provide a convenient user interface.

Managing a fleet is not trivial. Buses may experience technical issues or require maintenance. Ignoring these may result in financial losses and a reduced level of service.

Hence, BusVNext's core subdomains are:

- Routing
- Analysis
- Mobile app user experience
- Fleet management

Generic subdomains. The routing algorithm also uses traffic data and alerts provided by third-party companies—a generic subdomain. Moreover, BusVNext accepts payments from its customers, so it has to implement accounting and clearing functionalities. BusVNext's generic subdomains are:

- Traffic conditions
- Accounting
- Billing
- Authorization

Supporting subdomains. The module for managing promos and discounts supports the company's core business. That said, it's not a core subdomain by itself. Its management interface resembles a simple CRUD interface for managing active coupon codes. Therefore, this is a typical supporting subdomain.

Design decisions

Knowing the subdomains at play and the differences between their types, we can already make a number of strategic design decisions:

- The routing algorithm, data analysis, fleet management, and app usability have to be implemented in-house using the most elaborate technical tools and patterns.
- Implementation of the promotions management module can be outsourced.
- Identifying traffic conditions, authorizing users, and managing financial records and transactions can be offloaded to external service providers.

Who Are the Domain Experts?

Now that we have a clear understanding of business domains and subdomains, let's take a look at another DDD term that we will use often in the following chapters: *domain experts*. Domain experts are subject matter experts who know all the intricacies of the business that we are going to model and implement in code. In other words, domain experts are knowledge authorities in the software's business domain.

The domain experts are neither the analysts gathering the requirements nor the engineers designing the system. Domain experts represent the business. They are the people who identified the business problem in the first place and from whom all business knowledge originates. Systems analysts and engineers are transforming their mental models of the business domain into software requirements and source code.

As a rule of thumb, domain experts are either the people coming up with requirements or the software's end users. The software is supposed to solve their problems.

The domain experts' expertise can have different scopes. Some subject matter experts will have a detailed understanding of how the entire business domain operates, while others will specialize in particular subdomains. For example, in an online advertising agency, the domain experts would be campaign managers, media buyers, analysts, and other business stakeholders.

Conclusion

In this chapter, we covered domain-driven design tools for making sense of a company's business activity. As you've seen, it all starts with the business domain: the area the business operates in and the service it provides to its clients.

You also learned about the different building blocks required to achieve success in a business domain and differentiate the company from its competitors:

Core subdomains
> The interesting problems. These are the activities the company is performing differently from its competitors and from which it gains its competitive advantage.

Generic subdomains
> The solved problems. These are the things all companies are doing in the same way. There is no room or need for innovation here; rather than creating in-house implementations, it's more cost-effective to use existing solutions.

Supporting subdomains
> The problems with obvious solutions. These are the activities the company likely has to implement in-house, but that do not provide any competitive advantage.

Finally, you learned that domain experts are the business's subject matter experts. They have in-depth knowledge of the company's business domain or one or more of its subdomains and are critical to a project's success.

Exercises

1. Which of the subdomains provide(s) no competitive advantage?
   a. Core
   b. Generic
   c. Supporting
   d. B and C

2. For which subdomain might all competitors use the same solutions?
   a. Core.
   b. Generic.
   c. Supporting.
   d. None of the above. The company should always differentiate itself from its competitors.

3. Which subdomain is expected to change the most often?

    a. Core.

    b. Generic.

    c. Supporting.

    d. There is no difference in volatility of the different subdomain types.

Consider the description of WolfDesk (see the Preface), a company that provides a help desk ticket management system:

4. What is WolfDesk's business domain?

5. What is/are WolfDesk's core subdomain(s)?

6. What is/are WolfDesk's supporting subdomain(s)?

7. What is/are WolfDesk's generic subdomain(s)?

CHAPTER 2

Discovering Domain Knowledge

It's developers' (mis)understanding, not domain experts' knowledge, that gets released in production.
    —Alberto Brandolini

In the previous chapter, we started exploring business domains. You learned how to identify a company's business domains, or areas of activity, and analyze its strategy to compete in them; that is, its business subdomains' boundaries and types.

This chapter continues the topic of business domain analysis but in a different dimension: depth. It focuses on what happens inside a subdomain: its business function and logic. You will learn the domain-driven design tool for effective communication and knowledge sharing: the ubiquitous language. Here we will use it to learn the intricacies of business domains. Later in the book we will use it to model and implement their business logic in software.

Business Problems

The software systems we are building are solutions to business problems. In this context, the word *problem* doesn't resemble a mathematical problem or a riddle that you can solve and be done with. In the context of business domains, "problem" has a broader meaning. A business problem can be challenges associated with optimizing workflows and processes, minimizing manual labor, managing resources, supporting decisions, managing data, and so on.

Business problems appear both at the business domain and subdomain levels. A company's goal is to provide a solution for its customers' problems. Going back to the FedEx example in Chapter 1, that company's customers need to ship packages in limited time frames, so it optimizes the shipping process.

Subdomains are finer-grained problem domains whose goal is to provide solutions for specific business capabilities. A knowledge management subdomain optimizes the process of storing and retrieving information. A clearing subdomain optimizes the process of executing financial transactions. An accounting subdomain keeps track of the company's funds.

Knowledge Discovery

To design an effective software solution, we have to grasp at least the basic knowledge of the business domain. As we discussed in Chapter 1, this knowledge belongs to domain experts: it's their job to specialize in and comprehend all the intricacies of the business domain. By no means should we, nor can we, become domain experts. That said, it's crucial for us to understand domain experts and to use the same business terminology they use.

To be effective, the software has to mimic the domain experts' way of thinking about the problem—their mental models. Without an understanding of the business problem and the reasoning behind the requirements, our solutions will be limited to "translating" business requirements into source code. What if the requirements miss a crucial edge case? Or fail to describe a business concept, limiting our ability to implement a model that will support future requirements?

As Alberto Brandolini[1] says, software development is a learning process; working code is a side effect. A software project's success depends on the effectiveness of knowledge sharing between domain experts and software engineers. We have to understand the problem in order to solve it.

Effective knowledge sharing between domain experts and software engineers requires effective communication. Let's take a look at the common impediments to effective communication in software projects.

Communication

It's safe to say that almost all software projects require the collaboration of stakeholders in different roles: domain experts, product owners, engineers, UI and UX designers, project managers, testers, analysts, and others. As in any collaborative effort, the outcome depends on how well all those parties can work together. For example, do all stakeholders agree on what problem is being solved? What about the solution they are building—do they hold any conflicting assumptions about its functional and nonfunctional requirements? Agreement and alignment on all project-related matters are essential to a project's success.

---

1 Brandolini, Alberto. (n.d.). *Introducing EventStorming* (*https://www.eventstorming.com/book*). Leanpub.

Research into why software projects fail has shown that effective communication is essential for knowledge sharing and project success.[2] Yet, despite its importance, effective communication is rarely observed in software projects. Often, businesspeople and engineers have no direct interaction with one another. Instead, domain knowledge is pushed down from domain experts to engineers. It is delivered through people playing the role of mediators, or "translators," systems/business analysts, product owners, and project managers. Such common knowledge sharing flow is illustrated in Figure 2-1.

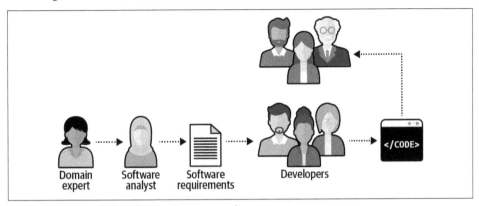

Figure 2-1. Knowledge sharing flow in a software project

During the traditional software development lifecycle, the domain knowledge is "translated" into an engineer-friendly form known as an *analysis model*, which is a description of the system's requirements rather than an understanding of the business domain behind it. While the intentions may be good, such mediation is hazardous to knowledge sharing. In any translation, information is lost; in this case, domain knowledge that is essential for solving business problems gets lost on its way to the software engineers. This is not the only such translation on a typical software project. The analysis model is translated into the software design model (a software design document, which is translated into an implementation model or the source code itself). As often happens, documents go out of date quickly. The source code is used to communicate business domain knowledge to software engineers who will maintain the project later. Figure 2-2 illustrates the different translations needed for domain knowledge to be implemented in code.

---

2 Sudhakar, Goparaju Purna. (2012). "A Model of Critical Success Factors for Software Projects." *Journal of Enterprise Information Management, 25*(6), 537–558.

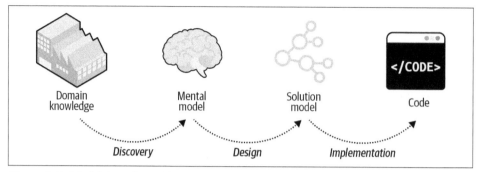

Figure 2-2. Model transformations

Such a software development process resembles the children's game Telephone:[3] the message, or domain knowledge, often becomes distorted. The information leads to software engineers implementing the wrong solution, or the right solution but to the wrong problems. In either case, the outcome is the same: a failed software project.

Domain-driven design proposes a better way to get the knowledge from domain experts to software engineers: by using a ubiquitous language.

What Is a Ubiquitous Language?

Using a ubiquitous language is the cornerstone practice of domain-driven design. The idea is simple and straightforward: if parties need to communicate efficiently, instead of relying on translations, they have to speak the same language.

Although this notion is borderline common sense, as Voltaire said, "common sense is not so common." The traditional software development lifecycle implies the following translations:

- Domain knowledge into an analysis model
- Analysis model into requirements
- Requirements into system design
- System design into source code

---

3 Players form a line, and the first player comes up with a message and whispers it into the ear of the second player. The second player repeats the message to the third player, and so on. The last player announces the message they heard to the entire group. The first player then compares the original message with the final version. Although the objective is to communicate the same message, it usually gets garbled and the last player receives a message that is significantly different from the original one.

Instead of continuously translating domain knowledge, domain-driven design calls for cultivating a single language for describing the business domain: the ubiquitous language.

All project-related stakeholders—software engineers, product owners, domain experts, UI/UX designers—should use the ubiquitous language when describing the business domain. Most importantly, domain experts must be comfortable using the ubiquitous language when reasoning about the business domain; this language will represent both the business domain and the domain experts' mental models.

Only through the continuous use of the ubiquitous language and its terms can a shared understanding among all of the project's stakeholders be cultivated.

Language of the Business

It's crucial to emphasize that the ubiquitous language is the language of the business. As such, it should consist of business domain–related terms only. No technical jargon! Teaching business domain experts about singletons and abstract factories is not your goal. The ubiquitous language aims to frame the domain experts' understanding and mental models of the business domain in terms that are easy to understand.

Scenarios

Let's say we are working on an advertising campaign management system. Consider the following statements:

- An advertising campaign can display different creative materials.
- A campaign can be published only if at least one of its placements is active.
- Sales commissions are accounted for after transactions are approved.

All of these statements are formulated in the language of the business. That is, they reflect the domain experts' view of the business domain.

On the other hand, the following statements are strictly technical and thus do not fit the notion of the ubiquitous language:

- The advertisement iframe displays an HTML file.
- A campaign can be published only if it has at least one associated record in the active-placements table.
- Sales commissions are based on correlated records from the transactions and approved-sales tables.

These latter statements are purely technical and will be unclear to domain experts. Suppose engineers are only familiar with this technical, solution-oriented view of the business domain. In that case, they won't be able to completely understand the business logic or why it operates the way it does, which will limit their ability to model and implement an effective solution.

Consistency

The ubiquitous language must be precise and consistent. It should eliminate the need for assumptions and should make the business domain's logic explicit.

Since ambiguity hinders communication, each term of the ubiquitous language should have one and only one meaning. Let's look at a few examples of unclear terminology and how it can be improved.

Ambiguous terms

Let's say that in some business domain, the term *policy* has multiple meanings: it can mean a regulatory rule or an insurance contract. The exact meaning can be worked out in human-to-human interaction, depending on the context. Software, however, doesn't cope well with ambiguity, and it can be cumbersome and challenging to model the "policy" entity in code.

Ubiquitous language demands a single meaning for each term, so "policy" should be modeled explicitly using the two terms *regulatory rule* and *insurance contract*.

Synonymous terms

Two terms cannot be used interchangeably in a ubiquitous language. For example, many systems use the term *user*. However, a careful examination of the domain experts' lingo may reveal that *user* and other terms are used interchangeably: for example, *user, visitor, administrator, account*, etc.

Synonymous terms can seem harmless at first. However, in most cases, they denote different concepts. In this example, both *visitor* and *account* technically refer to the system's users; however, in most systems, unregistered and registered users represent different roles and have different behaviors. For example, the "visitors" data is used mainly for analysis purposes, whereas "accounts" actually uses the system and its functionality.

It is preferable to use each term explicitly in its specific context. Understanding the differences between the terms in use allows for building simpler and clearer models and implementations of the business domain's entities.

Model of the Business Domain

Now let's look at the ubiquitous language from a different perspective: modeling.

What Is a Model?

> *A model is a simplified representation of a thing or phenomenon that intentionally emphasizes certain aspects while ignoring others. Abstraction with a specific use in mind.*
> —Rebecca Wirfs-Brock

A model is not a copy of the real world but a human construct that helps us make sense of real-world systems.

A canonical example of a model is a map. Any map is a model, including navigation maps, terrain maps, world maps, subway maps, and others, as shown in Figure 2-3.

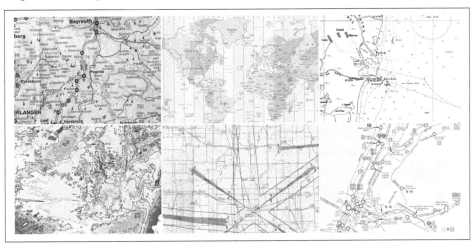

Figure 2-3. Different types of maps displaying different models of the earth: roads, time zones, nautical navigation, terrain, aeronautical navigation, and subway routes.

None of these maps represents all the details of our planet. Instead, each map contains just enough data to support its particular purpose: the problem it is supposed to solve.

Effective Modeling

All models have a purpose, and an effective model contains only the details needed to fulfill its purpose. For example, you won't see subway stops on a world map. On the other hand, you cannot use a subway map to estimate distances. Each map contains just the information it is supposed to provide.

This point is worth reiterating: a useful model is not a copy of the real world. Instead, a model is intended to solve a problem, and it should provide just enough information for that purpose. Or, as statistician George Box put it, "All models are wrong, but some are useful."

In its essence, a model is an abstraction. The notion of abstraction allows us to handle complexity by omitting unnecessary details and leaving only what's needed for solving the problem at hand. On the other hand, an ineffective abstraction removes necessary information or produces noise by leaving what's not required. As noted by Edsger W. Dijkstra in his paper "The Humble Programmer,"[4] the purpose of abstracting is not to be vague but to create a new semantic level in which one can be *absolutely precise*.

Modeling the Business Domain

When cultivating a ubiquitous language, we are effectively building a model of the business domain. The model is supposed to capture the domain experts' mental models—their thought processes about how the business works to implement its function. The model has to reflect the involved business entities and their behavior, cause and effect relationships, and invariants.

The ubiquitous language we use is not supposed to cover every possible detail of the domain. That would be equivalent to making every stakeholder a domain expert. Instead, the model is supposed to include just enough aspects of the business domain to make it possible to implement the required system; that is, to address the specific problem the software is intended to solve. In the following chapters, you will see how the ubiquitous language can drive low-level design and implementation decisions.

Effective communication between engineering teams and domain experts is vital. The importance of this communication grows with the complexity of the business domain. The more complex the business domain is, the harder it is to model and implement its business logic in code. Even a slight misunderstanding of a complicated business domain, or its underlying principles, will inadvertently lead to an implementation prone to severe bugs. The only reliable way to verify a business

---

4 Edsger W. Dijkstra, "The Humble Programmer" (*https://oreil.ly/LXd4W*).

domain's understanding is to converse with domain experts and do it in the language they understand: the language of the business.

Continuous Effort

Formulation of a ubiquitous language requires interaction with its natural holders, the domain experts. Only interactions with actual domain experts can uncover inaccuracies, wrong assumptions, or an overall flawed understanding of the business domain.

All stakeholders should consistently use the ubiquitous language in all project-related communications to spread knowledge about and foster a shared understanding of the business domain. The language should be continuously reinforced throughout the project: requirements, tests, documentation, and even the source code itself should use this language.

Most importantly, cultivation of a ubiquitous language is an ongoing process. It should be constantly validated and evolved. Everyday use of the language will, over time, reveal deeper insights into the business domain. When such breakthroughs happen, the ubiquitous language must evolve to keep pace with the newly acquired domain knowledge.

Tools

There are tools and technologies that can alleviate the processes of capturing and managing a ubiquitous language.

For example, a wiki can be used as a *glossary* to capture and document the ubiquitous language. Such a glossary alleviates the onboarding process of new team members, as it serves as a go-to place for information about the business domain's terminology.

It's important to make glossary maintenance a shared effort. When a ubiquitous language is changed, all team members should be encouraged to go ahead and update the glossary. That's contrary to a centralized approach, in which only team leaders or architects are in charge of maintaining the glossary.

Despite the obvious advantages of maintaining a glossary of project-related terminology, it has an inherent limitation. Glossaries work best for "nouns": names of entities, processes, roles, and so on. Although nouns are important, capturing the behavior is crucial. The behavior is not a mere list of verbs associated with nouns, but the actual business logic, with its rules, assumptions, and invariants. Such concepts are much harder to document in a glossary. Hence, glossaries are best used in tandem with other tools that are better suited to capture the behavior; for example, use cases or *Gherkin tests*.

Automated tests written in the Gherkin language (*https://oreil.ly/WJw3C*) are not only great tools for capturing the ubiquitous language but also act as an additional tool for bridging the gap between domain experts and software engineers. Domain experts can read the tests and verify the system's expected behavior.[5] For example, see the following test written in the Gherkin language:

```
Scenario: Notify the agent about a new support case
    Given Vincent Jules submits a new support case saying:
    """

    I need help configuring AWS Infinidash
    """

    When the ticket is assigned to Mr. Wolf
    Then the agent receives a notification about the new ticket
```

Managing a Gherkin-based test suite can be challenging at times, especially at the early stages of a project. However, it is definitely worth it for complex business domains.

Finally, there are even static code analysis tools that can verify the usage of a ubiquitous language's terms. A notable example for such a tool is NDepend.

While these tools are useful, they are secondary to the actual use of a ubiquitous language in day-to-day interactions. Use the tools to support the management of the ubiquitous language, but don't expect the documentation to replace the actual usage. As the Agile Manifesto says (*https://agilemanifesto.org*), "Individuals and interactions over processes and tools."

Challenges

In theory, cultivating a ubiquitous language sounds like a simple, straightforward process. In practice, it isn't. The only reliable way to gather domain knowledge is to converse with domain experts. Quite often, the most important knowledge is tacit. It's not documented or codified but resides only in the minds of domain experts. The only way to access it is to ask questions.

As you gain experience in this practice, you will notice that frequently, this process involves not merely discovering knowledge that is already there, but rather co-creating the model in tandem with domain experts. There may be ambiguities and even white spots in domain experts' own understanding of the business domain; for example, defining only the "happy path" scenarios but not considering edge cases that challenge the accepted assumptions. Furthermore, you may encounter business domain concepts that lack explicit definitions. Asking questions about the nature of the business domain often makes such implicit conflicts and white spots explicit. This

---

5 But please don't fall into the trap of thinking that domain experts will write Gherkin tests.

is especially common for core subdomains. In such a case, the learning process is mutual—you are helping the domain experts better understand their field.

When introducing domain-driven design practices to a brownfield project, you will notice that there is already a formed language for describing the business domain, and that the stakeholders use it. However, since DDD principles do not drive that language, it won't necessarily reflect the business domain effectively. For example, it may use technical terms, such as database table names. Changing a language that is already being used in an organization is not easy. The essential tool in such a situation is patience. You need to make sure the correct language is used where it's easy to control it: in the documentation and source code.

Finally, the question about the ubiquitous language that I am asked often at conferences is what language should we use if the company is not in an English-speaking country. My advice is to at least use English nouns for naming the business domain's entities. This will alleviate using the same terminology in code.

Conclusion

Effective communication and knowledge sharing are crucial for a successful software project. Software engineers have to understand the business domain in order to design and build a software solution.

Domain-driven design's ubiquitous language is an effective tool for bridging the knowledge gap between domain experts and software engineers. It fosters communication and knowledge sharing by cultivating a shared language that can be used by all the stakeholders throughout the project: in conversations, documentation, tests, diagrams, source code, and so on.

To ensure effective communication, the ubiquitous language has to eliminate ambiguities and implicit assumptions. All of a language's terms have to be consistent—no ambiguous terms and no synonymous terms.

Cultivating a ubiquitous language is a continuous process. As the project evolves, more domain knowledge will be discovered. It's important for such insights to be reflected in the ubiquitous language.

Tools such as wiki-based glossaries and Gherkin tests can greatly alleviate the process of documenting and maintaining a ubiquitous language. However, the main prerequisite for an effective ubiquitous language is usage: the language has to be used consistently in all project-related communications.

Exercises

1. Who should be able to contribute to the definition of a ubiquitous language?

   a. Domain experts

   b. Software engineers

   c. End users

   d. All of the project's stakeholders

2. Where should a ubiquitous language be used?

   a. In-person conversations

   b. Documentation

   c. Code

   d. All of the above

3. Please review the description of the fictional WolfDesk company in the Preface. What business domain terminology can you spot in the description?

4. Consider a software project you are working on at the moment or worked on in the past:

   a. Try to come up with concepts of the business domain that you could use in conversations with domain experts.

   b. Try to identify examples of inconsistent terms: business domain concepts that have either different meanings or identical concepts represented by different terms.

   c. Have you encountered software development inefficiencies that resulted from poor communication?

5. Assume you are working on a project and you notice that domain experts from different organizational units use the same term, for example, *policy*, to describe unrelated concepts of the business domain.

   The resultant ubiquitous language is based on domain experts' mental models but fails to fulfill the requirement of a term having a single meaning.

   Before you continue to the next chapter, how would you address such a conundrum?

CHAPTER 3

Managing Domain Complexity

As you saw in the previous chapter, to ensure a project's success it's crucial that you develop a ubiquitous language that can be used for communication by all stakeholders, from software engineers to domain experts. The language should reflect the domain experts' mental models of the business domain's inner workings and underlying principles.

Since our goal is to use ubiquitous language to drive software design decisions, the language must be clear and consistent. It should be free of ambiguity, implicit assumptions, and extraneous details. However, on an organizational scale, the domain experts' mental models can be inconsistent themselves. Different domain experts can use different models of the same business domain. Let's take a look at an example.

Inconsistent Models

Let's go back to the example of a telemarketing company from Chapter 2. The company's marketing department generates leads through online advertisements. Its sales department is in charge of soliciting prospective customers to buy its products or services, a chain that is shown in Figure 3-1.

Figure 3-1. Example business domain: telemarketing company

An examination of the domain experts' language reveals a peculiar observation. The term *lead* has different meanings in the marketing and sales departments:

Marketing department

> For the marketing people, a lead represents a notification that somebody is interested in one of the products. The event of receiving the prospective customer's contact details is considered a lead.

Sales department

> In the context of the sales department, a lead is a much more complex entity. It represents the entire lifecycle of the sales process. It's not a mere event, but a long-running process.

How do we formulate a ubiquitous language in the case of this telemarketing company?

On the one hand, we know the ubiquitous language has to be consistent—each term should have one meaning. On the other hand, we know the ubiquitous language has to reflect the domain experts' mental models. In this case, the mental model of the "lead" is inconsistent among the domain experts in the sales and marketing departments.

This ambiguity doesn't present that much of a challenge in person-to-person communications. Indeed, communication can be more challenging among people from different departments, but it's easy enough for humans to infer the exact meaning from the interaction's context.

However, it is more difficult to represent such a divergent model of the business domain in software. Source code doesn't cope well with ambiguity. If we were to bring the sales department's complicated model into marketing, it would introduce complexity where it's not needed— far more detail and behavior than marketing people need for optimizing advertising campaigns. But if we were to try to simplify the sales model according to the marketing world view, it wouldn't fit the sales subdomain's needs, because it's too simplistic for managing and optimizing the sales process. We'd have an overengineered solution in the first case and an under-engineered one in the second.

How do we solve this catch-22?

The traditional solution to this problem is to design a single model that can be used for all kinds of problems. Such models result in enormous entity relationship diagrams (ERDs) spanning whole office walls. Is Figure 3-2 an effective model?

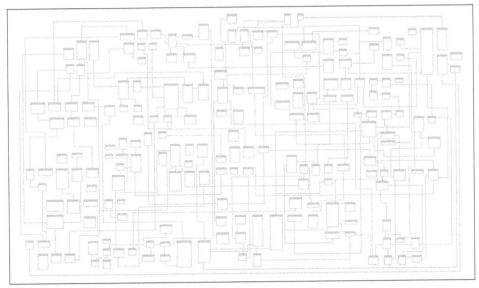

Figure 3-2. Enterprise-wide entity relationship diagram

As the saying goes, "jack of all trades, master of none." Such models are supposed to be suitable for everything but eventually are effective for nothing. No matter what you do, you are always facing complexity: the complexity of filtering out extraneous details, the complexity of finding what you do need, and most importantly, the complexity of keeping the data in a consistent state.

Another solution would be to prefix the problematic term with a definition of the context: "marketing lead" and "sales lead." That would allow the implementation of the two models in code. However, this approach has two main disadvantages. First, it induces cognitive load. When should each model be used? The closer the implementations of the conflicting models are, the easier it is to make a mistake. Second, the implementation of the model won't be aligned with the ubiquitous language. No one would use the prefixes in conversations. People don't need this extra information; they can rely on the conversation's context.

Let's turn to the domain-driven design pattern for tackling such scenarios: the bounded context pattern.

What Is a Bounded Context?

The solution in domain-driven design is trivial: divide the ubiquitous language into multiple smaller languages, then assign each one to the explicit context in which it can be applied: its *bounded context*.

In the preceding example, we can identify two bounded contexts: marketing and sales. The term *lead* exists in both bounded contexts, as shown in Figure 3-3. As long as it bears a single meaning in each bounded context, each fine-grained ubiquitous language is consistent and follows the domain experts' mental models.

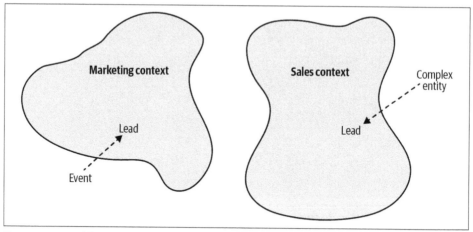

Figure 3-3. Tackling inconsistencies in the ubiquitous language by splitting it into bounded contexts

In a sense, terminology conflicts and implicit contexts are an inherent part of any decent-sized business. With the bounded context pattern, the contexts are modeled as an explicit and integral part of the business domain.

Model Boundaries

As we discussed in the previous chapter, a model is not a copy of the real world but a construct that helps us make sense of a complex system. The problem it is supposed to solve is an inherent part of a model—its purpose. A model cannot exist without a boundary; it will expand to become a copy of the real world. That makes defining a model's boundary—its bounded contexts—an intrinsic part of the modeling process.

Let's go back to the example of maps as models. We saw that each map has its specific context—aerial, nautical, terrain, subway, and so on. A map is useful and consistent only within the scope of its specific purpose.

Just as a subway map is useless for nautical navigation, a ubiquitous language in one bounded context can be completely irrelevant to the scope of another bounded context. Bounded contexts define the applicability of a ubiquitous language and of the model it represents. They allow defining distinct models according to different problem domains. In other words, bounded contexts are the consistency boundaries of ubiquitous languages. A language's terminology, principles, and business rules are only consistent inside its bounded context.

Ubiquitous Language Refined

Bounded contexts allow us to complete the definition of a ubiquitous language. A ubiquitous language is *not* "ubiquitous" in the sense that it should be used and applied "ubiquitously" throughout the organization. A ubiquitous language is *not* universal.

Instead, a ubiquitous language is ubiquitous only in the boundaries of its bounded context. The language is focused on describing only the model that is encompassed by the bounded context. As a model cannot exist without a problem it is supposed to address, a ubiquitous language cannot be defined or used without an explicit context of its applicability.

Scope of a Bounded Context

The example at the beginning of the chapter demonstrated an inherent boundary of the business domain. Different domain experts held conflicting mental models of the same business entity. To model the business domain, we had to divide the model and define a strict applicability context for each fine-grained model—its bounded context.

The consistency of the ubiquitous language only helps to identify the widest boundary of that language. It cannot be any larger, because then there will be inconsistent models and terminology. However, we can still further decompose the models into even smaller bounded contexts, as shown in Figure 3-4.

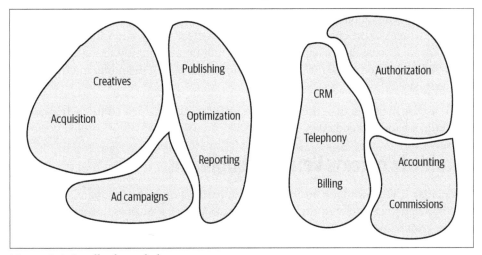

Figure 3-4. Smaller bounded contexts

Defining the scope of a ubiquitous language—its bounded context—is a strategic design decision. Boundaries can be wide, following the business domain's inherent contexts, or narrow, further dividing the business domain into smaller problem domains.

A bounded context's size, by itself, is not a deciding factor. Models shouldn't necessarily be big or small. Models need to be useful. The wider the boundary of the ubiquitous language is, the harder it is to keep it consistent. It may be beneficial to divide a large ubiquitous language into smaller, more manageable problem domains, but striving for small bounded contexts can backfire too. The smaller they are, the more integration overhead the design induces.

Hence, the decision for how big your bounded contexts should depend on the specific problem domain. Sometimes, using a wide boundary will be clearer, while at other times, decomposing it further will make more sense.

The reasons for extracting finer-grained bounded contexts out of a larger one include constituting new software engineering teams or addressing some of the system's nonfunctional requirements; for example, when you need to separate the development lifecycles of some of the components originally residing in a single bounded context. Another common reason for extracting one functionality is the ability to scale it independently from the rest of the bounded context's functionalities.

Therefore, keep your models useful and align the bounded contexts' sizes with your business needs and organizational constraints. One thing to beware of is splitting a coherent functionality into multiple bounded contexts. Such division will hinder the ability to evolve each context independently. Instead, the same business requirements and changes will simultaneously affect the bounded contexts and require simultaneous deployment of the changes. To avoid such ineffective decomposition, use the rule of thumb we discussed in Chapter 1 to find subdomains: identify sets of coherent use cases that operate on the same data and avoid decomposing them into multiple bounded contexts.

We'll discuss the topic of continuously optimizing the bounded contexts' boundaries further in Chapters 8 and 10.

Bounded Contexts Versus Subdomains

In Chapter 2, we saw that a business domain consists of multiple subdomains. So far in this chapter, we explored the notion of decomposing a business domain into a set of fine-grained problem domains or bounded contexts. At first, the two methods of decomposing business domains might seem redundant. However, that's not the case. Let's examine why we need both boundaries.

Subdomains

To comprehend a company's business strategy, we have to analyze its business domain. According to domain-driven design methodology, the analysis phase involves identifying the different subdomains (core, supporting, and generic). That's how the organization works and plans its competitive strategy.

As you learned in Chapter 1, a subdomain resembles a set of interrelated use cases. The use cases are defined by the business domain and the system's requirements. As software engineers, we do not define the requirements; that's the responsibility of the business. Instead, we are analyzing the business domain to identify the subdomains.

Bounded Contexts

Bounded contexts, on the other hand, are designed. Choosing models' boundaries is a strategic design decision. We decide how to divide the business domain into smaller, manageable problem domains.

The Interplay Between Subdomains and Bounded Contexts

Theoretically, though impractically, a single model could span the entire business domain. This strategy could work for a small system, as shown in Figure 3-5.

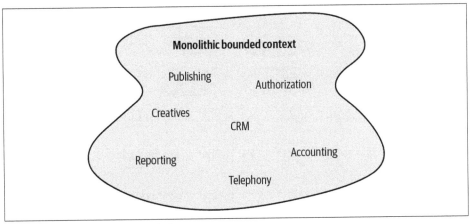

Figure 3-5. Monolithic bounded context

When conflicting models arise, we can follow the domain experts' mental models and decompose the systems into bounded contexts, as shown in Figure 3-6.

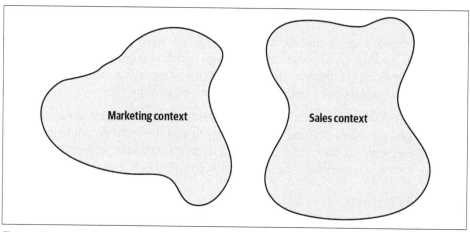

Figure 3-6. Bounded contexts driven by the consistency of the ubiquitous language

If the models are still large and hard to maintain, we can decompose them into even smaller bounded contexts; for example, by having a bounded context for each subdomain, as shown in Figure 3-7.

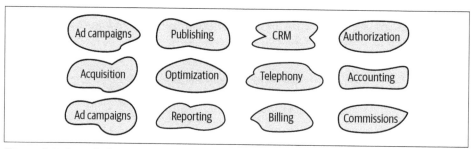

Figure 3-7. Bounded contexts aligned with subdomains' boundaries

Either way, this is a design decision. We design those boundaries as a part of the solution.

Having a one-to-one relationship between bounded contexts and subdomains can be perfectly reasonable in some scenarios. In others, however, different decomposition strategies can be more suitable.

It's crucial to remember that subdomains are discovered and bounded contexts are designed.[1] The subdomains are defined by the business strategy. However, we can design the software solution and its bounded contexts to address the specific project's context and constraints.

Finally, as you learned in Chapter 1, a model is intended to solve a specific problem. In some cases, it can be beneficial to use multiple models of the same concept simultaneously to solve different problems. As different types of maps provide different types of information about our planet, it may be reasonable to use different models of the same subdomain to solve different problems. Limiting the design to one-to-one relationships between bounded contexts would inhibit this flexibility and force us to use a single model of a subdomain in its bounded context.

Boundaries

As Ruth Malan says, architectural design is inherently about boundaries:

> Architectural design is system design. System design is contextual design—it is inherently about boundaries (what's in, what's out, what spans, what moves between), and about trade-offs. It reshapes what is outside, just as it shapes what is inside.[2]

The bounded context pattern is the domain-driven design tool for defining physical and ownership boundaries.

Physical Boundaries

Bounded contexts serve not only as model boundaries but also as physical boundaries of the systems implementing them. Each bounded context should be implemented as an individual service/project, meaning it is implemented, evolved, and versioned independently of other bounded contexts.

Clear physical boundaries between bounded contexts allow us to implement each bounded context with the technology stack that best fits its needs.

As we discussed earlier, a bounded context can contain multiple subdomains. In such a case, the bounded context is a physical boundary, while each of its subdomains is a logical boundary. Logical boundaries bear different names in different programming languages: namespaces, modules, or packages.

---

1 There is an exception here that is worth mentioning. Depending on the organization you are working in, you may be wearing two hats and be in charge of both software engineering and business development. As a result, you have the ability to affect both the software design (bounded contexts) and the business strategy (subdomains). Therefore, in the (bounded) context of our discussion here, we are focusing only on software engineering.

2 Bredemeyer Consulting, "What Is Software Architecture." Retrieved September 22, 2021, *https://www.brede meyer.com/who.htm*

Ownership Boundaries

Studies show that good fences do indeed make good neighbors. In software projects, we can leverage model boundaries—bounded contexts—for the peaceful coexistence of teams. The division of work between teams is another strategic decision that can be made using the bounded context pattern.

A bounded context should be implemented, evolved, and maintained by one team only. No two teams can work on the same bounded context. This segregation eliminates implicit assumptions that teams might make about one another's models. Instead, they have to define communication protocols for integrating their models and systems explicitly.

It's important to note that the relationship between teams and bounded contexts is one-directional: a bounded context should be owned by only one team. However, a single team can own multiple bounded contexts, as Figure 3-8 illustrates.

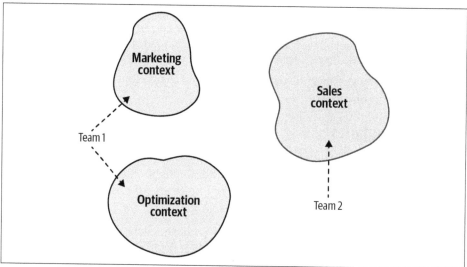

Figure 3-8. Team 1 working on the Marketing and Optimization bounded contexts, while Team 2 works on the Sales bounded context

Bounded Contexts in Real Life

In one of my domain driven-design classes, a participant once noted: "You said that DDD is about aligning software design with business domains. But where are the bounded contexts in real life? There are no bounded contexts in business domains."

Indeed, bounded contexts are not as evident as business domains and subdomains, but they are there, as domain experts' mental models are. You just have to be conscious about how domain experts think about the different business entities and processes.

I want to close this chapter by discussing examples demonstrating that not only are bounded contexts there when we are modeling business domains in software, but the notion of using different models in different contexts is widespread in life in general.

Semantic Domains

It can be said that domain-driven design's bounded contexts are based on the lexicographical notion of semantic domains (*https://oreil.ly/ugv75*). A *semantic domain* is defined as an area of meaning and the words used to talk about it. For example, the words *monitor*, *port*, and *processor* have different meanings in the software and hardware engineering semantic domains.

A rather peculiar example of different semantic domains is the meaning of the word *tomato*.

According to the botanic definition, a fruit is the plant's way of spreading its seeds. A fruit should grow from the plant's flower, and bear at least one seed. A vegetable, on the other hand, is a general term encompassing all other edible parts of a plant: roots, stems, and leaves. Based on this definition, the *tomato is a fruit*.

That definition, however, is of little use in the context of the culinary arts. In this context, fruits and vegetables are defined based on their flavor profiles. A fruit has a soft texture, is either sweet or sour, and can be enjoyed in its raw form, whereas a vegetable has a tougher texture, tastes blander, and often requires cooking. According to this definition, *the tomato is a vegetable*.

Hence, in the *bounded context of botany*, the tomato is a fruit, while in the *bounded context of the culinary arts*, it's a vegetable. But that's not all.

In 1883 the United States established a 10% tax on imported vegetables, but not fruits. The botanic definition of the tomato as a fruit allowed the importation of tomatoes to the United States without paying the import tax. To close the loophole, in 1893 the United States Supreme Court made the decision to classify the tomato as a vegetable. Therefore, in the *bounded context of taxation*, the tomato is a vegetable.

Furthermore, as my friend Romeu Moura says, *in the bounded context of theatrical performances*, the tomato is a feedback mechanism.

Science

As historian Yuval Noah Harari puts it, "Scientists generally agree that no theory is 100 percent correct. Thus, the real test of knowledge is not the truth, but utility." In other words, no scientific theory is correct in all cases. Different theories are useful in different contexts.

This notion can be demonstrated by the different models of gravity introduced by Sir Isaac Newton and Albert Einstein. According to Newton's laws of motion, space and time are absolute. They are the stage on which the motion of objects happens. In Einstein's theory of relativity, space and time are no longer absolute but different for different observers.

Even though the two models can be seen as contradictory, both are useful in their suitable (bounded) contexts.

Buying a Refrigerator

Finally, let's see a more earthbound example of real-life bounded contexts. What do you see in Figure 3-9?

Figure 3-9. A piece of cardboard

Is it just a piece of cardboard? No, it's a model. It's a model of the Siemens KG86NAI31L refrigerator. If you look it up, you may say the piece of cardboard doesn't look anything like that fridge. It has no doors, and even its color is different.

Although that's true, it's not relevant. As we've discussed, a model is not supposed to copy a real-world entity. Instead, it should have a purpose—a problem it is supposed to solve. Hence, the correct question to ask about the cardboard is, what problem does this model solve?

In our apartment, we do not have a standard entry into the kitchen. The cardboard was cut precisely to the size of the fridge's width and depth. The problem it solves is checking whether the refrigerator can fit through the kitchen door (see Figure 3-10).

Figure 3-10. The cardboard model in the kitchen doorway

Despite the cardboard not looking anything like the fridge, it proved extremely useful when we had to decide whether to buy this model or opt for a smaller one. Again, all models are wrong, but some are useful. Building a 3D model of the fridge would definitely be a fun project. But would it solve the problem any more efficiently than the cardboard? No. If the cardboard fits, the 3D model would fit as well, and vice versa. In software engineering terms, building a 3D model of the fridge would be gross overengineering.

But what about the refrigerator's height? What if the base fits, but it's too tall to fit in the doorway? Would that justify gluing together a 3D model of the fridge? No. The problem can be solved much more quickly and easily by using a simple tape measure to check the doorway's height. What is a tape measure in this case? Another simple model.

So, we ended up with two models of the same fridge. Using two models, each optimized for its specific task, reflects the DDD approach to modeling business domains. Each model has its strict bounded context: the cardboard verifying that the refrigerator's base can make it through the kitchen's entry, and the tape measure verifying that it's not too tall. *A model should omit the extraneous information irrelevant to the task at hand.* Also, there's no need to design a complex jack-of-all-trades model if multiple, much simpler models can effectively solve each problem individually.

A few days after I published this story on Twitter (*https://oreil.ly/rqnEy*), I received a reply saying that instead of fiddling with cardboard, I could have just used a mobile phone with a LiDAR scanner and an augmented reality (AR) application. Let's analyze this suggestion from the domain-driven design perspective.

The author of the comment says this is a problem that others have already solved, and the solution is readily available. Needless to say, both the scanning technology and the AR application are complex. In DDD lingo, that makes the problem of checking whether the refrigerator will fit through the doorway a generic subdomain.

Conclusion

Whenever we stumble upon an inherent conflict in the domain experts' mental models, we have to decompose the ubiquitous language into multiple bounded contexts. A ubiquitous language should be consistent within the scope of its bounded context. However, across bounded contexts, the same terms can have different meanings.

While subdomains are discovered, bounded contexts are designed. The division of the domain into bounded contexts is a strategic design decision.

A bounded context and its ubiquitous language can be implemented and maintained by one team. No two teams can share the work on the same bounded context. However, one team can work on multiple bounded contexts.

Bounded contexts decompose a system into physical components—services, subsystems, and so on. Each bounded context's lifecycle is decoupled from the rest. Each bounded context can evolve independently from the rest of the system. However, the bounded contexts have to work together to form a system. Some of the changes will inadvertently affect another bounded context. In the next chapter, we'll talk about the different patterns for integrating bounded contexts that can be used to protect them from cascading changes.

Exercises

1. What is the difference between subdomains and bounded contexts?

    a. Subdomains are designed, while bounded contexts are discovered.

    b. Bounded contexts are designed, while subdomains are discovered.

    c. Bounded contexts and subdomains are essentially the same.

    d. None of the above is true.

2. A bounded context is a boundary of:

    a. A model

    b. A lifecycle

    c. Ownership

    d. All of the above

3. Which of the following is true regarding the size of a bounded context?

    The smaller the bounded context is, the more flexible the system is.

    a. Bounded contexts should always be aligned with the boundaries of subdomains.

    b. The wider the bounded context is, the better.

    c. It depends.

4. Which of the following is true regarding team ownership of a bounded context?

    a. Multiple teams can work on the same bounded context.

    b. A single team can own multiple bounded contexts.

    c. A bounded context can be owned by one team only.

    d. B and C are correct.

5. Review the example of the WolfDesk company in the Preface and try to identify functionalities of the system that may require different models of a support ticket.

6. Try to find examples of real-life bounded contexts, in addition to those described in this chapter.

CHAPTER 4

Integrating Bounded Contexts

Not only does the bounded context pattern protect the consistency of a ubiquitous language, it also enables modeling. You cannot build a model without specifying its purpose—its boundary. The boundary divides the responsibility of languages. A language in one bounded context can model the business domain to solve a particular problem. Another bounded context can represent the same business entities but model them to solve a different problem.

Moreover, models in different bounded contexts can be evolved and implemented independently. That said, bounded contexts themselves are not independent. Just as a system cannot be built out of independent components—the components have to interact with one another to achieve the system's overarching goals—so, too, do the implementations in bounded contexts. Although they can evolve independently, they have to integrate with one another. As a result, there will always be touchpoints between bounded contexts. These are called *contracts*.

The need for contracts results from differences in bounded contexts' models and languages. Since each contract affects more than one party, they need to be defined and coordinated. Also, by definition, two bounded contexts are using different ubiquitous languages. Which language will be used for integration purposes? These integration concerns should be evaluated and addressed by the solution's design.

In this chapter, you will learn about domain-driven design patterns for defining relationships and integrations between bounded contexts. These patterns are driven by the nature of collaboration between teams working on bounded contexts. We will divide the patterns into three groups, each representing a type of team collaboration: cooperation, customer–supplier, and separate ways.

Cooperation

Cooperation patterns relate to bounded contexts implemented by teams with well-established communication.

In the simplest case, these are bounded contexts implemented by a single team. This also applies to teams with dependent goals, where one team's success depends on the success of the other, and vice versa. Again, the main criterion here is the quality of the teams' communication and collaboration.

Let's look at two DDD patterns suitable for cooperating teams: the partnership and shared kernel patterns.

Partnership

In the partnership model, the integration between bounded contexts is coordinated in an ad hoc manner. One team can notify a second team about a change in the API, and the second team will cooperate and adapt—no drama or conflicts (see Figure 4-1).

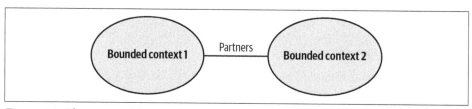

Figure 4-1. The partnership model

The coordination of integration here is two-way. No one team dictates the language that is used for defining the contracts. The teams can work out the differences and choose the most appropriate solution. Also, both sides cooperate in solving any integration issues that might come up. Neither team is interested in blocking the other one.

Well-established collaboration practices, high levels of commitment, and frequent synchronizations between teams are required for successful integration in this manner. From a technical perspective, continuous integration of the changes applied by both teams is needed to further minimize the integration feedback loop.

This pattern might not be a good fit for geographically distributed teams since it may present synchronization and communication challenges.

Shared Kernel

Despite bounded contexts being model boundaries, there still can be cases when the same model of a subdomain, or a part of it, will be implemented in multiple bounded contexts. It's crucial to stress that the shared model is designed according to the needs of all of the bounded contexts. Moreover, the shared model has to be consistent across all of the bounded contexts that are using it.

As an example, consider an enterprise system that uses a tailor-made model for managing users' permissions. Each user can have their permissions granted directly or inherited from one of the organizational units they belong to. Moreover, each bounded context can modify the authorization model, and the changes each bounded context applies have to affect all the other bounded contexts using the model (see Figure 4-2).

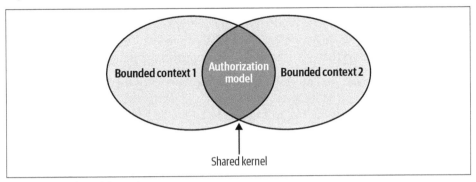

Figure 4-2. Shared kernel

Shared scope

The overlapping model couples the lifecycles of the participating bounded contexts. A change made to the shared model has an immediate effect on all the bounded contexts. Hence, to minimize the cascading effects of changes, the overlapping model should be limited, exposing only that part of the model that has to be implemented by both bounded contexts. Ideally, the shared kernel will consist only of integration contracts and data structures that are intended to be passed across the bounded contexts' boundaries.

Implementation

The shared kernel is implemented so that any modification to its source code is immediately reflected in all the bounded contexts using it.

If the organization uses the mono-repository approach, these can be the same source files referenced by multiple bounded contexts. If using a shared repository is not possible, the shared kernel can be extracted into a dedicated project and referenced in the bounded contexts as a linked library. Either way, each change to the shared kernel must trigger integration tests for all the affected bounded contexts.

The continuous integration of changes is required because the shared kernel belongs to multiple bounded contexts. Not propagating shared kernel changes to all related bounded contexts leads to inconsistencies in a model: bounded contexts may rely on stale implementations of the shared kernel, leading to data corruption and/or runtime issues.

When to use shared kernel

The overarching applicability criterion for the shared kernel pattern is the cost of duplication versus the cost of coordination. Since the pattern introduces a strong dependency between the participating bounded contexts, it should be applied only when the cost of duplication is higher than the cost of coordination—in other words, only when integrating changes applied to the shared model by both bounded contexts will require more effort than coordinating the changes in the shared codebase.

The difference between the integration and duplication costs depends on the volatility of the model. The more frequently it changes, the higher the integration costs will be. Therefore, the shared kernel will naturally be applied for the subdomains that change the most: the core subdomains.

In a sense, the shared kernel pattern contradicts the principles of bounded contexts introduced in the previous chapter. If the participating bounded contexts are not implemented by the same team, introducing a shared kernel contradicts the principle that a single team should own a bounded context. The overlapping model—the shared kernel—is, in effect, being developed by multiple teams.

That's the reason why the use of a shared kernel has to be justified. It's a pragmatic exception that should be considered carefully. A common use case for implementing a shared kernel is when communication or collaboration issues prevent implementing the partnership pattern—for example, because of geographical constraints or organizational politics. Implementing a closely related functionality without proper coordination will result in integration issues, desynchronized models, and arguments about which model is better designed. Minimizing the shared kernel's scope controls the scope of cascading changes, and triggering integration tests for each change is a way to enforce early detection of integration issues.

Another common use case for applying the shared kernel pattern, albeit a temporary one, is the gradual modernization of a legacy system. In such a scenario, the shared codebase can be a pragmatic intermediate solution for gradually decomposing the system into bounded contexts.

Finally, a shared kernel can be a good fit for integrating bounded contexts owned and implemented by the same team. In such a case, an ad hoc integration of the bounded contexts—a partnership—can "wash out" the contexts' boundaries over time. A shared kernel can be used for explicitly defining the bounded contexts' integration contracts.

Customer–Supplier

The second group of collaboration patterns we'll examine is the customer–supplier patterns. As shown in Figure 4-3, one of the bounded contexts—the supplier—provides a service for its customers. The service provider is "upstream" and the customer or consumer is "downstream."

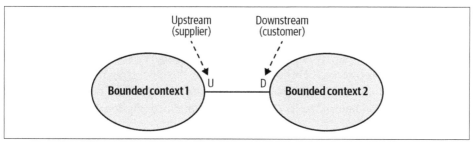

Figure 4-3. Customer–supplier relationship

Unlike in the cooperation case, both teams (upstream and downstream) can succeed independently. Consequently, in most cases we have an imbalance of power: either the upstream or the downstream team can dictate the integration contract.

This section will discuss three patterns addressing such power differences: the conformist, anticorruption layer, and open-host service patterns.

Conformist

In some cases, the balance of power favors the upstream team, which has no real motivation to support its clients' needs. Instead, it just provides the integration contract, defined according to its own model—take it or leave it. Such power imbalances can be caused by integration with service providers that are external to the organization or simply by organizational politics.

If the downstream team can accept the upstream team's model, the bounded contexts' relationship is called *conformist*. The downstream conforms to the upstream bounded context's model, as shown in Figure 4-4.

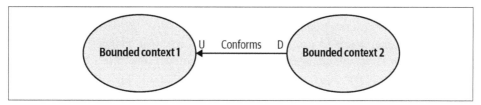

Figure 4-4. Conformist relationship

The downstream team's decision to give up some of its autonomy can be justified in multiple ways. For example, the contract exposed by the upstream team may be an industry-standard, well-established model, or it may just be good enough for the downstream team's needs.

The next pattern addresses the case in which a consumer is not willing to accept the supplier's model.

Anticorruption Layer

As in the conformist pattern, the balance of power in this relationship is still skewed toward the upstream service. However, in this case, the downstream bounded context is not willing to conform. Instead, it can translate the upstream bounded context's model into a model tailored to its own needs via an anticorruption layer, as shown in Figure 4-5.

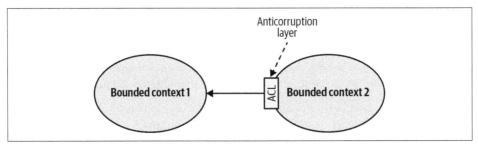

Figure 4-5. Integration through an anticorruption layer

The anticorruption layer pattern addresses scenarios in which it is not desirable or worth the effort to conform to the supplier's model, such as the following:

When the downstream bounded context contains a core subdomain
A core subdomain's model requires extra attention, and adhering to the supplier's model might impede the modeling of the problem domain.

When the upstream model is inefficient or inconvenient for the consumer's needs
If a bounded context conforms to a mess, it risks becoming a mess itself. That is often the case when integrating with legacy systems.

When the supplier's contract changes often
The consumer wants to protect its model from frequent changes. With an anticorruption layer, the changes in the supplier's model only affect the translation mechanism.

From a modeling perspective, the translation of the supplier's model isolates the downstream consumer from foreign concepts that are not relevant to its bounded context. Hence, it simplifies the consumer's ubiquitous language and model.

In Chapter 9, we will explore the different ways to implement an anticorruption layer.

Open-Host Service

This pattern addresses cases in which the power is skewed toward the consumers. The supplier is interested in protecting its consumers and providing the best service possible.

To protect the consumers from changes in its implementation model, the upstream supplier decouples the implementation model from the public interface. This decoupling allows the supplier to evolve its implementation and public models at different rates, as shown in Figure 4-6.

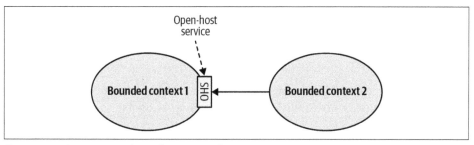

Figure 4-6. Integration through an open-host service

The supplier's public interface is not intended to conform to its ubiquitous language. Instead, it is intended to expose a protocol convenient for the consumers, expressed in an integration-oriented language. As such, the public protocol is called the *published language*.

In a sense, the open-host service pattern is a reversal of the anticorruption layer pattern: instead of the consumer, the supplier implements the translation of its internal model.

Decoupling the bounded context's implementation and integration models gives the upstream bounded context the freedom to evolve its implementation without affecting the downstream contexts. Of course, that's only possible if the modified implementation model can be translated into the published language the consumers are already using.

Furthermore, the integration model's decoupling allows the upstream bounded context to simultaneously expose multiple versions of the published language, allowing the consumer to migrate to the new version gradually (see Figure 4-7).

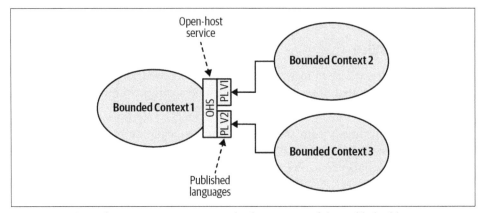

Figure 4-7. Open-host service exposing multiple versions of the published language

Separate Ways

The last collaboration option is not to collaborate at all. This pattern can arise for different reasons, in cases where the teams are unwilling or unable to collaborate. We'll look at a few of them here.

Communication Issues

A common reason for avoiding collaboration is communication difficulties driven by the organization's size or internal politics. When teams have a hard time collaborating and agreeing, it may be more cost-effective to go their separate ways and duplicate functionality in multiple bounded contexts.

Generic Subdomains

The nature of the duplicated subdomain can also be a reason for teams to go their separate ways. When the subdomain in question is generic, and if the generic solution is easy to integrate, it may be more cost-effective to integrate it locally in each bounded context. An example is a logging framework; it would make little sense for one of the bounded contexts to expose it as a service. The added complexity of integrating such a solution would outweigh the benefit of not duplicating the functionality in multiple contexts. Duplicating the functionality would be less expensive than collaborating.

Model Differences

Differences in the bounded contexts' models can also be a reason to go with a separate ways collaboration. The models may be so different that a conformist relationship is impossible, and implementing an anticorruption layer would be more expensive than duplicating the functionality. In such a case, it is again more cost-effective for the teams to go their separate ways.

 The separate ways pattern should be avoided when integrating core subdomains. Duplicating the implementation of such subdomains would defy the company's strategy to implement them in the most effective and optimized way.

Context Map

After analyzing the integration patterns between a system's bounded contexts, we can plot them on a context map, as shown in Figure 4-8.

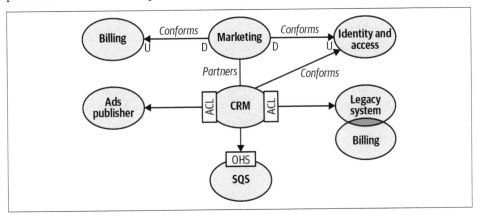

Figure 4-8. Context map

The context map is a visual representation of the system's bounded contexts and the integrations between them. This visual notation gives valuable strategic insight on multiple levels:

High-level design
A context map provides an overview of the system's components and the models they implement.

Communication patterns
A context map depicts the communication patterns among teams—for example, which teams are collaborating and which prefer "less intimate" integration patterns, such as the anticorruption layer and separate ways patterns.

Organizational issues
A context map can give insight into organizational issues. For example, what does it mean if a certain upstream team's downstream consumers all resort to

implementing an anticorruption layer, or if all implementations of the separate ways pattern are concentrated around the same team?

Maintenance

Ideally, a context map should be introduced into a project right from the get-go, and be updated to reflect additions of new bounded contexts and modifications to the existing one.

Since the context map potentially contains information originating from the work of multiple teams, it's best to define the maintenance of the context map as a shared effort: each team is responsible for updating its own integrations with other bounded contexts.

A context map can be managed and maintained as code, using a tool like Context Mapper (*https://contextmapper.org*).

Limitations

It's important to note that charting a context map can be a challenging task. When a system's bounded contexts encompass multiple subdomains, there can be multiple integration patterns at play. For example, in Figure 4-9, you can see two bounded contexts with two integration patterns: partnership and anticorruption layer.

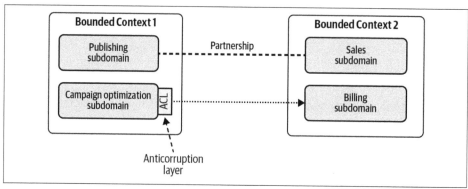

Figure 4-9. Complicated context map

Moreover, even if bounded contexts are limited to a single subdomain, there still can be multiple integration patterns at play—for example, if the subdomains' modules require different integration strategies.

Conclusion

Bounded contexts are not independent. They have to interact with one another. The following patterns define different ways bounded contexts can be integrated:

Partnership
Bounded contexts are integrated in an ad hoc manner.

Shared kernel
Two or more bounded contexts are integrated by sharing a limited overlapping model that belongs to all participating bounded contexts.

Conformist
The consumer conforms to the service provider's model.

Anticorruption layer
The consumer translates the service provider's model into a model that fits the consumer's needs.

Open-host service
The service provider implements a published language—a model optimized for its consumers' needs.

Separate ways
It's less expensive to duplicate particular functionality than to collaborate and integrate it.

The integrations among the bounded contexts can be plotted on a context map. This tool gives insight into the system's high-level design, communication patterns, and organizational issues.

Now that you have learned about the domain-driven design tools and techniques for analyzing and modeling business domains, we will shift our perspective from strategy to tactics. In Part II, you'll learn different ways to implement domain logic, organize high-level architecture, and coordinate communication between a system's components.

Exercises

1. Which integration pattern should never be used for a core subdomain?

   a. Shared kernel

   b. Open-host service

   c. Anticorruption layer

   d. Separate ways

2. Which downstream subdomain is more likely to implement an anticorruption layer?

    a. Core subdomain

    b. Supporting subdomain

    c. Generic subdomain

    d. B and C

3. Which upstream subdomain is more likely to implement an open-host service?

    a. Core subdomain

    b. Supporting subdomain

    c. Generic subdomain

    d. A and B

4. Which integration pattern, in a sense, violates bounded contexts' ownership boundaries?

    a. Partnership.

    b. Shared kernel.

    c. Separate ways.

    d. No integration pattern should ever break the bounded contexts' ownership boundaries.

PART II

Tactical Design

In Part I, we discussed the "what" and "why" of software: you learned to analyze business domains, identify subdomains and their strategic value, and turn the knowledge of business domains into the design of bounded contexts—software components implementing different models of the business domain.

In this part of the book, we will turn from strategy to tactics: the "how" of software design:

- In Chapters 5 through 7, you will learn business logic implementation patterns that allow the code to speak the ubiquitous language of its bounded context. Chapter 5 introduces two patterns that accommodate a relatively simple business logic: transaction script and active record. Chapter 6 moves to more challenging cases and presents the domain model pattern: DDD's way of implementing complex business logic. In Chapter 7, you will learn to expand the domain model pattern by modeling the dimension of time.

- In Chapter 8, we will explore the different ways to organize a bounded context's architecture: the layered architecture, ports & adapters, and CQRS patterns. You will learn the essence of each architectural pattern and in which cases each pattern should be used.

- Chapter 9 will discuss technical concerns and implementation strategies for orchestrating the interactions among components of a system. You will learn patterns supporting the implementation of bounded context integration patterns, how to implement reliable publishing of messages, and patterns for defining complex, cross-component workflows.

Implementing Simple Business Logic

Business logic is the most important part of software. It's the reason the software is being implemented in the first place. A system's user interface can be sexy and its database can be blazing fast and scalable. But if the software is not useful for the business, it's nothing but an expensive technology demo.

As we saw in Chapter 2, not all business subdomains are created equal. Different subdomains have different levels of strategic importance and complexity. This chapter begins our exploration of the different ways to model and implement business logic code. We will start with two patterns suited for rather simple business logic: transaction script and active record.

Transaction Script

Organizes business logic by procedures where each procedure handles a single request from the presentation.
—Martin Fowler[1]

A system's public interface can be seen as a collection of business transactions that consumers can execute, as shown in Figure 5-1. These transactions can retrieve information managed by the system, modify it, or both. The pattern organizes the system's business logic based on procedures, where each procedure implements an operation that is executed by the system's consumer via its public interface. In effect, the system's public operations are used as encapsulation boundaries.

---

1 Fowler, M. (2002). *Patterns of Enterprise Application Architecture*. Boston: Addison-Wesley.

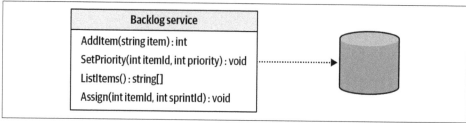

Figure 5-1. Transaction script interface

Implementation

Each procedure is implemented as a simple, straightforward procedural script. It can use a thin abstraction layer for integrating with storage mechanisms, but it is also free to access the databases directly.

The only requirement procedures have to fulfill is transactional behavior. *Each operation should either succeed or fail but can never result in an invalid state.* Even if execution of a transaction script fails at the most inconvenient moment, the system should remain consistent—either by rolling back any changes it has made up until the failure or by executing compensating actions. The transactional behavior is reflected in the pattern's name: transaction script.

Here is an example of a transaction script that converts batches of JSON files into XML files:

```
DB.StartTransaction();

var job = DB.LoadNextJob();
var json = LoadFile(job.Source);
var xml = ConvertJsonToXml(json);
WriteFile(job.Destination, xml.ToString());
DB.MarkJobAsCompleted(job);

DB.Commit()
```

It's Not That Easy!

When I introduce the transaction script pattern in my domain-driven design classes, my students often raise their eyebrows, and some even ask, "Is it worth our time? Aren't we here for the more advanced patterns and techniques?"

The thing is, the transaction script pattern is a *foundation* for the more advanced business logic implementation patterns you will learn in the forthcoming chapters. Furthermore, despite its apparent simplicity, it is the easiest pattern to get wrong. A considerable number of production issues I have helped to debug and fix, in one way or another, often boiled down to a misimplementation of the transactional behavior of the system's business logic.

Let's take a look at three common, real-life examples of data corruption that results from failing to correctly implement a transaction script.

Lack of transactional behavior

A trivial example of failing to implement transactional behavior is to issue multiple updates without an overarching transaction. Consider the following method that updates a record in the Users table and inserts a record into the VisitsLog table:

```
01  public class LogVisit
02  {
03      ...
04
05      public void Execute(Guid userId, DataTime visitedOn)
06      {
07          _db.Execute("UPDATE Users SET last_visit=@p1 WHERE user_id=@p2",
08              visitedOn, userId);
09          _db.Execute(@"INSERT INTO VisitsLog(user_id, visit_date)
10                      VALUES(@p1, @p2)", userId, visitedOn);
11      }
12  }
```

If any issue occurs after the record in the Users table was updated (line 7) but before appending the log record on line 9 succeeds, the system will end up in an inconsistent state. The Users table will be updated but no corresponding record will be written to the VisitsLog table. The issue can be due to anything from a network outage to a database timeout or deadlock, or even a crash of the server executing the process.

This can be fixed by introducing a proper transaction encompassing both data changes:

```
public class LogVisit
{
    ...

    public void Execute(Guid userId, DataTime visitedOn)
    {
        try
        {
            _db.StartTransaction();

            _db.Execute(@"UPDATE Users SET last_visit=@p1
                        WHERE user_id=@p2",
                        visitedOn, userId);

            _db.Execute(@"INSERT INTO VisitsLog(user_id, visit_date)
                        VALUES(@p1, @p2)",
                        userId, visitedOn);

            _db.Commit();
        } catch {
```

```
                    _db.Rollback();
                    throw;
                }
            }
        }
```

The fix is easy to implement due to relational databases' native support of transactions spanning multiple records. Things get more complicated when you have to issue multiple updates in a database that doesn't support multirecord transactions, or when you are working with multiple storage mechanisms that are impossible to unite in a distributed transaction. Let's see an example of the latter case.

Distributed transactions

In modern distributed systems, it's a common practice to make changes to the data in a database and then notify other components of the system about the changes by publishing messages into a message bus. Consider that in the previous example, instead of logging a visit in a table, we have to publish it to a message bus:

```
01  public class LogVisit
02  {
03      ...
04
05      public void Execute(Guid userId, DataTime visitedOn)
06      {
07          _db.Execute("UPDATE Users SET last_visit=@p1 WHERE user_id=@p2",
08                      visitedOn,userId);
09          _messageBus.Publish("VISITS_TOPIC",
10                      new { UserId = userId, VisitDate = visitedOn });
11      }
12  }
```

As in the previous example, any failure occurring after line 7 but before line 9 succeeds will corrupt the system's state. The Users table will be updated but the other components won't be notified as publishing to the message bus has failed.

Unfortunately, fixing the issue is not as easy as in the previous example. Distributed transactions spanning multiple storage mechanisms are complex, hard to scale, error prone, and therefore are usually avoided. In Chapter 8, you will learn how to use the CQRS architectural pattern to populate multiple storage mechanisms. In addition, Chapter 9 will introduce the outbox pattern, which enables reliable publishing of messages after committing changes to another database.

Let's see a more intricate example of improper implementation of transactional behavior.

Implicit distributed transactions

Consider the following deceptively simple method:

```
public class LogVisit
{
    ...

    public void Execute(Guid userId)
    {
        _db.Execute("UPDATE Users SET visits=visits+1 WHERE user_id=@p1",
                userId);
    }
}
```

Instead of tracking the last visit date as in the previous examples, this method maintains a counter of visits for each user. Calling the method increases the corresponding counter's value by 1. All the method does is update one value, in one table, residing in one database. Yet this is still a distributed transaction that can potentially lead to inconsistent state.

This example constitutes a distributed transaction because it communicates information to the databases and the external process that called the method, as demonstrated in Figure 5-2.

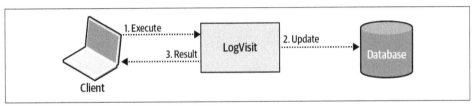

Figure 5-2. The LogVisit operation updating the data and notifying the caller of the operation's success or failure

Although the execute method is of type void, that is, it doesn't return any data, it still communicates whether the operation has succeeded or failed: if it failed, the caller will get an exception. What if the method succeeds, but the communication of the result to the caller fails? For example:

- If LogVisit is part of a REST service and there is a network outage; or
- If both LogVisit and the caller are running in the same process, but the process fails before the caller gets to track successful execution of the LogVisit action?

In both cases, the consumer will assume failure and try calling LogVisit again. Executing the LogVisit logic again will result in an incorrect increase of the counter's value. Overall, it will be increased by 2 instead of 1. As in the previous two examples, the code fails to implement the transaction script pattern correctly, and inadvertently leads to corrupting the system's state.

As in the previous example, there is no simple fix for this issue. It all depends on the business domain and its needs. In this specific example, one way to ensure transactional behavior is to make the operation *idempotent*: that is, leading to the same result even if the operation repeated multiple times.

For example, we can ask the consumer to pass the value of the counter. To supply the counter's value, the caller will have to read the current value first, increase it locally, and then provide the updated value as a parameter. Even if the operation will be executed multiple times, it won't change the end result:

```
public class LogVisit
{
    ...

    public void Execute(Guid userId, long visits)
    {
        _db.Execute("UPDATE Users SET visits = @p1 WHERE user_id=@p2",
                visits, userId);
    }
}
```

Another way to address such an issue is to use optimistic concurrency control: prior to calling the LogVisit operation, the caller has read the counter's current value and passed it to LogVisit as a parameter. LogVisit will update the counter's value only if it equals the one initially read by the caller:

```
public class LogVisit
{
    ...

    public void Execute(Guid userId, long expectedVisits)
    {
        _db.Execute(@"UPDATE Users SET visits=visits+1
                    WHERE user_id=@p1 and visits = @p2",
                    userId, visits);
    }
}
```

Subsequent executions of LogVisit with the same input parameters won't change the data, as the WHERE...visits = @prm2 condition won't be fulfilled.

When to Use Transaction Script

The transaction script pattern is well adapted to the most straightforward problem domains in which the business logic resembles simple procedural operations. For example, in extract-transform-load (ETL) operations, each operation extracts data from a source, applies transformation logic to convert it into another form, and loads the result into the destination store. This process is shown in Figure 5-3.

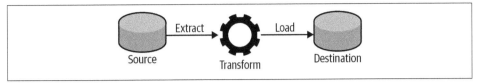

Figure 5-3. Extract-transform-load data flow

The transaction script pattern naturally fits supporting subdomains where, by definition, the business logic is simple. It can also be used as an adapter for integration with external systems—for example, generic subdomains, or as a part of an anticorruption layer (more on that in Chapter 9).

The main advantage of the transaction script pattern is its simplicity. It introduces minimal abstractions and minimizes the overhead both in runtime performance and in understanding the business logic. That said, this simplicity is also the pattern's disadvantage. The more complex the business logic gets, the more it's prone to duplicate business logic across transactions, and consequently, to result in inconsistent behavior—when the duplicated code goes out of sync. As a result, transaction script should never be used for core subdomains, as this pattern won't cope with the high complexity of a core subdomain's business logic.

This simplicity earned the transaction script a dubious reputation. Sometimes the pattern is even treated as an antipattern. After all, if complex business logic is implemented as a transaction script, sooner rather than later it's going to turn into an unmaintainable, big ball of mud. It should be noted, however, that despite the simplicity, the transaction script pattern is ubiquitous in software development. All the business logic implementation patterns that we will discuss in this and the following chapters, in one way or another, are based on the transaction script pattern.

Active Record

> *An object that wraps a row in a database table or view, encapsulates the database access, and adds domain logic on that data.*
>   —Martin Fowler[2]

Like the transaction script pattern, active record supports cases where the business logic is simple. Here, however, the business logic may operate on more complex data structures. For example, instead of flat records, we can have more complicated object trees and hierarchies, as shown in Figure 5-4.

---

2 Fowler, M. (2002). *Patterns of Enterprise Application Architecture*. Boston: Addison-Wesley.

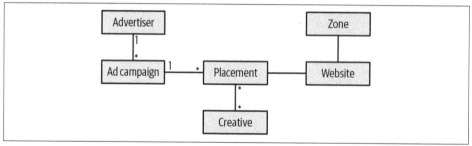

Figure 5-4. A more complicated data model with one-to-many and many-to-many relationships

Operating on such data structures via a simple transaction script would result in lots of repetitive code. The mapping of the data to an in-memory representation would be duplicated all over.

Implementation

Consequently, this pattern uses dedicated objects, known as active records, to represent complicated data structures. Apart from the data structure, these objects also implement data access methods for creating, reading, updating, and deleting records—the so-called CRUD operations. As a result, the active record objects are coupled to an object-relational mapping (ORM) or some other data access framework. The pattern's name is derived from the fact that each data structure is "active"; that is, it implements data access logic.

As in the previous pattern, the system's business logic is organized in a transaction script. The difference between the two patterns is that in this case, instead of accessing the database directly, the transaction script manipulates active record objects. When it completes, the operation has to either complete or fail as an atomic transaction:

```
public class CreateUser
{
    ...

    public void Execute(userDetails)
    {
        try
        {
            _db.StartTransaction();

            var user = new User();
            user.Name = userDetails.Name;
            user.Email = userDetails.Email;
            user.Save();
```

```
            _db.Commit();
        } catch {
            _db.Rollback();
            throw;
        }
    }
}
```

The pattern's goal is to encapsulate the complexity of mapping the in-memory object to the database's schema. In addition to being responsible for persistence, the active record objects can contain business logic; for example, validating new values assigned to the fields, or even implementing business-related procedures that manipulate an object's data. That said, the distinctive feature of an active record object is the separation of data structures and behavior (business logic). Usually, an active record's fields have public getters and setters that allow external procedures to modify its state.

When to Use Active Record

Because an active record is essentially a transaction script that optimizes access to databases, this pattern can only support relatively simple business logic, such as CRUD operations, which, at most, validate the user's input.

Accordingly, as in the case of the transaction script pattern, the active record pattern lends itself to supporting subdomains, integration of external solutions for generic subdomains, or model transformation tasks. The difference between the patterns is that active record addresses the complexity of mapping complicated data structures to a database's schema.

The active record pattern is also known as an *anemic domain model antipattern*; in other words, an improperly designed domain model. I prefer to restrain from the negative connotation of the words *anemic* and *antipattern*. This pattern is a tool. Like any tool, it can solve problems, but it can potentially introduce more harm than good when applied in the wrong context. There is nothing wrong with using active records when the business logic is simple. Furthermore, using a more elaborate pattern when implementing simple business logic will also result in harm by introducing accidental complexity. In the next chapter, you will learn what a domain model is and how it differs from an active record pattern.

 It's important to stress that in this context, *active record* refers to the design pattern, not the Active Record framework. The pattern name was coined in *Patterns of Enterprise Application Architecture* by Martin Fowler. The framework came later as one way to implement the pattern. In our context, we are talking about the design pattern and the concepts behind it, not a specific implementation.

Be Pragmatic

Although business data is important and the code we design and build should protect its integrity, there are cases in which a pragmatic approach is more desirable.

Especially at high levels of scale, there are cases when data consistency guarantees can be relaxed. Check whether corrupting the state of one record out of 1 million is really a showstopper for the business and whether it can negatively affect the performance and profitability of the business. For example, let's assume you are building a system that ingests billions of events per day from IoT devices. Is it a big deal if 0.001% of the events will be duplicated or lost?

As always, there are no universal laws. It all depends on the business domain you are working in. It's OK to "cut corners" where possible; just make sure you evaluate the risks and business implications.

Conclusion

In this chapter, we covered two patterns for implementing business logic:

Transaction script
> This pattern organizes the system's operations as simple, straightforward procedural scripts. The procedures ensure that each operation is transactional—either it succeeds or it fails. The transaction script pattern lends itself to supporting subdomains, with business logic resembling simple, ETL-like operations.

Active record
> When the business logic is simple but operates on complicated data structures, you can implement those data structures as active records. An active record object is a data structure that provides simple CRUD data access methods.

The two patterns discussed in this chapter are oriented toward cases of rather simple business logic. In the next chapter, we will turn to more complex business logic and discuss how to tackle the complexity using the domain model pattern.

Exercises

1. Which of the discussed patterns should be used for implementing a core subdomain's business logic?

   a. Transaction script.

   b. Active record.

   c. Neither of these patterns can be used to implement a core subdomain.

   d. Both can be used to implement a core subdomain.

2. Consider the following code:

```
public void CreateTicket(TicketData data)
{
    var agent = FindLeastBusyAgent();

    agent.ActiveTickets = agent.ActiveTickets + 1;
    agent.Save();

    var ticket = new Ticket();
    ticket.Id = Guid.New();
    ticket.Data = data;
    ticket.AssignedAgent = agent;
    ticket.Save();

    _alerts.Send(agent, "You have a new ticket!");
}
```

Assuming there is no high-level transaction mechanism, what potential data consistency issues can you spot here?

a. On receiving a new ticket, the assigned agent's counter of active tickets can be increased by more than 1.

b. An agent's counter of active tickets can be increased by 1 but the agent won't get assigned any new tickets.

c. An agent can get a new ticket but won't be notified about it.

d. All of the above issues are possible.

3. In the preceding code, there is at least one more possible edge case that can corrupt the system's state. Can you spot it?

4. Going back to the example of WolfDesk in the book's Preface, what parts of the system could potentially be implemented as a transaction script or an active record?

CHAPTER 6

Tackling Complex Business Logic

The previous chapter discussed two patterns addressing cases of relatively simple business logic: transaction script and active record. This chapter continues the topic of implementing business logic and introduces a pattern oriented for complicated business logic: the domain model pattern.

History

As with both the transaction script and active record patterns, the domain model pattern was introduced initially in Martin Fowler's book *Patterns of Enterprise Application Architecture*. Fowler concluded his discussion of the pattern by saying, "Eric Evans is currently writing a book on building Domain Models." The referenced book is Evans's seminal work, *Domain-Driven Design: Tackling Complexity in the Heart of Software*.

In his book, Evans presents a set of patterns aimed at tightly relating the code to the underlying model of the business domain: aggregate, value objects, repositories, and others. These patterns closely follow where Fowler left off in his book and resemble an effective set of tools for implementing the domain model pattern.

The patterns that Evans introduced are often referred to as *tactical domain-driven design*. To eliminate the confusion of thinking that implementing domain-driven design necessarily entails the use of these patterns to implement business logic, I prefer to stick with Fowler's original terminology. The pattern is "domain model," and the aggregates and value objects are its building blocks.

Domain Model

The domain model pattern is intended to cope with cases of complex business logic. Here, instead of CRUD interfaces, we deal with complicated state transitions, business rules, and invariants: rules that have to be protected at all times.

Let's assume we are implementing a help desk system. Consider the following excerpt from the requirements that describes the logic controlling the lifecycles of support tickets:

- Customers open support tickets describing issues they are facing.
- Both the customer and the support agent append messages, and all the correspondence is tracked by the support ticket.
- Each ticket has a priority: low, medium, high, or urgent.
- An agent should offer a solution within a set time limit (SLA) that is based on the ticket's priority.
- If the agent doesn't reply within the SLA, the customer can escalate the ticket to the agent's manager.
- Escalation reduces the agent's response time limit by 33%.
- If the agent didn't open an escalated ticket within 50% of the response time limit, it is automatically reassigned to a different agent.
- Tickets are automatically closed if the customer doesn't reply to the agent's questions within seven days.
- Escalated tickets cannot be closed automatically or by the agent, only by the customer or the agent's manager.
- A customer can reopen a closed ticket only if it was closed in the past seven days.

These requirements form an entangled net of dependencies among the different rules, all affecting the support ticket's lifecycle management logic. This is not a CRUD data entry screen, as we discussed in the previous chapter. Attempting to implement this logic using active record objects will make it easy to duplicate the logic and corrupt the system's state by misimplementing some of the business rules.

Implementation

A domain model is an object model of the domain that incorporates both behavior and data.[1] DDD's tactical patterns—aggregates, value objects, domain events, and domain services—are the building blocks of such an object model.[2]

All of these patterns share a common theme: they put the business logic first. Let's see how the domain model addresses different design concerns.

Complexity

The domain's business logic is already inherently complex, so the objects used for modeling it should not introduce any additional accidental complexities. The model should be devoid of any infrastructural or technological concerns, such as implementing calls to databases or other external components of the system. This restriction requires the model's objects to be *plain old objects*, objects implementing business logic without relying on or directly incorporating any infrastructural components or frameworks.[3]

Ubiquitous language

The emphasis on business logic instead of technical concerns makes it easier for the domain model's objects to follow the terminology of the bounded context's ubiquitous language. In other words, this pattern allows the code to "speak" the ubiquitous language and to follow the domain experts' mental models.

Building Blocks

Let's look at the central domain model building blocks, or tactical patterns, offered by DDD: value objects, aggregates, and domain services.

Value object

A value object is an object that can be identified by the composition of its values. For example, consider a color object:

```
class Color
{
    int _red;
    int _green;
```

---

1 Fowler, M. (2002). *Patterns of Enterprise Application Architecture*. Boston: Addison-Wesley.

2 All the code samples in this chapter will use an object-oriented programming language. However, the discussed concepts are not limited to OOP and are as relevant for the functional programming paradigm.

3 POCOs in .NET, POJOs in Java, POPOs in Python, etc.

```
    int _blue;
}
```

The composition of the values of the three fields red, green, and blue defines a color. Changing the value of one of the fields will result in a new color. No two colors can have the same values. Also, two instances of the same color must have the same values. Therefore, no explicit identification field is needed to identify colors.

The ColorId field shown in Figure 6-1 is not only redundant, but actually creates an opening for bugs. You could create two rows with the same values of red, green, and blue, but comparing the values of ColorId would not reflect that this is the same color.

Colors

color-id	red	green	blue
1	255	255	0
2	0	128	128
3	0	0	255
4	0	0	255

Figure 6-1. Redundant ColorId field, making it possible to have two rows with the same values

Ubiquitous language. Relying exclusively on the language's standard library's primitive data types—such as strings, integers, or dictionaries—to represent concepts of the business domain is known as the primitive obsession[4] code smell. For example, consider the following class:

```
class Person
{
    private int    _id;
    private string _firstName;
    private string _lastName;
    private string _landlinePhone;
    private string _mobilePhone;
    private string _email;
    private int    _heightMetric;
    private string _countryCode;

    public Person(...) {...}
```

---

4 "Primitive Obsession." (n.d.) Retrieved June 13, 2021, from *https://wiki.c2.com/?PrimitiveObsession*.

```
    }

    static void Main(string[] args)
    {
        var dave = new Person(
            id: 30217,
            firstName: "Dave",
            lastName: "Ancelovici",
            landlinePhone: "023745001",
            mobilePhone: "0873712503",
            email: "dave@learning-ddd.com",
            heightMetric: 180,
            countryCode: "BG");
    }
```

In the preceding implementation of the Person class, most of the values are of type String and they are assigned based on convention. For example, the input to the landlinePhone should be a valid landline phone number, and the countryCode should be a valid, two-letter, uppercased country code. Of course, the system cannot trust the user to always supply correct values, and as a result, the class has to validate all input fields.

This approach presents multiple design risks. First, the validation logic tends to be duplicated. Second, it's hard to enforce calling the validation logic before the values are used. It will become even more challenging in the future, when the codebase will be evolved by other engineers.

Compare the following alternative design of the same object, this time leveraging value objects:

```
    class Person {
        private PersonId     _id;
        private Name         _name;
        private PhoneNumber  _landline;
        private PhoneNumber  _mobile;
        private EmailAddress _email;
        private Height       _height;
        private CountryCode  _country;

        public Person(...) { ... }
    }

    static void Main(string[] args)
    {
        var dave = new Person(
            id:       new PersonId(30217),
            name:     new Name("Dave", "Ancelovici"),
            landline: PhoneNumber.Parse("023745001"),
            mobile:   PhoneNumber.Parse("0873712503"),
            email:    Email.Parse("dave@learning-ddd.com"),
            height:   Height.FromMetric(180),
```

```
        country:  CountryCode.Parse("BG"));
    }
```

First, notice the increased clarity. Take, for example, the country variable. There is no need to elaborately call it "countryCode" to communicate the intent of it holding a country code and not, for example, a full country name. The value object makes the intent clear, even with shorter variable names.

Second, there is no need to validate the values before the assignment, as the validation logic resides in the value objects themselves. However, a value object's behavior is not limited to mere validation. Value objects shine brightest when they centralize the business logic that manipulates the values. The cohesive logic is implemented in one place and is easy to test. Most importantly, value objects express the business domain's concepts: they make the code speak the ubiquitous language.

Let's see how representing the concepts of height, phone numbers, and colors as value objects makes the resultant type system rich and intuitive to use.

Compared to an integer-based value, the Height value object both makes the intent clear and decouples the measurement from a specific measurement unit. For example, the Height value object can be initialized using both metric and imperial units, making it easy to convert from one unit to another, generating string representation, and comparing values of different units:

```
var heightMetric = Height.Metric(180);
var heightImperial = Height.Imperial(5, 3);

var string1 = heightMetric.ToString();           // "180cm"
var string2 = heightImperial.ToString();          // "5 feet 3 inches"
var string3 = heightMetric.ToImperial().ToString(); // "5 feet 11 inches"

var firstIsHigher = heightMetric > heightImperial; // true
```

The PhoneNumber value object can encapsulate the logic of parsing a string value, validating it, and extracting different attributes of the phone number; for example, the country it belongs to and the phone number's type—landline or mobile:

```
var phone = PhoneNumber.Parse("+359877123503");
var country = phone.Country;                      // "BG"
var phoneType = phone.PhoneType;                  // "MOBILE"
var isValid = PhoneNumber.IsValid("+972120266680"); // false
```

The following example demonstrates the power of a value object when it encapsulates all of the business logic that manipulates the data and produces new instances of the value object:

```
var red = Color.FromRGB(255, 0, 0);
var green = Color.Green;
var yellow = red.MixWith(green);
var yellowString = yellow.ToString();             // "#FFFF00"
```

As you can see in the preceding examples, value objects eliminate the need for conventions—for example, the need to keep in mind that this string is an email and the other string is a phone number—and instead makes using the object model less error prone and more intuitive.

Implementation. Since a change to any of the fields of a value object results in a different value, value objects are implemented as immutable objects. A change to one of the value object's fields conceptually creates a different value—a different instance of a value object. Therefore, when an executed action results in a new value, as in the following case, which uses the MixWith method, it doesn't modify the original instance but instantiates and returns a new one:

```
public class Color
{
    public readonly byte Red;
    public readonly byte Green;
    public readonly byte Blue;

    public Color(byte r, byte g, byte b)
    {
        this.Red = r;
        this.Green = g;
        this.Blue = b;
    }

    public Color MixWith(Color other)
    {
        return new Color(
            r: (byte) Math.Min(this.Red + other.Red, 255),
            g: (byte) Math.Min(this.Green + other.Green, 255),
            b: (byte) Math.Min(this.Blue + other.Blue, 255)
        );
    }

    ...
}
```

Since the equality of value objects is based on their values rather than on an id field or reference, it's important to override and properly implement the equality checks. For example, in C#:[5]

```
public class Color
{
    ...

    public override bool Equals(object obj)
```

---

5 In C# 9.0, the new type record implements value-based equality and thus doesn't require overriding the equality operators.

```
    {
        var other = obj as Color;
        return other != null &&
            this.Red == other.Red &&
            this.Green == other.Green &&
            this.Blue == other.Blue;
    }

    public static bool operator == (Color lhs, Color rhs)
    {
        if (Object.ReferenceEquals(lhs, null)) {
            return Object.ReferenceEquals(rhs, null);
        }
        return lhs.Equals(rhs);
    }

    public static bool operator != (Color lhs, Color rhs)
    {
        return !(lhs == rhs);
    }

    public override int GetHashCode()
    {
        return ToString().GetHashCode();
    }

    ...
}
```

Although using a core library's Strings to represent domain-specific values contradicts the notion of value objects, in .NET, Java, and other languages the string type is implemented exactly as a value object. Strings are immutable, as all operations result in a new instance. Moreover, the string type encapsulates a rich behavior that creates new instances by manipulating the values of one or more strings: trim, concatenate multiple strings, replace characters, substring, and other methods.

When to use value objects.   The simple answer is, whenever you can. Not only do value objects make the code more expressive and encapsulate business logic that tends to spread apart, but the pattern makes the code safer. Since value objects are immutable, the value objects' behavior is free of side effects and is thread safe.

From a business domain perspective, a useful rule of thumb is to use value objects for the domain's elements that describe properties of other objects. This namely applies to properties of entities, which are discussed in the next section. The examples you saw earlier used value objects to describe a person, including their ID, name, phone numbers, email, and so on. Other examples of using value objects include various statuses, passwords, and more business domain–specific concepts that can be identified by their values and thus do not require an explicit identification field. An especially important opportunity to introduce a value object is when modeling money and

---

other monetary values. Relying on primitive types to represent money not only limits your ability to encapsulate all money-related business logic in one place, but also often leads to dangerous bugs, such as rounding errors and other precision-related issues.

Entities

An *entity* is the opposite of a value object. It requires an explicit identification field to distinguish between the different instances of the entity. A trivial example of an entity is a person. Consider the following class:

```
class Person
{
    public Name Name { get; set; }

    public Person(Name name)
    {
        this.Name = name;
    }
}
```

The class contains only one field: name (a value object). This design, however, is suboptimal because different people can be namesakes and can have exactly the same names. That, of course, doesn't make them the same person. Hence, an identification field is needed to properly identify people:

```
class Person
{
    public readonly PersonId Id;
    public Name Name { get; set; }

    public Person(PersonId id, Name name)
    {
        this.Id = id;
        this.Name = name;
    }
}
```

In the preceding code, we introduced the identification field Id of type PersonId. PersonId is a value object, and it can use any underlying data types that fit the business domain's needs. For example, the Id can be a GUID, a number, a string, or a domain-specific value such as a Social Security number.

The central requirement for the identification field is that it should be unique for each instance of the entity: for each person, in our case (Figure 6-2). Furthermore, except for very rare exceptions, the value of an entity's identification field should remain immutable throughout the entity's lifecycle. This brings us to the second conceptual difference between value objects and entities.

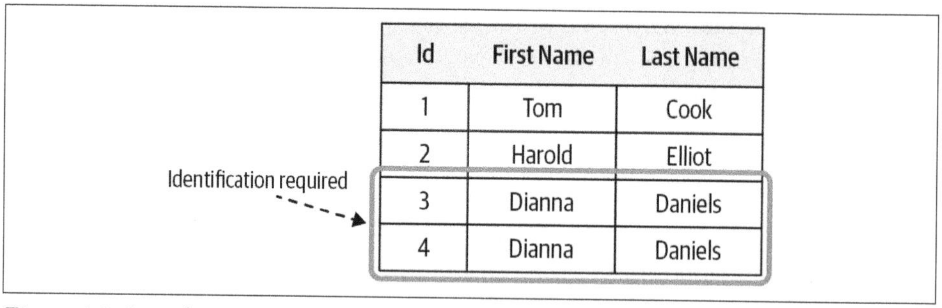

Id	First Name	Last Name
1	Tom	Cook
2	Harold	Elliot
3	Dianna	Daniels
4	Dianna	Daniels

Identification required →

Figure 6-2. Introducing an explicit identification field, allowing differentiating instances of the object even if the values of all other fields are identical

Contrary to value objects, entities are not immutable and are expected to change. Another difference between entities and value objects is that value objects describe an entity's properties. Earlier in the chapter, you saw an example of the entity `Person` and it had two value objects describing each instance: `PersonId` and `Name`.

Entities are an essential building block of any business domain. That said, you may have noticed that earlier in the chapter I didn't include "entity" in the list of the domain model's building blocks. That's not a mistake. The reason "entity" was omitted is because we don't implement entities independently, but only in the context of the aggregate pattern.

Aggregates

An aggregate is an *entity*: it requires an explicit identification field and its state is expected to change during an instance's lifecycle. However, it is much more than just an entity. The goal of the pattern is to protect the consistency of its data. Since an aggregate's data is mutable, there are implications and challenges that the pattern has to address to keep its state consistent at all times.

Consistency enforcement. Since an aggregate's state can be mutated, it creates an opening for multiple ways in which its data can become corrupted. To enforce consistency of the data, the aggregate pattern draws a clear boundary between the aggregate and its outer scope: the aggregate is a consistency enforcement boundary. The aggregate's logic has to validate all incoming modifications and ensure that the changes do not contradict its business rules.

From an implementation perspective, the consistency is enforced by allowing only the aggregate's business logic to modify its state. All processes or objects external to the aggregate are only allowed to read the aggregate's state. Its state can only be mutated by executing corresponding methods of the aggregate's public interface.

The state-modifying methods exposed as an aggregate's public interface are often referred to as *commands*, as in "a command to do something." A command can be implemented in two ways. First, it can be implemented as a plain public method of the aggregate object:

```
public class Ticket
{
    ...

    public void AddMessage(UserId from, string body)
    {
        var message = new Message(from, body);
        _messages.Append(message);
    }

    ...
}
```

Alternatively, a command can be represented as a parameter object (*https://oreil.ly/ 4hNtn*) that encapsulates all the input required for executing the command:

```
public class Ticket
{
    ...

    public void Execute(AddMessage cmd)
    {
        var message = new Message(cmd.from, cmd.body);
        _messages.Append(message);
    }

    ...
}
```

How commands are expressed in an aggregate's code is a matter of preference. I prefer the more explicit way of defining command structures and passing them polymorphically to the relevant Execute method.

An aggregate's public interface is responsible for validating the input and enforcing all of the relevant business rules and invariants. This strict boundary also ensures that all business logic related to the aggregate is implemented in one place: the aggregate itself.

This makes the application layer[6] that orchestrates operations on aggregates rather simple:[7] all it has to do is load the aggregate's current state, execute the required action, persist the modified state, and return the operation's result to the caller:

```
01  public ExecutionResult Escalate(TicketId id, EscalationReason reason)
02  {
03      try
04      {
05          var ticket = _ticketRepository.Load(id);
06          var cmd = new Escalate(reason);
07          ticket.Execute(cmd);
08          _ticketRepository.Save(ticket);
09          return ExecutionResult.Success();
10      }
11      catch (ConcurrencyException ex)
12      {
13          return ExecutionResult.Error(ex);
14      }
15  }
```

Pay attention to the concurrency check in the preceding code (line 11). It's vital to protect the consistency of an aggregate's state.[8] If multiple processes are concurrently updating the same aggregate, we have to prevent the latter transaction from blindly overwriting the changes committed by the first one. In such a case, the second process has to be notified that the state on which it had based its decisions is out of date, and it has to retry the operation.

Hence, the database used for storing aggregates has to support concurrency management. In its simplest form, an aggregate should hold a version field that will be incremented after each update:

```
class Ticket
{
    TicketId _id;
    int      _version;

    ...
}
```

When committing a change to the database, we have to ensure that the version that is being overwritten matches the one that was originally read. For example, in SQL:

---

6 Also known as a service layer, the part of the system that forwards public API actions to the domain model.

7 In essence, the application layer's operations implement the transaction script pattern. It has to orchestrate the operation as an atomic transaction. The changes to the whole aggregate either succeed or fail, but never commit a partially updated state.

8 Recall that the application layer is a collection of transaction scripts, and as we discussed in Chapter 5, concurrency management is essential to prevent competing updates from corrupting the system's data.

```
01  UPDATE tickets
02  SET ticket_status = @new_status,
03  agg_version = agg_version + 1
04  WHERE ticket_id=@id and agg_version=@expected_version;
```

This SQL statement applies changes made to the aggregate instance's state (line 2), and increases its version counter (line 3) but only if the current version equals the one that was read prior to applying changes to the aggregate's state (line 4).

Of course, concurrency management can be implemented elsewhere besides a relational database. Furthermore, document databases lend themselves more toward working with aggregates. That said, it's crucial to ensure that the database used for storing an aggregate's data supports concurrency management.

Transaction boundary. Since an aggregate's state can only be modified by its own business logic, the aggregate also acts as a transactional boundary. All changes to the aggregate's state should be committed transactionally as one atomic operation. If an aggregate's state is modified, either all the changes are committed or none of them is.

Furthermore, no system operation can assume a multi-aggregate transaction. A change to an aggregate's state can only be committed individually, one aggregate per database transaction.

The one aggregate instance per transaction forces us to carefully design an aggregate's boundaries, ensuring that the design addresses the business domain's invariants and rules. The need to commit changes in multiple aggregates signals a wrong transaction boundary, and hence, wrong aggregate boundaries.

This seems to impose a modeling limitation. What if we need to modify multiple objects in the same transaction? Let's see how the pattern addresses such situations.

Hierarchy of entities. As we discussed earlier in the chapter, we don't use entities as an independent pattern, only as part of an aggregate. Let's see the fundamental difference between entities and aggregates, and why entities are a building block of an aggregate rather than of the overarching domain model.

There are business scenarios in which multiple objects should share a transactional boundary; for example, when both can be modified simultaneously or the business rules of one object depend on the state of another object.

DDD prescribes that a system's design should be driven by its business domain. Aggregates are no exception. To support changes to multiple objects that have to be applied in one atomic transaction, the aggregate pattern resembles a hierarchy of entities, all sharing transactional consistency, as shown in Figure 6-3.

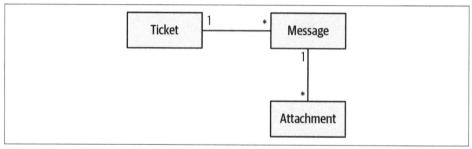

Figure 6-3. Aggregate as a hierarchy of entities

The hierarchy contains both entities and value objects, and all of them belong to the same aggregate if they are bound by the domain's business logic.

That's why the pattern is named "aggregate": it aggregates business entities and value objects that belong to the same transaction boundary.

The following code sample demonstrates a business rule that spans multiple entities belonging to the aggregate's boundary—"If an agent didn't open an escalated ticket within 50% of the response time limit, it is automatically reassigned to a different agent":

```
01   public class Ticket
02   {
03       ...
04       List<Message> _messages;
05       ...
06
07       public void Execute(EvaluateAutomaticActions cmd)
08       {
09           if (this.IsEscalated && this.RemainingTimePercentage < 0.5 &&
10               GetUnreadMessagesCount(for: AssignedAgent) > 0)
11           {
12               _agent = AssignNewAgent();
13           }
14       }
15
16       public int GetUnreadMessagesCount(UserId id)
17       {
18           return _messages.Where(x => x.To == id && !x.WasRead).Count();
19       }
20
21       ...
22   }
```

The method checks the ticket's values to see whether it is escalated and whether the remaining processing time is less than the defined threshold of 50% (line 9). Furthermore, it checks for messages that were not yet read by the current agent (line 10). If all conditions are met, the ticket is requested to be reassigned to a different agent.

The aggregate ensures that all the conditions are checked against strongly consistent data, and it won't change after the checks are completed by ensuring that all changes to the aggregate's data are performed as one atomic transaction.

Referencing other aggregates. Since all objects contained by an aggregate share the same transactional boundary, performance and scalability issues may arise if an aggregate grows too large.

The consistency of the data can be a convenient guiding principle for designing an aggregate's boundaries. Only the information that is required by the aggregate's business logic to be strongly consistent should be a part of the aggregate. All information that can be eventually consistent should reside outside of the aggregate's boundary; for example, as a part of another aggregate, as shown in Figure 6-4.

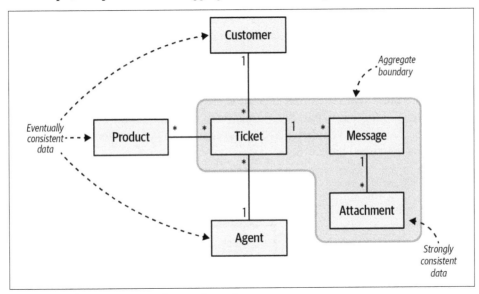

Figure 6-4. Aggregate as consistency boundary

The rule of thumb is to keep the aggregates as small as possible and include only objects that are required to be in a strongly consistent state by the aggregate's business logic:

```
public class Ticket
{
    private UserId          _customer;
    private List<ProductId> _products;
    private UserId          _assignedAgent;
    private List<Message>   _messages;

    ...
}
```

In the preceding example, the Ticket aggregate references a collection of messages, which belong to the aggregate's boundary. On the other hand, the customer, the collection of products that are relevant to the ticket, and the assigned agent do not belong to the aggregate and therefore are referenced by its ID.

The reasoning behind referencing external aggregates by ID is to reify that these objects do not belong to the aggregate's boundary, and to ensure that each aggregate has its own transactional boundary.

To decide whether an entity belongs to an aggregate or not, examine whether the aggregate contains business logic that can lead to an invalid system state if it will work on eventually consistent data. Let's go back to the previous example of reassigning the ticket if the current agent didn't read the new messages within 50% of the response time limit. What if the information about read/unread messages would be eventually consistent? In other words, it would be reasonable to receive reading acknowledgment after a certain delay. In that case, it's safe to expect a considerable number of tickets to be unnecessarily reassigned. That, of course, would corrupt the system's state. Therefore, the data in the messages belongs to the aggregate's boundary.

The aggregate root.   We saw earlier that an aggregate's state can only be modified by executing one of its commands. Since an aggregate represents a hierarchy of entities, only one of them should be designated as the aggregate's public interface—the aggregate root, as shown in Figure 6-5.

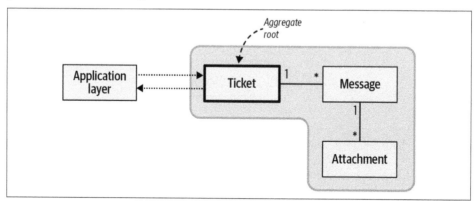

Figure 6-5. Aggregate root

Consider the following excerpt of the Ticket aggregate:

```
public class Ticket
{
    ...
    List<Message> _messages;
    ...
```

```
public void Execute(AcknowledgeMessage cmd)
{
    var message = _messages.Where(x => x.Id == cmd.id).First();
    message.WasRead = true;
}
...
}
```

In this example, the aggregate exposes a command that allows marking a specific message as read. Although the operation modifies an instance of the Message entity, it is accessible only through its aggregate root: Ticket.

In addition to the aggregate root's public interface, there is another mechanism through which the outer world can communicate with aggregates: domain events.

Domain events. A domain event is a message describing a significant event that has occurred in the business domain. For example:

- Ticket assigned
- Ticket escalated
- Message received

Since domain events describe something that has already happened, their names should be formulated in the past tense.

The goal of a domain event is to describe what has happened in the business domain and provide all the necessary data related to the event. For example, the following domain event communicates that the specific ticket was escalated, at what time, and for what reason:

```
{
    "ticket-id": "c9d286ff-3bca-4f57-94d4-4d4e490867d1",
    "event-id": 146,
    "event-type": "ticket-escalated",
    "escalation-reason": "missed-sla",
    "escalation-time": 1628970815
}
```

As with almost everything in software engineering, naming is important. Make sure the names of the domain events succinctly reflect exactly what has happened in the business domain.

Domain events are part of an aggregate's public interface. An aggregate publishes its domain events. Other processes, aggregates, or even external systems can subscribe to and execute their own logic in response to the domain events, as shown in Figure 6-6.

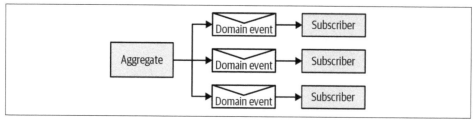

Figure 6-6. Domain events publishing flow

In the following excerpt from the `Ticket` aggregate, a new domain event is instanti-ated (line 12) and appended to the collection of the ticket's domain events (line 13):

```
01  public class Ticket
02  {
03      ...
04      private List<DomainEvent> _domainEvents;
05      ...
06
07      public void Execute(RequestEscalation cmd)
08      {
09          if (!this.IsEscalated && this.RemainingTimePercentage <= 0)
10          {
11              this.IsEscalated = true;
12              var escalatedEvent = new TicketEscalated(_id, cmd.Reason);
13              _domainEvents.Append(escalatedEvent);
14          }
15      }
16
17      ...
18  }
```

In Chapter 9, we will discuss how domain events can be reliably published to interes-ted subscribers.

Ubiquitous language.   Last but not least, aggregates should reflect the ubiquitous lan-guage. The terminology that is used for the aggregate's name, its data members, its actions, and its domain events all should be formulated in the bounded context's ubiquitous language. As Eric Evans put it, the code must be based on the same lan-guage the developers use when they speak with one another and with domain experts. This is especially important for implementing complex business logic.

Now let's take a look at the third and final building block of a domain model.

Domain services

Sooner or later, you may encounter business logic that either doesn't belong to any aggregate or value object, or that seems to be relevant to multiple aggregates. In such cases, domain-driven design proposes to implement the logic as a *domain service*.

A *domain service* is a stateless object that implements the business logic. In the vast majority of cases, such logic orchestrates calls to various components of the system to perform some calculation or analysis.

Let's go back to the example of the ticket aggregate. Recall that the assigned agent has a limited time frame in which to propose a solution to the customer. The time frame depends not only on the ticket's data (its priority and escalation status), but also on the agent's department policy regarding the SLAs for each priority and the agent's work schedule (shifts)—we can't expect the agent to respond during off-hours.

The response time frame calculation logic requires information from multiple sources: the ticket, the assigned agent's department, and the work schedule. That makes it an ideal candidate to be implemented as a domain service:

```
public class ResponseTimeFrameCalculationService
{
    ...

    public ResponseTimeframe CalculateAgentResponseDeadline(UserId agentId,
        Priority priority, bool escalated, DateTime startTime)
    {
        var policy = _departmentRepository.GetDepartmentPolicy(agentId);
        var maxProcTime = policy.GetMaxResponseTimeFor(priority);

        if (escalated) {
            maxProcTime = maxProcTime * policy.EscalationFactor;
        }

        var shifts = _departmentRepository.GetUpcomingShifts(agentId,
            startTime, startTime.Add(policy.MaxAgentResponseTime));

        return CalculateTargetTime(maxProcTime, shifts);
    }

    ...

}
```

Domain services make it easy to coordinate the work of multiple aggregates. However, it is important to always keep in mind the aggregate pattern's limitation of modifying only one instance of an aggregate in one database transaction. Domain services are not a loophole around this limitation. The rule of one instance per transaction still holds true. Instead, domain services lend themselves to implementing calculation logic that requires *reading* the data of multiple aggregates.

It is also important to point out that domain services have nothing to do with microservices, service-oriented architecture, or almost any other use of the word *service* in software engineering. It is just a stateless object used to host business logic.

Managing Complexity

As noted in this chapter's introduction, the aggregate and value object patterns were introduced as a means for tackling complexity in the implementation of business logic. Let's see the reasoning behind this.

In his book *The Choice*, business management guru Eliyahu M. Goldratt outlines a succinct yet powerful definition of system complexity. According to Goldratt, when discussing the complexity of a system we are interested in evaluating the difficulty of controlling and predicting the system's behavior. These two aspects are reflected by the system's degrees of freedom.

A system's degrees of freedom are the data points needed to describe its state. Consider the following two classes:

```
public class ClassA
{
    public int A { get; set; }
    public int B { get; set; }
    public int C { get; set; }
    public int D { get; set; }
    public int E { get; set; }
}

public class ClassB
{
    private int _a, _d;

    public int A
    {
        get => _a;
        set {
            _a = value;
            B = value / 2;
            C = value / 3;
        }
    }

    public int B { get; private set; }

    public int C { get; private set; }

    public int D
    {
        get => _d;
        set {
            _d = value;
            E = value * 2
        }
    }
}
```

```
        public int E { get; private set; }
    }
```

At first glance, it seems that ClassB is much more complex than ClassA. It has the same number of variables, but on top of that, it implements additional calculations. Is it more complex than ClassA?

Let's analyze both classes from the degrees-of-freedom perspective. How many data elements do you need to describe the state of ClassA? The answer is five: its five variables. Hence, ClassA has five degrees of freedom.

How many data elements do you need to describe the state of ClassB? If you look at the assignment logic for properties A and D, you will notice that the values of B, C, and E are functions of the values of A and D. If you know what A and D are, then you can deduce the values of the rest of the variables. Therefore, ClassB has only two degrees of freedom. You need only two values to describe its state.

Going back to the original question, which class is more difficult in terms of controlling and predicting its behavior? The answer is the one with more degrees of freedom, or ClassA. The invariants introduced in ClassB reduce its complexity. That's what both aggregate and value object patterns do: encapsulate invariants and thus reduce complexity.

All the business logic related to the state of a value object is located in its boundaries. The same is true for aggregates. An aggregate can only be modified by its own methods. Its business logic encapsulates and protects business invariants, thus reducing the degrees of freedom.

Since the domain model pattern is applied only for subdomains with complex business logic, it's safe to assume that these are core subdomains—the heart of the software.

Conclusion

The domain model pattern is aimed at cases of complex business logic. It consists of three main building blocks:

Value objects
> Concepts of the business domain that can be identified exclusively by their values and thus do not require an explicit ID field. Since a change in one of the fields semantically creates a new value, value objects are immutable.
>
> Value objects model not only data, but behavior as well: methods manipulating the values and thus initializing new value objects.

Aggregates

A hierarchy of entities sharing a transactional boundary. All of the data included in an aggregate's boundary has to be strongly consistent to implement its business logic.

The state of the aggregate, and its internal objects, can only be modified through its public interface, by executing the aggregate's commands. The data fields are read-only for external components for the sake of ensuring that all the business logic related to the aggregate resides in its boundaries.

The aggregate acts as a transactional boundary. All of its data, including all of its internal objects, has to be committed to the database as one atomic transaction.

An aggregate can communicate with external entities by publishing domain events—messages describing important business events in the aggregate's lifecycle. Other components can subscribe to the events and use them to trigger the execution of business logic.

Domain services

A stateless object that hosts business logic that naturally doesn't belong to any of the domain model's aggregates or value objects.

The domain model's building blocks tackle the complexity of the business logic by encapsulating it in the boundaries of value objects and aggregates. The inability to modify the objects' state externally ensures that all the relevant business logic is implemented in the boundaries of aggregates and value objects and won't be duplicated in the application layer.

In the next chapter, you will learn the advanced way to implement the domain model pattern, this time making the dimension of time an inherent part of the model.

Exercises

1. Which of the following statements is true?

    a. Value objects can only contain data.

    b. Value objects can only contain behavior.

    c. Value objects are immutable.

    d. Value objects' state can change.

2. What is the general guiding principle for designing the boundary of an aggregate?

   a. An aggregate can contain only one entity as only one instance of an aggregate can be included in a single database transaction.

   b. Aggregates should be designed to be as small as possible, as long as the business domain's data consistency requirements are intact.

   c. An aggregate represents a hierarchy of entities. Therefore, to maximize the consistency of the system's data, aggregates should be designed to be as wide as possible.

   d. It depends: for some business domains small aggregates are best, while in others it's more efficient to work with aggregates that are as large as possible.

3. Why can only one instance of an aggregate be committed in one transaction?

   a. To ensure that the model can perform under high load.

   b. To ensure correct transactional boundaries.

   c. There is no such requirement; it depends on the business domain.

   d. To make it possible to work with databases that do not support multirecord transactions, such as key–value and document stores.

4. Which of the following statements best describes the relationships between the building blocks of a domain model?

   a. Value objects describe entities' properties.

   b. Value objects can emit domain events.

   c. An aggregate contains one or more entities.

   d. A and C.

5. Which of the following statements is correct about differences between active records and aggregates?

   a. Active records contain only data, whereas aggregates also contain behavior.

   b. An aggregate encapsulates all of its business logic, but business logic manipulating an active record can be located outside of its boundary.

   c. Aggregates contain only data, whereas active records contain both data and behavior.

   d. An aggregate contains a set of active records.

CHAPTER 7

Modeling the Dimension of Time

In the previous chapter, you learned about the domain model pattern: its building blocks, purpose, and application context. The event-sourced domain model pattern is based on the same premise as the domain model pattern. Again, the business logic is complex and belongs to a core subdomain. Moreover, it uses the same tactical patterns as the domain model: value objects, aggregates, and domain events.

The difference between these implementation patterns lies in the way the aggregates' state is persisted. The event-sourced domain model uses the event sourcing pattern to manage the aggregates' states: instead of persisting an aggregate's state, the model generates domain events describing each change and uses them as the source of truth for the aggregate's data.

This chapter starts by introducing the notion of event sourcing. Then it covers how event sourcing can be combined with the domain model pattern, making it an event-sourced domain model.

Event Sourcing

Show me your flowchart and conceal your tables, and I shall continue to be mystified. Show me your tables, and I won't usually need your flowchart; it'll be obvious.
—Fred Brooks[1]

Let's use Fred Brooks's reasoning to define the event sourcing pattern and understand how it differs from traditional modeling and persisting of data. Examine Table 7-1 and analyze what you can learn from this data about the system it belongs to.

---

1 Brooks, F. P. Jr. (1974). *The Mythical Man-Month: Essays on Software Engineering*. Reading, MA: Addison-Wesley.

Table 7-1. State-based model

lead-id	first-name	last-name	status	phone-number	followup-on	created-on	updated-on
1	Sean	Callahan	CONVERTED	555-1246		2019-01-31T 10:02:40.32Z	2019-01-31T 10:02:40.32Z
2	Sarah	Estrada	CLOSED	555-4395		2019-03-29T 22:01:41.44Z	2019-03-29T 22:01:41.44Z
3	Stephanie	Brown	CLOSED	555-1176		2019-04-15T 23:08:45.59Z	2019-04-15T 23:08:45.59Z
4	Sami	Calhoun	CLOSED	555-1850		2019-04-25T 05:42:17.07Z	2019-04-25T 05:42:17.07Z
5	William	Smith	CONVERTED	555-3013		2019-05-14T 04:43:57.51Z	2019-05-14T 04:43:57.51Z
6	Sabri	Chan	NEW_LEAD	555-2900		2019-06-19T 15:01:49.68Z	2019-06-19T 15:01:49.68Z
7	Samantha	Espinosa	NEW_LEAD	555-8861		2019-07-17T 13:09:59.32Z	2019-07-17T 13:09:59.32Z
8	Hani	Cronin	CLOSED	555-3018		2019-10-09T 11:40:17.13Z	2019-10-09T 11:40:17.13Z
9	Sian	Espinoza	FOLLOWUP_SET	555-6461	2019-12-04T 01:49:08.05Z	2019-12-04T 01:49:08.05Z	2019-12-04T 01:49:08.05Z
10	Sophia	Escamilla	CLOSED	555-4090		2019-12-06T 09:12:32.56Z	2019-12-06T 09:12:32.56Z
11	William	White	FOLLOWUP_SET	555-1187	2020-01-23T 00:33:13.88Z	2020-01-23T 00:33:13.88Z	2020-01-23T 00:33:13.88Z
12	Casey	Davis	CONVERTED	555-8101		2020-05-20T 09:52:55.95Z	2020-05-27T 12:38:44.12Z
13	Walter	Connor	NEW_LEAD	555-4753		2020-04-20T 06:52:55.95Z	2020-04-20T 06:52:55.95Z
14	Sophie	Garcia	CONVERTED	555-1284		2020-05-06T 18:47:04.70Z	2020-05-06T 18:47:04.70Z
15	Sally	Evans	PAYMENT_FAILED	555-3230		2020-06-04T 14:51:06.15Z	2020-06-04T 14:51:06.15Z
16	Scott	Chatman	NEW_LEAD	555-6953		2020-06-09T 09:07:05.23Z	2020-06-09T 09:07:05.23Z
17	Stephen	Pinkman	CONVERTED	555-2326		2020-07-20T 00:56:59.94Z	2020-07-20T 00:56:59.94Z
18	Sara	Elliott	PENDING_PAYMENT	555-2620		2020-08-12T 17:39:43.25Z	2020-08-12T 17:39:43.25Z
19	Sadie	Edwards	FOLLOWUP_SET	555-8163	2020-10-22T 12:40:03.98Z	2020-10-22T 12:40:03.98Z	2020-10-22T 12:40:03.98Z
20	William	Smith	PENDING_PAYMENT	555-9273		2020-11-13T 08:14:07.17Z	2020-11-13T 08:14:07.17Z

It's evident that the table is used to manage potential customers, or leads, in a tele-marketing system. For each lead, you can see their ID, their first and last names, when the record was created and updated, their phone number, and the lead's current status.

By examining the various statuses, we can also assume the processing cycle each potential customer goes through:

- The sales flow starts with the potential customer in the NEW_LEAD status.
- A sales call can end with the person not being interested in the offer (the lead is CLOSED), scheduling a follow-up call (FOLLOWUP_SET), or accepting the offer (PENDING_PAYMENT).
- If the payment is successful, the lead is CONVERTED into a customer. Conversely, the payment can fail—PAYMENT_FAILED.

That's quite a lot of information that we can gather just by analyzing a table's schema and the data stored in it. We can even assume what ubiquitous language was used when modeling the data. But what information is missing from that table?

The table's data documents the leads' current states, but it misses the story of how each lead got to their current state. We can't analyze what was happening during the lifecycles of leads. We don't know how many calls were made before a lead became CONVERTED. Was a purchase made right away, or was there a lengthy sales journey? Based on the historical data, is it worth trying to contact a person after multiple follow-ups, or is it more efficient to close the lead and move to a more promising prospect? None of that information is there. All we know are the leads' current states.

These questions reflect business concerns essential for optimizing the sales process. From a business standpoint, it's crucial to analyze the data and optimize the process based on the experience. One of the ways to fill in the missing information is to use event sourcing.

The event sourcing pattern introduces the dimension of time into the data model. Instead of the schema reflecting the aggregates' current state, an event sourcing–based system persists events documenting every change in an aggregate's lifecycle.

Consider the CONVERTED customer on line 12 in Table 7-1. The following listing dem-onstrates how the person's data would be represented in an event-sourced system:

```
{
    "lead-id": 12,
    "event-id": 0,
    "event-type": "lead-initialized",
    "first-name": "Casey",
    "last-name": "David",
    "phone-number": "555-2951",
```

```
        "timestamp": "2020-05-20T09:52:55.95Z"
    },
    {
        "lead-id": 12,
        "event-id": 1,
        "event-type": "contacted",
        "timestamp": "2020-05-20T12:32:08.24Z"
    },
    {
        "lead-id": 12,
        "event-id": 2,
        "event-type": "followup-set",
        "followup-on": "2020-05-27T12:00:00.00Z",
        "timestamp": "2020-05-20T12:32:08.24Z"
    },
    {
        "lead-id": 12,
        "event-id": 3,
        "event-type": "contact-details-updated",
        "first-name": "Casey",
        "last-name": "Davis",
        "phone-number": "555-8101",
        "timestamp": "2020-05-20T12:32:08.24Z"
    },
    {
        "lead-id": 12,
        "event-id": 4,
        "event-type": "contacted",
        "timestamp": "2020-05-27T12:02:12.51Z"
    },
    {
        "lead-id": 12,
        "event-id": 5,
        "event-type": "order-submitted",
        "payment-deadline": "2020-05-30T12:02:12.51Z",
        "timestamp": "2020-05-27T12:02:12.51Z"
    },
    {
        "lead-id": 12,
        "event-id": 6,
        "event-type": "payment-confirmed",
        "status": "converted",
        "timestamp": "2020-05-27T12:38:44.12Z"
    }
}
```

The events in the listing tell the customer's story. The lead was created in the system (event 0) and was contacted by a sales agent about two hours later (event 1). During the call, it was agreed that the sales agent would call back a week later (event 2), but to a different phone number (event 3). The sales agent also fixed a typo in the last name (event 3). The lead was contacted on the agreed date and time (event 4) and submitted an order (event 5). The order was to be paid in three days (event 5), but the payment was received about half an hour later (event 6), and the lead was converted into a new customer.

As we saw earlier, the customer's state can easily be projected out from these domain events. All we have to do is apply simple transformation logic sequentially to each event:

```
public class LeadSearchModelProjection
{
    public long LeadId { get; private set; }
    public HashSet<string> FirstNames { get; private set; }
    public HashSet<string> LastNames { get; private set; }
    public HashSet<PhoneNumber> PhoneNumbers { get; private set; }
    public int Version { get; private set; }

    public void Apply(LeadInitialized @event)
    {
        LeadId = @event.LeadId;
        FirstNames = new HashSet<string>();
        LastNames = new HashSet<string>();
        PhoneNumbers = new HashSet<PhoneNumber>();
        FirstNames.Add(@event.FirstName);
        LastNames.Add(@event.LastName);
        PhoneNumbers.Add(@event.PhoneNumber);
        Version = 0;
    }

    public void Apply(ContactDetailsChanged @event)
    {
        FirstNames.Add(@event.FirstName);
        LastNames.Add(@event.LastName);
        PhoneNumbers.Add(@event.PhoneNumber);
        Version += 1;
    }

    public void Apply(Contacted @event)
    {
        Version += 1;
    }

    public void Apply(FollowupSet @event)
    {
        Version += 1;
    }

    public void Apply(OrderSubmitted @event)
    {
        Version += 1;
    }

    public void Apply(PaymentConfirmed @event)
    {
```

```
            Version += 1;
        }
    }
```

Iterating an aggregate's events and feeding them sequentially into the appropriate overrides of the `Apply` method will produce precisely the state representation modeled in the table in Table 7-1.

Pay attention to the `Version` field that is incremented after applying each event. Its value represents the total number of modifications made to the business entity. Moreover, suppose we apply a subset of events. In that case, we can "travel through time": we can project the entity's state at any point of its lifecycle by applying only the relevant events. For example, if we need the entity's state in version 5, we can apply only the first five events.

Finally, we are not limited to projecting only a single state representation of the events! Consider the following scenarios.

Search

You have to implement a search. However, since a lead's contact information can be updated—first name, last name, and phone number—sales agents may not be aware of the changes applied by other agents and may want to locate leads using their contact information, including historical values. We can easily project the historical information:

```
public class LeadSearchModelProjection
{
    public long LeadId { get; private set; }
    public HashSet<string> FirstNames { get; private set; }
    public HashSet<string> LastNames { get; private set; }
    public HashSet<PhoneNumber> PhoneNumbers { get; private set; }
    public int Version { get; private set; }

    public void Apply(LeadInitialized @event)
    {
        LeadId = @event.LeadId;
        FirstNames = new HashSet<string>();
        LastNames = new HashSet<string>();
        PhoneNumbers = new HashSet<PhoneNumber>();

        FirstNames.Add(@event.FirstName);
        LastNames.Add(@event.LastName);
        PhoneNumbers.Add(@event.PhoneNumber);

        Version = 0;
    }

    public void Apply(ContactDetailsChanged @event)
    {
```

```
            FirstNames.Add(@event.FirstName);
            LastNames.Add(@event.LastName);
            PhoneNumbers.Add(@event.PhoneNumber);

            Version += 1;
        }

        public void Apply(Contacted @event)
        {
        Version += 1;
        }

        public void Apply(FollowupSet @event)
        {
        Version += 1;
        }

        public void Apply(OrderSubmitted @event)
        {
        Version += 1;
        }

        public void Apply(PaymentConfirmed @event)
        {
        Version += 1;
        }
    }
```

The projection logic uses the `LeadInitialized` and `ContactDetailsChanged` events to populate the respective sets of the lead's personal details. Other events are ignored since they do not affect the specific model's state.

Applying this projection logic to Casey Davis's events from the earlier example will result in the following state:

```
LeadId: 12
FirstNames: ['Casey']
LastNames: ['David', 'Davis']
PhoneNumbers: ['555-2951', '555-8101']
Version: 6
```

Analysis

Your business intelligence department asks you to provide a more analysis-friendly representation of the leads data. For their current research, they want to get the number of follow-up calls scheduled for different leads. Later they will filter the converted and closed leads data and use the model to optimize the sales process. Let's project the data they are asking for:

```
public class AnalysisModelProjection
{
```

```
public long LeadId { get; private set; }
public int Followups { get; private set; }
public LeadStatus Status { get; private set; }
public int Version { get; private set; }

public void Apply(LeadInitialized @event)
{
    LeadId = @event.LeadId;
    Followups = 0;
    Status = LeadStatus.NEW_LEAD;
    Version = 0;
}

public void Apply(Contacted @event)
{
    Version += 1;
}

public void Apply(FollowupSet @event)
{
    Status = LeadStatus.FOLLOWUP_SET;
    Followups += 1;
    Version += 1;
}

public void Apply(ContactDetailsChanged @event)
{
    Version += 1;
}

public void Apply(OrderSubmitted @event)
{
    Status = LeadStatus.PENDING_PAYMENT;
    Version += 1;
}

public void Apply(PaymentConfirmed @event)
{
    Status = LeadStatus.CONVERTED;
    Version += 1;
}
}
```

The preceding logic maintains a counter of the number of times follow-up events appeared in the lead's events. If we were to apply this projection to the example of the aggregate's events, it would generate the following state:

```
LeadId: 12
Followups: 1
Status: Converted
Version: 6
```

The logic implemented in the preceding examples projects the search-optimized and analysis-optimized models in-memory. However, to actually implement the required functionality, we have to persist the projected models in a database. In Chapter 8, you will learn about a pattern that allows us to do that: command-query responsibility segregation (CQRS).

Source of Truth

For the event sourcing pattern to work, all changes to an object's state should be represented and persisted as events. These events become the system's source of truth (hence the name of the pattern). This process is shown in Figure 7-1.

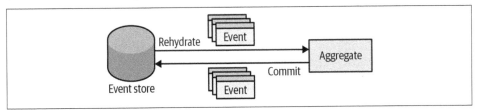

Figure 7-1. Event-sourced aggregate

The database that stores the system's events is the only strongly consistent storage: the system's source of truth. The accepted name for the database that is used for persisting events is *event store*.

Event Store

The event store should not allow modifying or deleting the events[2] since it's append-only storage. To support implementation of the event sourcing pattern, at a minimum the event store has to support the following functionality: fetch all events belonging to a specific business entity and append the events. For example:

```
interface IEventStore
{
    IEnumerable<Event> Fetch(Guid instanceId);
    void Append(Guid instanceId, Event[] newEvents, int expectedVersion);
}
```

The `expectedVersion` argument in the `Append` method is needed to implement optimistic concurrency management: when you append new events, you also specify the version of the entity on which you are basing your decisions. If it's *stale*, that is, new events were added after the expected version, the event store should raise a concurrency exception.

---

2 Except for exceptional cases, such as data migration.

In most systems, additional endpoints are needed for implementing the CQRS pattern, as we will discuss in the next chapter.

 In essence, the event sourcing pattern is nothing new. The financial industry uses events to represent changes in a ledger. A ledger is an append-only log that documents transactions. A current state (e.g., account balance) can always be deduced by "projecting" the ledger's records.

Event-Sourced Domain Model

The original domain model maintains a state representation of its aggregates and emits select domain events. The event-sourced domain model uses domain events exclusively for modeling the aggregates' lifecycles. All changes to an aggregate's state have to be expressed as domain events.

Each operation on an event-sourced aggregate follows this script:

- Load the aggregate's domain events.
- Reconstitute a state representation—project the events into a state representation that can be used to make business decisions.
- Execute the aggregate's command to execute the business logic, and consequently, produce new domain events.
- Commit the new domain events to the event store.

Going back to the example of the Ticket aggregate from Chapter 6, let's see how it would be implemented as an event-sourced aggregate.

The application service follows the script described earlier: it loads the relevant ticket's events, rehydrates the aggregate instance, calls the relevant command, and persists changes back to the database:

```
01  public class TicketAPI
02  {
03      private ITicketsRepository _ticketsRepository;
04      ...
05
06      public void RequestEscalation(TicketId id, EscalationReason reason)
07      {
08          var events = _ticketsRepository.LoadEvents(id);
09          var ticket = new Ticket(events);
10          var originalVersion = ticket.Version;
11          var cmd = new RequestEscalation(reason);
12          ticket.Execute(cmd);
13          _ticketsRepository.CommitChanges(ticket, originalVersion);
14      }
```

```
15
16      ...
17  }
```

The `Ticket` aggregate's rehydration logic in the constructor (lines 27 through 31) instantiates an instance of the state projector class, `TicketState`, and sequentially calls its `AppendEvent` method for each of the ticket's events:

```
18  public class Ticket
19  {
20      ...
21      private List<DomainEvent> _domainEvents = new List<DomainEvent>();
22      private TicketState _state;
23      ...
24
25      public Ticket(IEnumerable<IDomainEvents> events)
26      {
27          _state = new TicketState();
28          foreach (var e in events)
29          {
30              AppendEvent(e);
31          }
32      }
```

The `AppendEvent` passes the incoming events to the `TicketState` projection logic, thus generating the in-memory representation of the ticket's current state:

```
33      private void AppendEvent(IDomainEvent @event)
34      {
35          _domainEvents.Append(@event);
36          // Dynamically call the correct overload of the "Apply" method.
37          ((dynamic)state).Apply((dynamic)@event);
38      }
```

Contrary to the implementation we saw in the previous chapter, the event-sourced aggregate's `RequestEscalation` method doesn't explicitly set the `IsEscalated` flag to true. Instead, it instantiates the appropriate event and passes it to the `AppendEvent` method (lines 43 and 44):

```
39      public void Execute(RequestEscalation cmd)
40      {
41          if (!_state.IsEscalated && _state.RemainingTimePercentage <= 0)
42          {
43              var escalatedEvent = new TicketEscalated(_id, cmd.Reason);
44              AppendEvent(escalatedEvent);
45          }
46      }
47
48      ...
49  }
```

All events added to the aggregate's events collection are passed to the state projection logic in the TicketState class, where the relevant fields' values are mutated according to the events' data:

```
50  public class TicketState
51  {
52      public TicketId Id { get; private set; }
53      public int Version { get; private set; }
54      public bool IsEscalated { get; private set; }
55      ...
56      public void Apply(TicketInitialized @event)
57      {
58          Id = @event.Id;
59          Version = 0;
60          IsEscalated = false;
61          ....
62      }
63
64      public void Apply(TicketEscalated @event)
65      {
66          IsEscalated = true;
67          Version += 1;
68      }
69
70      ...
71  }
```

Now let's look at some of the advantages of leveraging event sourcing when implementing complex business logic.

Why "Event-Sourced Domain Model"?

I feel obliged to explain why I use the term *event-sourced domain model* rather than just *event sourcing*. Using events to represent state transitions—the event sourcing pattern—is possible with or without the domain model's building blocks. Therefore, I prefer the longer term to explicitly state that we are using event sourcing to represent changes in the lifecycles of the domain model's aggregates.

Advantages

Compared to the more traditional model, in which the aggregates' current states are persisted in a database, the event-sourced domain model requires more effort to model the aggregates. However, this approach brings significant advantages that make the pattern worth considering in many scenarios:

Time traveling

Just as the domain events can be used to reconstitute an aggregate's current state, they can also be used to restore all past states of the aggregate. In other words, you can always reconstitute all the past states of an aggregate.

This is often done when analyzing the system's behavior, inspecting the system's decisions, and optimizing the business logic.

Another common use case for reconstituting past states is retroactive debugging: you can revert the aggregate to the exact state it was in when a bug was observed.

Deep insight

In Part I of this book, we saw that optimizing core subdomains is strategically important for the business. Event sourcing provides deep insight into the system's state and behavior. As you learned earlier in this chapter, event sourcing provides the flexible model that allows for transforming the events into different state representations—you can always add new projections that will leverage the existing events' data to provide additional insights.

Audit log

The persisted domain events represent a strongly consistent audit log of everything that has happened to the aggregates' states. Laws oblige some business domains to implement such audit logs, and event sourcing provides this out of the box.

This model is especially convenient for systems managing money or monetary transactions. It allows us to easily trace the system's decisions and the flow of funds between accounts.

Advanced optimistic concurrency management

The classic optimistic concurrency model raises an exception when the read data becomes stale—overwritten by another process—while it is being written.

When using event sourcing, we can gain deeper insight into exactly what has happened between reading the existing events and writing the new ones. You can query the exact events that were concurrently appended to the event store and make a business domain–driven decision as to whether the new events collide with the attempted operation or the additional events are irrelevant and it's safe to proceed.

Disadvantages

So far it may seem that the event-sourced domain model is the ultimate pattern for implementing business logic and thus should be used as often as possible. Of course, that would contradict the principle of letting the business domain's needs drive the design decisions. So, let's discuss some of the challenges presented by the pattern:

Learning curve

The obvious disadvantage of the pattern is its sharp difference from the traditional techniques of managing data. Successful implementation of the pattern demands training of the team and time to get used to the new way of thinking. Unless the team already has experience implementing event-sourced systems, the learning curve has to be taken into account.

Evolving the model

Evolving an event-sourced model can be challenging. The strict definition of event sourcing says that events are immutable. But what if you need to adjust the event's schema? The process is not as simple as changing a table's schema. In fact, a whole book was written on this subject alone: *Versioning in an Event Sourced System* (*https://leanpub.com/esversioning*) by Greg Young.

Architectural complexity

Implementation of event sources introduces numerous architectural "moving parts," making the overall design more complicated. This topic will be covered in more detail in the next chapter, when we discuss the CQRS architecture.

All of these challenges are even more acute if the task at hand doesn't justify the use of the pattern and instead can be addressed by a simpler design. In Chapter 10, you will learn simple rules of thumb that can help you decide which business logic implementation pattern to use.

Frequently Asked Questions

When engineers are introduced to the event sourcing pattern, they often ask several common questions, so I find it obligatory to address them in this chapter.

Performance

Reconstituting an aggregate's state from events will negatively affect the system's performance. It will degrade as events are added. How can this even work?

Projecting events into a state representation indeed requires compute power, and that need will grow as more events are added to an aggregate's list.

It's important to benchmark a projection's impact on performance: the effect of working with hundreds or thousands of events. The results should be compared with the expected lifespan of an aggregate—the number of events expected to be recorded during an average lifespan.

In most systems, the performance hit will be noticeable only after 10,000+ events per aggregate. That said, in the vast majority of systems, an aggregate's average lifespan won't go over 100 events.

In the rare cases when projecting states does become a performance issue, another pattern can be implemented: snapshot. This pattern, shown in Figure 7-2, implements the following steps:

- A process continuously iterates new events in the event store, generates corresponding projections, and stores them in a cache.
- An in-memory projection is needed to execute an action on the aggregate. In this case:
  — The process fetches the current state projection from the cache.
  — The process fetches the events that came after the snapshot version from the event store.
  — The additional events are applied in-memory to the snapshot.

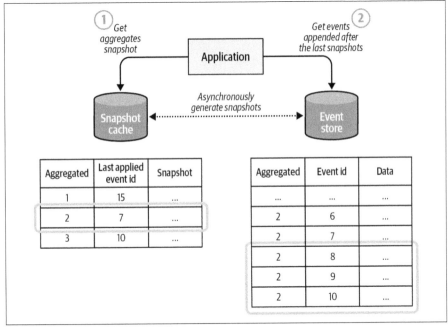

Figure 7-2. Snapshotting an aggregate's events

It's worth reiterating that the snapshot pattern is an optimization that has to be justified. If the aggregates in your system won't persist 10,000+ events, implementing the snapshot pattern is just an accidental complexity. But before you go ahead and implement the snapshot pattern, I recommend that you take a step back and double-check the aggregate's boundaries.

This model generates enormous amounts of data. Can it scale?

The event-sourced model is easy to scale. Since all aggregate-related operations are done in the context of a single aggregate, the event store can be sharded by aggregate IDs: all events belonging to an instance of an aggregate should reside in a single shard (see Figure 7-3).

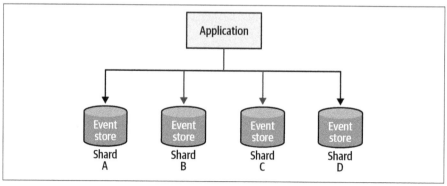

Figure 7-3. Sharding the event store

Deleting Data

The event store is an append-only database, but what if I do need to delete data physically; for example, to comply with GDPR?[3]

This need can be addressed with the forgettable payload pattern: all sensitive information is included in the events in encrypted form. The encryption key is stored in an external key–value store: the key storage, where the key is a specific aggregate's ID and the value is the encryption key. When the sensitive data has to be deleted, the encryption key is deleted from the key storage. As a result, the sensitive information contained in the events is no longer accessible.

Why Can't I Just...?

Why can't I just write logs to a text file and use it as an audit log?

Writing data both to an operational database and to a logfile is an error-prone operation. In its essence, it's a transaction against two storage mechanisms: the database and the file. If the first one fails, the second one has to be rolled back. For example, if a database transaction fails, no one cares to delete the prior log messages. Hence, such logs are not consistent, but rather, eventually inconsistent.

---

3 General Data Protection Regulation. (n.d.) Retrieved June 14, 2021, from Wikipedia (*https://oreil.ly/08px7*).

Why can't I keep working with a state-based model, but in the same database transaction, append logs to a logs table?

From an infrastructural perspective, this approach does provide consistent synchronization between the state and the log records. However, it is still error prone. What if the engineer who will be working on the codebase in the future forgets to append an appropriate log record?

Furthermore, when the state-based representation is used as the source of truth, the additional log table's schema usually degrades into chaos quickly. There is no way to enforce that all required information is written and that it is written in the correct format.

Why can't I just keep working with a state-based model but add a database trigger that will take a snapshot of the record and copy it into a dedicated "history" table?

This approach overcomes the previous one's drawback: no explicit manual calls are needed to append records to the log table. That said, the resultant history only includes the dry facts: what fields were changed. It misses the business contexts: why the fields were changed. The lack of "why" drastically limits the ability to project additional models.

Conclusion

This chapter explained the event sourcing pattern and its application for modeling the dimension of time in the domain model's aggregates.

In an event-sourced domain model, all changes to an aggregate's state are expressed as a series of domain events. That's in contrast to the more traditional approaches in which a state change just updates a record in the databases. The resultant domain events can be used to project the aggregate's current state. Moreover, the event-based model gives us the flexibility to project the events into multiple representation models, each optimized for a specific task.

This pattern fits cases in which it's crucial to have deep insight into the system's data, whether for analysis and optimization or because an audit log is required by law.

This chapter completes our exploration of the different ways to model and implement business logic. In the next chapter, we will shift our attention to patterns belonging to a higher scope: architectural patterns.

Exercises

1. Which of the following statements is correct regarding the relationship between domain events and value objects?

   a. Domain events use value objects to describe what has happened in the business domain.

   b. When implementing an event-sourced domain model, value objects should be refactored into event-sourced aggregates.

   c. Value objects are relevant for the domain model pattern, and are replaced by domain events in the event-sourced domain model.

   d. All of the statements are incorrect.

2. Which of the following statements is correct regarding the options of projecting state from a series of events?

   a. A single state representation can be projected from an aggregate's events.

   b. Multiple state representations can be projected, but the domain events have to be modeled in a way that supports multiple projections.

   c. Multiple state representations can be projected and you can always add additional projections in the future.

   d. All of the statements are incorrect.

3. Which of the following statements is correct regarding the difference between state-based and event-sourced aggregates?

   a. An event-sourced aggregate can produce domain events, while a state-based aggregate cannot produce domain events.

   b. Both variants of the aggregate pattern produce domain events, but only event-sourced aggregates use domain events as the source of truth.

   c. Event-sourced aggregates ensure that domain events are generated for every state transition.

   d. Both B and C are correct.

4. Going back to the WolfDesk company described in the book's Preface, which functionality of the system lends itself to be implemented as an event-sourced domain model?

CHAPTER 8

Architectural Patterns

The tactical patterns discussed up to this point in the book defined the different ways to model and implement business logic. In this chapter, we will explore tactical design decisions in a broader context: the different ways to orchestrate the interactions and dependencies between a system's components.

Business Logic Versus Architectural Patterns

Business logic is the most important part of software; however, it is not the only part of a software system. To implement functional and nonfunctional requirements, the codebase has to fulfill more responsibilities. It has to interact with users to gather input and provide output, and it has to use different storage mechanisms to persist state and integrate with external systems and information providers.

The variety of concerns that a codebase has to take care of makes it easy for its business logic to become diffused among the different components: that is, for some of the logic to be implemented in the user interface or database, or be duplicated in different components. Lacking strict organization in implementation concerns makes the codebase hard to change. When the business logic has to change, it may not be evident what parts of the codebase have to be affected by the change. The change may have unexpected effects on seemingly unrelated parts of the system. Conversely, it may be easy to miss code that has to be modified. All of these issues dramatically increase the cost of maintaining the codebase.

Architectural patterns introduce organizational principles for the different aspects of a codebase and present clear boundaries between them: how the business logic is wired to the system's input, output, and other infrastructural components. This affects how these components interact with each other: what knowledge they share and how the components reference each other.

Choosing the appropriate way to organize the codebase, or the correct architectural pattern, is crucial to support implementation of the business logic in the short term and alleviate maintenance in the long term. Let's explore three predominant application architecture patterns and their use cases: layered architecture, ports & adapters, and CQRS.

Layered Architecture

Layered architecture is one of the most common architectural patterns. It organizes the codebase into horizontal layers, with each layer addressing one of the following technical concerns: interaction with the consumers, implementing business logic, and persisting the data. You can see this represented in Figure 8-1.

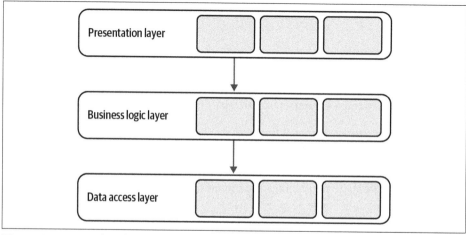

Figure 8-1. Layered architecture

In its classic form, the layered architecture consists of three layers: the presentation layer (PL), the business logic layer (BLL), and the data access layer (DAL).

Presentation Layer

The presentation layer, shown in Figure 8-2, implements the program's user interface for interactions with its consumers. In the pattern's original form, this layer denotes a graphical interface, such as a web interface or a desktop application.

In modern systems, however, the presentation layer has a broader scope: that is, all means for triggering the program's behavior, both synchronous and asynchronous. For example:

- Graphical user interface (GUI)
- Command-line interface (CLI)

- API for programmatic integration with other systems
- Subscription to events in a message broker
- Message topics for publishing outgoing events

All of these are the means for the system to receive requests from the external environment and communicate the output. Strictly speaking, the presentation layer is the program's public interface.

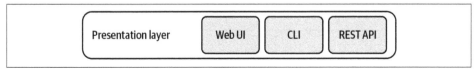

Figure 8-2. Presentation layer

Business Logic Layer

As the name suggests, this layer is responsible for implementing and encapsulating the program's business logic. This is the place where business decisions are implemented. As Eric Evans says,[1] this layer is the heart of software.

This layer is where the business logic patterns described in Chapters 5–7 are implemented—for example, active records or a domain model (see Figure 8-3).

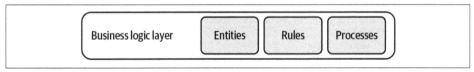

Figure 8-3. Business logic layer

Data Access Layer

The data access layer provides access to persistence mechanisms. In the pattern's original form, this referred to the system's database. However, as in the case of the presentation layer, the layer's responsibility is broader for modern systems.

First, ever since the NoSQL revolution broke out, it is common for a system to work with multiple databases. For example, a document store can act as the operational database, a search index for dynamic queries, and an in-memory database for performance-optimized operations.

---

1 Evans, E. (2003). *Domain-Driven Design: Tackling Complexity in the Heart of Software*. Boston: Addison-Wesley.

Second, traditional databases are not the only medium for storing information. For example, cloud-based object storage[2] can be used to store the system's files, or a message bus can be used to orchestrate communication between the program's different functions.[3]

Finally, this layer also includes integration with the various external information providers needed to implement the program's functionality: APIs provided by external systems, or cloud vendors' managed services, such as language translation, stock market data, and audio transcription (see Figure 8-4).

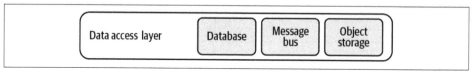

Figure 8-4. Data access layer

Communication Between Layers

The layers are integrated in a top-down communication model: each layer can hold a dependency only on the layer directly beneath it, as shown in Figure 8-5. This enforces decoupling of implementation concerns and reduces the knowledge shared between the layers. In Figure 8-5, the presentation layer references only the business logic layer. It has no knowledge of the design decisions made in the data access layer.

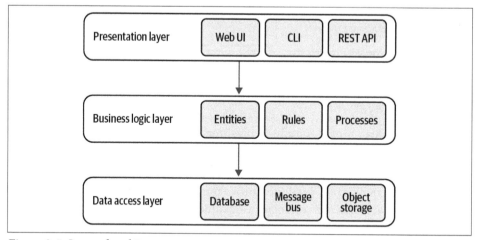

Figure 8-5. Layered architecture

---

2 Such as AWS S3 or Google Cloud Storage.

3 In this context, the message bus is used for the system's internal needs. If it were exposed publicly, it would belong to the presentation layer.

Variation

It's common to see the layered architecture pattern extended with an additional layer: the service layer.

Service layer

Defines an application's boundary with a layer of services that establishes a set of available operations and coordinates the application's response in each operation.
—Patterns of Enterprise Application Architecture[4]

The service layer acts as an intermediary between the program's presentation and business logic layers. Consider the following code:

```
namespace MvcApplication.Controllers
{
    public class UserController: Controller
    {
        ...

        [AcceptVerbs(HttpVerbs.Post)]
        public ActionResult Create(ContactDetails contactDetails)
        {
            OperationResult result = null;

            try
            {
                _db.StartTransaction();

                var user = new User();
                user.SetContactDetails(contactDetails)
                user.Save();

                _db.Commit();
                result = OperationResult.Success;
            } catch (Exception ex) {
                _db.Rollback();
                result = OperationResult.Exception(ex);
            }

            return View(result);
        }
    }
}
```

The MVC controller in this example belongs to the presentation layer. It exposes an endpoint that creates a new user. The endpoint uses the User active record object to

---

4 Fowler, M. (2002). *Patterns of Enterprise Application Architecture*. Boston: Addison-Wesley.

create a new instance and save it. Moreover, it orchestrates a database transaction to ensure that a proper response is generated in case of an error.

To further decouple the presentation layer from the underlying business logic, such orchestration logic can be moved into a service layer, as shown in Figure 8-6.

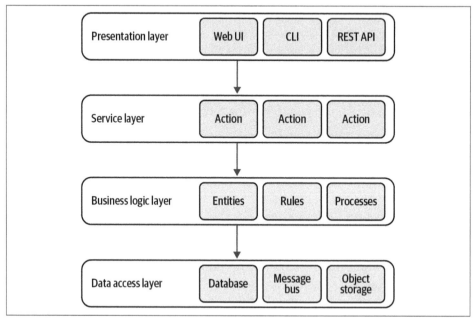

Figure 8-6. Service layer

It's important to note that in the context of the architectural pattern, the service layer is a logical boundary. It is not a physical service.

The service layer acts as a façade for the business logic layer: it exposes an interface that corresponds with the public interface's methods, encapsulating the required orchestration of the underlying layers. For example:

```
interface CampaignManagementService
{
    OperationResult CreateCampaign(CampaignDetails details);
    OperationResult Publish(CampaignId id, PublishingSchedule schedule);
    OperationResult Deactivate(CampaignId id);
    OperationResult AddDisplayLocation(CampaignId id, DisplayLocation newLocation);
    ...
}
```

All of the preceding methods correspond to the system's public interface. However, they lack presentation-related implementation details. The presentation layer's responsibility becomes limited to providing the required input to the service layer and communicating its responses back to the caller.

Let's refactor the preceding example and extract the orchestration logic into a service layer:

```
namespace ServiceLayer
{
    public class UserService
    {
        ...

        public OperationResult Create(ContactDetails contactDetails)
        {
            OperationResult result = null;

            try
            {
                _db.StartTransaction();

                var user = new User();
                user.SetContactDetails(contactDetails)
                user.Save();

                _db.Commit();
                result = OperationResult.Success;
            } catch (Exception ex) {
                _db.Rollback();
                result = OperationResult.Exception(ex);
            }

            return result;
        }

        ...
    }
}

namespace MvcApplication.Controllers
{
    public class UserController: Controller
    {
        ...

        [AcceptVerbs(HttpVerbs.Post)]
        public ActionResult Create(ContactDetails contactDetails)
        {
            var result = _userService.Create(contactDetails);
            return View(result);
        }
    }
}
```

Having an explicit service level has a number of advantages:

- We can reuse the same service layer to serve multiple public interfaces; for example, a graphical user interface and an API. No duplication of the orchestration logic is required.
- It improves modularity by gathering all related methods in one place.
- It further decouples the presentation and business logic layers.
- It makes it easier to test the business functionality.

That said, a service layer is not always necessary. For example, when the business logic is implemented as a transaction script, it essentially is a service layer, as it already exposes a set of methods that form the system's public interface. In such a case, the service layer's API would just repeat the transaction scripts' public interfaces, without abstracting or encapsulating any complexity. Hence, either a service layer or a business logic layer will suffice.

On the other hand, the service layer is required if the business logic pattern requires external orchestration, as in the case of the active record pattern. In this case, the service layer implements the transaction script pattern, while the active records it operates on are located in the business logic layer.

Terminology

Elsewhere, you may encounter other terms used for the layered architecture:

- Presentation layer = user interface layer
- Service layer = application layer
- Business logic layer = domain layer = model layer
- Data access layer = infrastructure layer

To eliminate confusion, I present the pattern using the original terminology. That said, I prefer "user interface layer" and "infrastructure layer" as these terms better reflect the responsibilities of modern systems and an application layer to avoid confusion with the physical boundaries of services.

When to Use Layered Architecture

The dependency between the business logic and the data access layers makes this architectural pattern a good fit for a system with its business logic implemented using the transaction script or active record pattern.

However, the pattern makes it challenging to implement a domain model. In a domain model, the business entities (aggregates and value objects) should have no dependency and no knowledge of the underlying infrastructure. The layered architecture's top-down dependency requires jumping through some hoops to fulfill this requirement. It is still possible to implement a domain model in a layered architecture, but the pattern we will discuss next fits much better.

Optional: Layers Versus Tiers

The layers architecture is often confused with the N-Tier architecture, and vice versa. Despite the similarities between the two patterns, layers and tiers are conceptually different: a layer is a logical boundary, whereas a tier is a physical boundary. All layers in the layered architecture are bound by the same lifecycle: they are implemented, evolved, and deployed as one single unit. On the other hand, a tier is an independently deployable service, server, or system. For example, consider the N-Tier system in Figure 8-7.

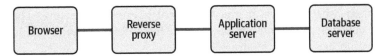

Figure 8-7. N-Tier system

The system depicts the integration between physical services involved in a web-based system. The consumer uses a browser, which can run on a desktop computer or a mobile device. The browser interacts with a reverse proxy that forwards the requests to the actual web application. The web application runs on a web server and communicates with a database server. All of these components may run on the same physical server, such as containers, or be distributed among multiple servers. However, since each component can be deployed and managed independent of the rest, these are tiers and not layers.

Layers, on the other hand, are logical boundaries inside the web application.

Ports & Adapters

The ports & adapters architecture addresses the shortcomings of the layered architecture and is a better fit for implementation of more complex business logic. Interestingly, both patterns are quite similar. Let's "refactor" the layered architecture into ports & adapters.

Terminology

Essentially, both the presentation layer and data access layer represent integration with external components: databases, external services, and user interface frameworks. These technical implementation details do not reflect the system's business logic; so, let's unify all such infrastructural concerns into a single "infrastructure layer," as shown in Figure 8-8.

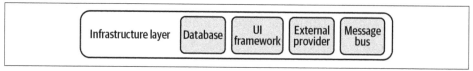

Figure 8-8. Presentation and data access layers combined into an infrastructure layer

Dependency Inversion Principle

The dependency inversion principle (DIP) states that high-level modules, which implement the business logic, should not depend on low-level modules. However, that's precisely what happens in the traditional layered architecture. The business logic layer depends on the infrastructure layer. To conform with the DIP, let's reverse the relationship, as shown in Figure 8-9.

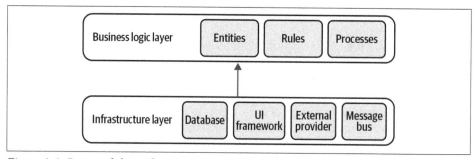

Figure 8-9. Reversed dependencies

Instead of being sandwiched between the technological concerns, now the business logic layer takes the central role. It doesn't depend on any of the system's infrastructural components.

Finally, let's add an application[5] layer as a façade for the system's public interface. As the service layer in the layered architecture, it describes all the operations exposed by the system and orchestrates the system's business logic for executing them. The resultant architecture is depicted in Figure 8-10.

---

5 Since we are not in the context of the layered architecture, I will take the freedom to use the term *application layer* instead of *service layer*, as it better reflects the purpose.

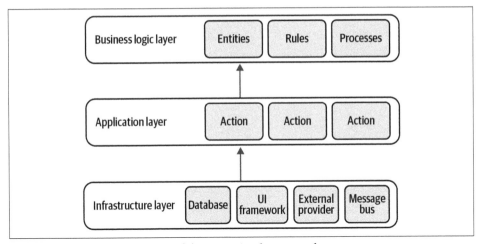

Figure 8-10. Traditional layers of the ports & adapters architecture

The architecture depicted in Figure 8-10 is the ports & adapters architectural pattern. The business logic doesn't depend on any of the underlying layers, as required for implementing the domain model and event-sourced domain model patterns.

Why is this pattern called ports & adapters? To answer this question, let's see how the infrastructural components are integrated with the business logic.

Integration of Infrastructural Components

The core goal of the ports & adapters architecture is to decouple the system's business logic from its infrastructural components.

Instead of referencing and calling the infrastructural components directly, the business logic layer defines "ports" that have to be implemented by the infrastructure layer. The infrastructure layer implements "adapters": concrete implementations of the ports' interfaces for working with different technologies (see Figure 8-11).

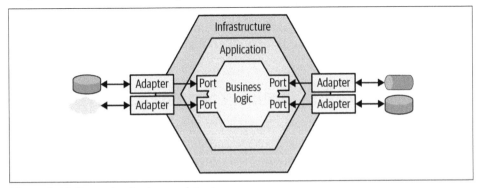

Figure 8-11. Ports & adapters architecture

The abstract ports are resolved into concrete adapters in the infrastructure layer, either through dependency injection or by bootstrapping.

For example, here is a possible port definition and a concrete adapter for a message bus:

```
namespace App.BusinessLogicLayer
{
    public interface IMessaging
    {
        void Publish(Message payload);
        void Subscribe(Message type, Action callback);
    }
}

namespace App.Infrastructure.Adapters
{
    public class SQSBus: IMessaging { ... }
}
```

Variants

The ports & adapters architecture is also known as hexagonal architecture, onion architecture, and clean architecture. All of these patterns are based on the same design principles, have the same components, and have the same relationships between them, but as in the case of the layered architecture, the terminology may differ:

- Application layer = service layer = use case layer
- Business logic layer = domain layer = core layer

Despite that, these patterns can be mistakenly treated as conceptually different. That's just another example of the importance of a ubiquitous language.

When to Use Ports & Adapters

The decoupling of the business logic from all technological concerns makes the ports & adapters architecture a perfect fit for business logic implemented with the domain model pattern.

Command-Query Responsibility Segregation

The command-query responsibility segregation (CQRS) pattern is based on the same organizational principles for business logic and infrastructural concerns as ports & adapters. It differs, however, in the way the system's data is managed. This pattern enables representation of the system's data in multiple persistent models.

Let's see why we might need such a solution and how to implement it.

Polyglot Modeling

In many cases, it may be difficult, if not impossible, to use a single model of the system's business domain to address all of the system's needs. For example, as discussed in Chapter 7, online transaction processing (OLTP) and online analytical processing (OLAP) may require different representations of the system's data.

Another reason for working with multiple models may have to do with the notion of polyglot persistence. There is no perfect database. Or, as Greg Young[6] says, all databases are flawed, each in its own way: we often have to balance the needs for scale, consistency, or supported querying models. An alternative to finding a perfect database is the polyglot persistence model: using multiple databases to implement different data-related requirements. For example, a single system might use a document store as its operational database, a column store for analytics/reporting, and a search engine for implementing robust search capabilities.

Finally, the CQRS pattern is closely related to event sourcing. Originally, CQRS was defined to address the limited querying possibilities of an event-sourced model: it is only possible to query events of one aggregate instance at a time. The CQRS pattern provides the possibility of materializing projected models into physical databases that can be used for flexible querying options.

That said, this chapter "decouples" CQRS from event sourcing. I intend to show that CQRS is useful even if the business logic is implemented using any of the other business logic implementation patterns.

Let's see how CQRS allows the use of multiple storage mechanisms for representing different models of the system's data.

Implementation

As the name suggests, the pattern segregates the responsibilities of the system's models. There are two types of models: the command execution model and the read models.

Command execution model

CQRS devotes a single model to executing operations that modify the system's state (system commands). This model is used to implement the business logic, validate rules, and enforce invariants.

---

6 *Polyglot data by Greg Young.* (n.d.). Retrieved June 14, 2021, from YouTube (*https://oreil.ly/3CdMw*).

The command execution model is also the only model representing strongly consistent data—the system's source of truth. It should be possible to read the strongly consistent state of a business entity and have optimistic concurrency support when updating it.

Read models (projections)

The system can define as many models as needed to present data to users or supply information to other systems.

A read model is a precached projection. It can reside in a durable database, flat file, or in-memory cache. Proper implementation of CQRS allows for wiping out all data of a projection and regenerating it from scratch. This also enables extending the system with additional projections in the future—models that couldn't have been foreseen originally.

Finally, read models are read-only. None of the system's operations can directly modify the read models' data.

Projecting Read Models

For the read models to work, the system has to project changes from the command execution model to all its read models. This concept is illustrated in Figure 8-12.

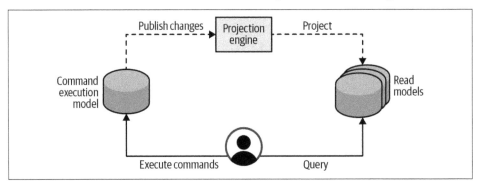

Figure 8-12. CQRS architecture

The projection of read models is similar to the notion of a materialized view in relational databases: whenever source tables are updated, the changes have to be reflected in the precached views.

Next, let's see two ways to generate projections: synchronously and asynchronously.

Synchronous projections

Synchronous projections fetch changes to the OLTP data through the catch-up subscription model:

- The projection engine queries the OLTP database for added or updated records after the last processed checkpoint.

- The projection engine uses the updated data to regenerate/update the system's read models.

- The projection engine stores the checkpoint of the last processed record. This value will be used during the next iteration for getting records added or modified after the last processed record.

This process is illustrated in Figure 8-13 and shown as a sequence diagram in Figure 8-14.

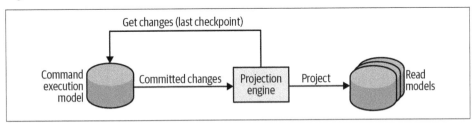

Figure 8-13. Synchronous projection model

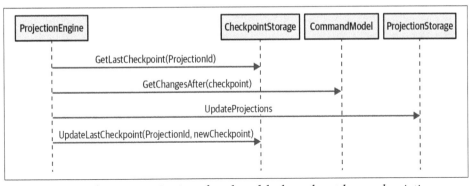

Figure 8-14. Synchronous projection of read models through catch-up subscription

For the catch-up subscription to work, the command execution model has to checkpoint all the appended or updated database records. The storage mechanism should also support the querying of records based on the checkpoint.

The checkpoint can be implemented using the databases' features. For example, SQL Server's "rowversion" column can be used to generate unique, incrementing numbers upon inserting or updating a row, as illustrated in Figure 8-15. In databases that lack such functionality, a custom solution can be implemented that increments a running counter and appends it to each modified record. It's important to ensure that the checkpoint-based query returns consistent results. If the last returned record has a checkpoint value of 10, on the next execution no new requests should have values lower than 10. Otherwise, these records will be skipped by the projection engine, which will result in inconsistent models.

Id	First Name	Last Name	Checkpoint
1	Tom	Cook	0x0000000000001792
2	Harold	Elliot	0x0000000000001793
3	Dianna	Daniels	0x0000000000001796
4	Dianna	Daniels	0x0000000000001795

Figure 8-15. Auto-generated checkpoint column in a relational database

The synchronous projection method makes it trivial to add new projections and regenerate existing ones from scratch. In the latter case, all you have to do is reset the checkpoint to 0; the projection engine will scan the records and rebuild the projections from the ground up.

Asynchronous projections

In the asynchronous projection scenario, the command execution model publishes all committed changes to a message bus. The system's projection engines can subscribe to the published messages and use them to update the read models, as shown in Figure 8-16.

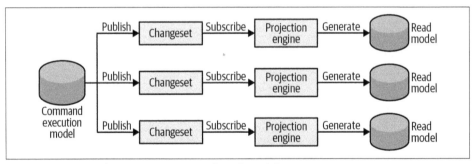

Figure 8-16. Asynchronous projection of read models

Challenges

Despite the apparent scaling and performance advantages of the asynchronous projection method, it is more prone to the challenges of distributed computing. If the messages are processed out of order or duplicated, inconsistent data will be projected into the read models.

This method also makes it more challenging to add new projections or regenerate existing ones.

For these reasons, it's advisable to always implement synchronous projection and, optionally, an additional asynchronous projection on top of it.

Model Segregation

In the CQRS architecture, the responsibilities of the system's models are segregated according to their type. A command can only operate on the strongly consistent command execution model. A query cannot directly modify any of the system's persisted state—neither the read models nor the command execution model.

A common misconception about CQRS-based systems is that a command can only modify data, and data can be fetched for display only through a read model. In other words, the command executing the methods should never return any data. This is wrong. This approach produces accidental complexities and leads to a bad user experience.

A command should always let the caller know whether it has succeeded or failed. If it has failed, why did it fail? Was there a validation or technical issue? The caller has to know how to fix the command. *Therefore, a command can—and in many cases should—return data;* for example, if the system's user interface has to reflect the modifications resulting from the command. Not only does this make it easier for consumers to work with the system since they immediately receive feedback for their actions, but the returned values can be used further in the consumers' workflows, eliminating the need for unnecessary data round trips.

The only limitation here is that the returned data should originate from the strongly consistent model—the command execution model—as we cannot expect the projections, which will eventually be consistent, to be refreshed immediately.

When to Use CQRS

The CQRS pattern can be useful for applications that need to work with the same data in multiple models, potentially stored in different kinds of databases. From an operational perspective, the pattern supports domain-driven design's core value of working with the most effective models for the task at hand, and continuously improving the model of the business domain. From an infrastructural perspective, CQRS allows for leveraging the strength of the different kinds of databases; for example, using a relational database to store the command execution model, a search index for full text search, and prerendered flat files for fast data retrieval, with all the storage mechanisms reliably synchronized.

Moreover, CQRS naturally lends itself to event-sourced domain models. The event-sourcing model makes it impossible to query records based on the aggregates' states, but CQRS enables this by projecting the states into queryable databases.

Scope

The patterns we've discussed—layered architecture, ports & adapters architecture, and CQRS—should not be treated as systemwide organizational principles. These are not necessarily high-level architecture patterns for a whole bounded context either.

Consider a bounded context encompassing multiple subdomains, as shown in Figure 8-17. The subdomains can be of different types: core, supporting, or generic. Even subdomains of the same type may require different business logic and architectural patterns (that's the topic of Chapter 10). Enforcing a single, bounded, context-wide architecture will inadvertently lead to accidental complexity.

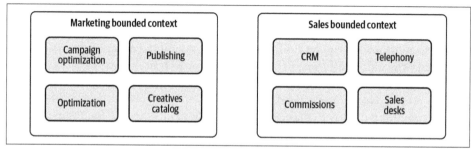

Figure 8-17. Bounded contexts spanning multiple subdomains

Our goal is to drive design decisions according to the actual needs and business strategy. In addition to the layers that partition the system horizontally, we can introduce additional vertical partitioning. It's crucial to define logical boundaries for modules encapsulating distinct business subdomains and use the appropriate tools for each, as demonstrated in Figure 8-18.

Appropriate vertical boundaries make a monolithic bounded context a modular one and help to prevent it from becoming a big ball of mud. As we will discuss in Chapter 11, these logical boundaries can be refactored later into physical boundaries of finer-grained bounded contexts.

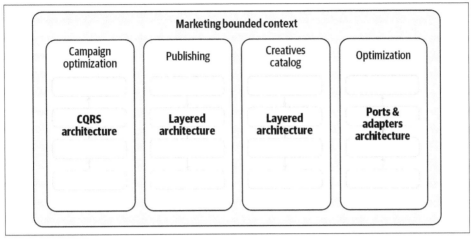

Figure 8-18. Architectural slices

Conclusion

The layered architecture decomposes the codebase based on its technological concerns. Since this pattern couples business logic with data access implementation, it's a good fit for active record–based systems.

The ports & adapters architecture inverts the relationships: it puts the business logic at the center and decouples it from all infrastructural dependencies. This pattern is a good fit for business logic implemented with the domain model pattern.

The CQRS pattern represents the same data in multiple models. Although this pattern is obligatory for systems based on the event-sourced domain model, it can also be used in any systems that need a way of working with multiple persistent models.

The patterns we will discuss in the next chapter address architectural concerns from a different perspective: how to implement reliable interaction between different components of a system.

Exercises

1. Which of the discussed architectural patterns can be used with business logic implemented as the active record pattern?

   a. Layered architecture

   b. Ports & adapters

   c. CQRS

   d. A and C

2. Which of the discussed architectural patterns decouples the business logic from infrastructural concerns?

   a. Layered architecture

   b. Ports & adapters

   c. CQRS

   d. B and C

3. Assume you are implementing the ports & adapters pattern and need to integrate a cloud provider's managed message bus. In which layer should the integration be implemented?

   a. Business logic layer

   b. Application layer

   c. Infrastructure layer

   d. Any layer

4. Which of the following statements is true regarding the CQRS pattern?

   a. Asynchronous projections are easier to scale.

   b. Either synchronous or asynchronous projection can be used, but not both at the same time.

   c. A command cannot return any information to the caller. The caller should always use the read models to get the results of the executed actions.

   d. A command can return information as long as it originates from a strongly consistent model.

   e. A and D.

5. The CQRS pattern allows for representing the same business objects in multiple persistent models, and thus allows working with multiple models in the same bounded context. Does it contradict the bounded context's notion of being a model boundary?

CHAPTER 9

Communication Patterns

Chapters 5–8 presented tactical design patterns that define the different ways to implement a system's components: how to model the business logic and how to organize the internals of a bounded context architecturally. In this chapter, we will step beyond the boundaries of a single component and discuss the patterns for organizing the flow of communication across a system's elements.

The patterns you will learn about in this chapter facilitate cross-bounded context communication, address the limitations imposed by aggregate design principles, and orchestrate business processes spanning multiple system components.

Model Translation

A bounded context is the boundary of a model—a ubiquitous language. As you learned in Chapter 3, there are different patterns for designing communication across different bounded contexts. Suppose the teams implementing two bounded contexts are communicating effectively and willing to collaborate. In this case, the bounded contexts can be integrated in a partnership: the protocols can be coordinated in an ad hoc manner, and any integration issues can be effectively addressed through communication between the teams. Another cooperation-driven integration method is *shared kernel*: the teams extract and co-evolve a limited portion of a model; for example, extracting the bounded contexts' integration contracts into a co-owned repository.

In a customer–supplier relationship, the balance of power tips toward either the upstream (supplier) or the downstream (consumer) bounded context. Suppose the downstream bounded context cannot conform to the upstream bounded context's model. In this case, a more elaborate technical solution is required that can facilitate communication by translating the bounded contexts' models.

This translation can be handled by one, or sometimes both, sides: the downstream bounded context can adapt the upstream bounded context's model to its needs using an anticorruption layer (ACL), while the upstream bounded context can act as an open-host service (OHS) and protect its consumers from changes to its implementation model by using an integration-specific published language. Since the translation logic is similar for both the anticorruption layer and the open-host service, this chapter covers the implementation options without differentiating between the patterns and mentions the differences only in exceptional cases.

The model's translation logic can be either stateless or stateful. *Stateless translation* happens on the fly, as incoming (OHS) or outgoing (ACL) requests are issued, while *stateful translation* involves a more complicated translation logic that requires a database. Let's see design patterns for implementing both types of model translation.

Stateless Model Translation

For stateless model translation, the bounded context that owns the translation (OHS for upstream, ACL for downstream) implements the proxy design pattern (*https://oreil.ly/A1nb2*) to interject the incoming and outgoing requests and map the source model to the bounded context's target model. This is depicted in Figure 9-1.

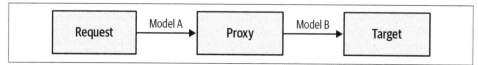

Figure 9-1. Model translation by a proxy

Implementation of the proxy depends on whether the bounded contexts are communicating synchronously or asynchronously.

Synchronous

The typical way to translate models used in synchronous communication is to embed the transformation logic in the bounded context's codebase, as shown in Figure 9-2. In an open-host service, translation to the public language takes place when processing incoming requests, and in an anticorruption layer, it occurs when calling the upstream bounded context.

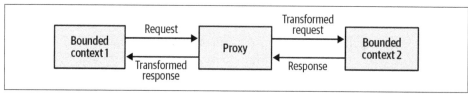

Figure 9-2. Synchronous communication

In some cases, it can be more cost-effective and convenient to offload the translation logic to an external component such as an API gateway pattern. The API gateway component can be an open source software-based solution such as Kong or KrakenD, or it can be a cloud vendor's managed service such as AWS API Gateway, Google Apigee, or Azure API Management.

For bounded contexts implementing the open-host pattern, the API gateway is responsible for converting the internal model into the integration-optimized published language. Moreover, having an explicit API gateway can alleviate the process of managing and serving multiple versions of the bounded context's API, as depicted in Figure 9-3.

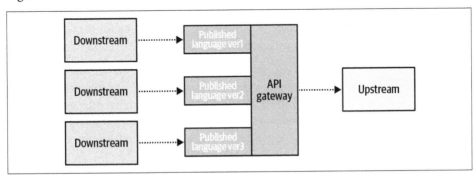

Figure 9-3. Exposing different versions of the published language

Anticorruption layers implemented using an API gateway can be consumed by multiple downstream bounded contexts. In such cases, the anticorruption layer acts as an integration-specific bounded context, as shown in Figure 9-4.

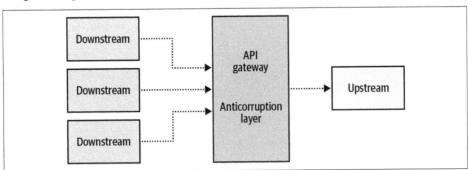

Figure 9-4. Shared anticorruption layer

Such bounded contexts, which are mainly in charge of transforming models for more convenient consumption by other components, are often referred to as *interchange contexts*.

Asynchronous

To translate models used in asynchronous communication you can implement a *message proxy*: an intermediary component subscribing to messages coming from the source bounded context. The proxy will apply the required model transformations and forward the resultant messages to the target subscriber (see Figure 9-5).

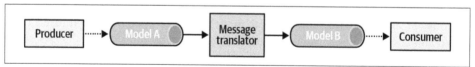

Figure 9-5. Translating models in asynchronous communication

In addition to translating the messages' model, the intercepting component can also reduce the noise on the target bounded context by filtering out irrelevant messages.

Asynchronous model translation is essential when implementing an open host service. It's a common mistake to design and expose a published language for the model's objects and allow domain events to be published as they are, thereby exposing the bounded context's implementation model. Asynchronous translation can be used to intercept the domain events and convert them into a published language, thus providing better encapsulation of the bounded context's implementation details (see Figure 9-6).

Moreover, translating messages to the published language enables differentiating between private events that are intended for the bounded context's internal needs and public events that are designed for integration with other bounded contexts. We'll revisit and expand on the topic of private/public events in Chapter 15, where we discuss the relationship between domain-driven design and event-driven architecture.

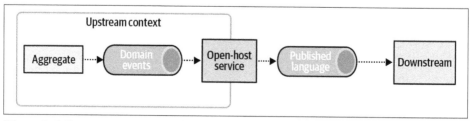

Figure 9-6. Domain events in a published language

Stateful Model Translation

For more significant model transformations—for example, when the translation mechanism has to aggregate the source data or unify data from multiple sources into a single model—a stateful translation may be required. Let's discuss each of these use cases in detail.

Aggregating incoming data

Let's say a bounded context is interested in aggregating incoming requests and processing them in batches for performance optimization. In this case, aggregation may be required both for synchronous and asynchronous requests (see Figure 9-7).

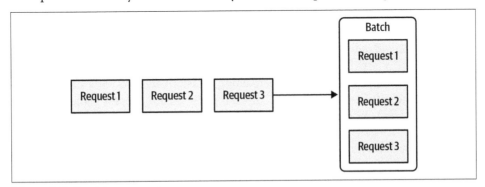

Figure 9-7. Batching requests

Another common use case for aggregation of source data is combining multiple fine-grained messages into a single message containing the unified data, as depicted in Figure 9-8.

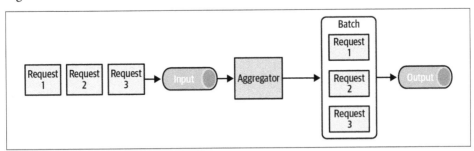

Figure 9-8. Unifying incoming events

Model transformation that aggregates incoming data cannot be implemented using an API gateway, and thus requires more elaborate, stateful processing. To track the incoming data and process it accordingly, the translation logic requires its own persistent storage (see Figure 9-9).

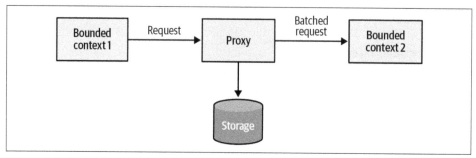

Figure 9-9. Stateful model transformation

In some use cases, you can avoid implementing a custom solution for a stateful translation by using off-the-shelf products; for example, a stream-process platform (Kafka, AWS Kinesis, etc.), or a batching solution (Apache NiFi, AWS Glue, Spark, etc.).

Unifying multiple sources

A bounded context may need to process data aggregates from multiple sources, including other bounded contexts. A typical example for this is the backend-for-frontend pattern,[1] in which the user interface has to combine data originating from multiple services.

Another example is a bounded context that must process data from multiple other contexts and implement complex business logic to process all the data. In this case, it can be beneficial to decouple the integration and business logic complexities by fronting the bounded context with an anticorruption layer that aggregates data from all other bounded contexts, as shown in Figure 9-10.

---

1 Richardson, C. (2019). *Microservice Patterns: With Examples in Java*. New York: Manning Publications.

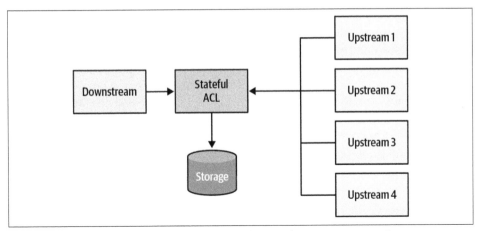

Figure 9-10. Simplifying the integration model using the anticorruption layer pattern

Integrating Aggregates

In Chapter 6, we discussed that one of the ways aggregates communicate with the rest of the system is by publishing domain events. External components can subscribe to these domain events and execute their logic. But how are domain events published to a message bus?

Before we get to the solution, let's examine a few common mistakes in the event publishing process and the consequences of each approach. Consider the following code:

```
01  public class Campaign
02  {
03      ...
04      List<DomainEvent> _events;
05      IMessageBus _messageBus;
06      ...
07
08      public void Deactivate(string reason)
09      {
10          for (l in _locations.Values())
11          {
12              l.Deactivate();
13          }
14
15          IsActive = false;
16
17          var newEvent = new CampaignDeactivated(_id, reason);
18          _events.Append(newEvent);
19          _messageBus.Publish(newEvent);
20      }
21  }
```

On line 17, a new event is instantiated. On the following two lines, it is appended to the aggregate's internal list of domain events (line 18), and the event is published to the message bus (line 19). This implementation of publishing domain events is simple but wrong. Publishing the domain event right from the aggregate is bad for two reasons. First, the event will be dispatched before the aggregate's new state is committed to the database. A subscriber may receive the notification that the campaign was deactivated, but it would contradict the campaign's state. Second, what if the database transaction fails to commit because of a race condition, subsequent aggregate logic rendering the operation invalid, or simply a technical issue in the database? Even though the database transaction is rolled back, the event is already published and pushed to subscribers, and there is no way to retract it.

Let's try something else:

```
01   public class ManagementAPI
02   {
03       ...
04       private readonly IMessageBus _messageBus;
05       private readonly ICampaignRepository _repository;
06       ...
07       public ExecutionResult DeactivateCampaign(CampaignId id, string reason)
08       {
09           try
10           {
11               var campaign = repository.Load(id);
12               campaign.Deactivate(reason);
13               _repository.CommitChanges(campaign);
14
15               var events = campaign.GetUnpublishedEvents();
16               for (IDomainEvent e in events)
17               {
18                   _messageBus.publish(e);
19               }
20               campaign.ClearUnpublishedEvents();
21           }
22           catch(Exception ex)
23           {
24               ...
25           }
26       }
27   }
```

In the preceding listing, the responsibility of publishing new domain events is shifted to the application layer. On lines 11 through 13, the relevant instance of the Campaign aggregate is loaded, its Deactivate command is executed, and only after the updated state is successfully committed to the database, on lines 15 through 20, are the new domain events published to the message bus. Can we trust this code? No.

In this case, the process running the logic for some reason fails to publish the domain events. Perhaps the message bus is down. Or the server running the code fails right after committing the database transaction, but before publishing the events the system will still end in an inconsistent state, which means that the database transaction is committed, but the domain events will never be published.

These edge cases can be addressed using the outbox pattern.

Outbox

The outbox pattern (Figure 9-11) ensures reliable publishing of domain events using the following algorithm:

- Both the updated aggregate's state and the new domain events are committed in the same atomic transaction.
- A message relay fetches newly committed domain events from the database.
- The relay publishes the domain events to the message bus.
- Upon successful publishing, the relay either marks the events as published in the database or deletes them completely.

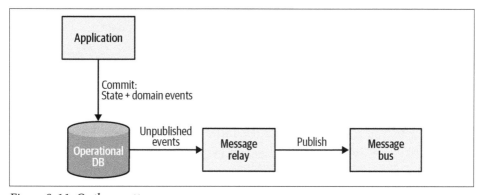

Figure 9-11. Outbox pattern

When using a relational database, it's convenient to leverage the database's ability to commit to two tables atomically and use a dedicated table for storing the messages, as shown in Figure 9-12.

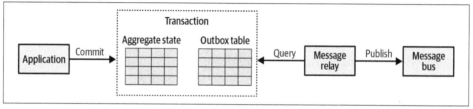

Figure 9-12. Outbox table

When using a NoSQL database that doesn't support multidocument transactions, the outgoing domain events have to be embedded in the aggregate's record. For example:

```
{
    "campaign-id": "364b33c3-2171-446d-b652-8e5a7b2be1af",
    "state": {
        "name": "Autumn 2017",
        "publishing-state": "DEACTIVATED",
        "ad-locations": [
            ...
        ]
        ...
    },
    "outbox": [
        {
            "campaign-id": "364b33c3-2171-446d-b652-8e5a7b2be1af",
            "type": "campaign-deactivated",
            "reason": "Goals met",
            "published": false
        }
    ]
}
```

In this sample, you can see the JSON document's additional property, outbox, containing a list of domain events that have to be published.

Fetching unpublished events

The publishing relay can fetch the new domain events in either a pull-based or push-based manner:

Pull: polling publisher

> The relay can continuously query the database for unpublished events. Proper indexes have to be in place to minimize the load on the database induced by the constant polling.

Push: transaction log tailing
> Here we can leverage the database's feature set to proactively call the publishing relay when new events are appended. For example, some relational databases enable getting notifications about updated/inserted records by tailing the database's transaction log. Some NoSQL databases expose committed changes as streams of events (e.g., AWS DynamoDB Streams).

It's important to note that the outbox pattern guarantees delivery of the messages at least once: if the relay fails right after publishing a message but before marking it as published in the database, the same message will be published again in the next iteration.

Next, we'll take a look at how we can leverage the reliable publishing of domain events to overcome some of the limitations imposed by aggregate design principles.

Saga

One of the core aggregate design principles is to limit each transaction to a single instance of an aggregate. This ensures that an aggregate's boundaries are carefully considered and encapsulate a coherent set of business functionality. But there are cases when you have to implement a business process that spans multiple aggregates.

Consider the following example: when an advertising campaign is activated, it should automatically submit the campaign's advertising materials to its publisher. Upon receiving the confirmation from the publisher, the campaign's publishing state should change to Published. In the case of rejection by the publisher, the campaign should be marked as Rejected.

This flow spans two business entities: advertising campaign and publisher. Co-locating the entities in the same aggregate boundary would definitely be overkill, as these are clearly different business entities that have different responsibilities and may belong to different bounded contexts. Instead, this flow can be implemented as a saga.

A saga is a long-running business process. It's long running not necessarily in terms of time, as sagas can run from seconds to years, but rather in terms of transactions: a business process that spans multiple transactions. The transactions can be handled not only by aggregates but by any component emitting domain events and responding to commands. The saga listens to the events emitted by the relevant components and issues subsequent commands to the other components. If one of the execution steps fails, the saga is in charge of issuing relevant compensating actions to ensure the system state remains consistent.

Let's see how the advertising campaign publishing flow from the preceding example can be implemented as a saga, as shown in Figure 9-13.

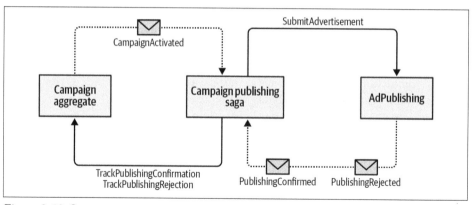

Figure 9-13. Saga

To implement the publishing process, the saga has to listen to the Campaign Act
ivated event from the Campaign aggregate and the PublishingConfirmed and Pub
lishingRejected events from the AdPublishing bounded context. The saga has to
execute the SubmitAdvertisement command on AdPublishing, and the TrackPub
lishingConfirmation and TrackPublishingRejection commands on the Campaign
aggregate. In this example, the TrackPublishingRejection command acts as a com-
pensation action that will ensure that the advertising campaign is not listed as active.
Here is the code:

```
public class CampaignPublishingSaga
{
    private readonly ICampaignRepository _repository;
    private readonly IPublishingServiceClient _publishingService;
    ...

    public void Process(CampaignActivated @event)
    {
        var campaign = _repository.Load(@event.CampaignId);
        var advertisingMaterials = campaign.GenerateAdvertisingMaterials();
        _publishingService.SubmitAdvertisement(@event.CampaignId,
                                        advertisingMaterials);
    }

    public void Process(PublishingConfirmed @event)
    {
        var campaign = _repository.Load(@event.CampaignId);
        campaign.TrackPublishingConfirmation(@event.ConfirmationId);
        _repository.CommitChanges(campaign);
    }

    public void Process(PublishingRejected @event)
    {
        var campaign = _repository.Load(@event.CampaignId);
        campaign.TrackPublishingRejection(@event.RejectionReason);
```

```
            _repository.CommitChanges(campaign);
        }
    }
```

The preceding example relies on the messaging infrastructure to deliver the relevant
events, and it reacts to the events by executing the relevant commands. This is an
example of a relatively simple saga: it has no state. You will encounter sagas that do
require state management; for example, to track the executed operations so that relevant compensating actions can be issued in case of a failure. In such a situation, the
saga can be implemented as an event-sourced aggregate, persisting the complete history of received events and issued commands. However, the command execution
logic should be moved out of the saga itself and executed asynchronously, similar to
the way domain events are dispatched in the outbox pattern:

```
public class CampaignPublishingSaga
{
    private readonly ICampaignRepository _repository;
    private readonly IList<IDomainEvent> _events;
    ...

    public void Process(CampaignActivated activated)
    {
        var campaign = _repository.Load(activated.CampaignId);
        var advertisingMaterials = campaign.GenerateAdvertisingMaterials();
        var commandIssuedEvent = new CommandIssuedEvent(
            target: Target.PublishingService,
            command: new SubmitAdvertisementCommand(activated.CampaignId,
            advertisingMaterials));

        _events.Append(activated);
        _events.Append(commandIssuedEvent);
    }

    public void Process(PublishingConfirmed confirmed)
    {
        var commandIssuedEvent = new CommandIssuedEvent(
            target: Target.CampaignAggregate,
            command: new TrackConfirmation(confirmed.CampaignId,
                                           confirmed.ConfirmationId));

        _events.Append(confirmed);
        _events.Append(commandIssuedEvent);
    }

    public void Process(PublishingRejected rejected)
    {
        var commandIssuedEvent = new CommandIssuedEvent(
            target: Target.CampaignAggregate,
            command: new TrackRejection(rejected.CampaignId,
                                        rejected.RejectionReason));
```

```
            _events.Append(rejected);
            _events.Append(commandIssuedEvent);
        }
    }
```

In this example, the outbox relay will have to execute the commands on relevant end-points for each instance of CommandIssuedEvent. As in the case of publishing domain events, separating the transition of the saga's state from the execution of commands ensures that the commands will be executed reliably, even if the process fails at any stage.

Consistency

Although the saga pattern orchestrates a multicomponent transaction, the states of the involved components are eventually consistent. And although the saga will eventually execute the relevant commands, no two transactions can be considered atomic. This correlates with another aggregate design principle:

> *Only the data within an aggregate's boundaries can be considered strongly consistent. Everything outside is eventually consistent.*

Use this as a guiding principle to make sure you are not abusing sagas to compensate for improper aggregate boundaries. Business operations that have to belong to the same aggregate require strongly consistent data.

The saga pattern is often confused with another pattern: process manager. Although the implementation is similar, these are different patterns. In the next section, we'll discuss the purpose of the process manager pattern and how it differs from the saga pattern.

Process Manager

The saga pattern manages simple, linear flow. Strictly speaking, a saga matches events to the corresponding commands. In the examples we used to demonstrate saga implementations, we actually implemented simple matching of events to commands:

- CampaignActivated event to PublishingService.SubmitAdvertisement command

- PublishingConfirmed event to Campaign.TrackConfirmation command

- PublishingRejected event to Campaign.TrackRejection command

The process manager pattern, shown in Figure 9-14, is intended to implement a business-logic-based process. It is defined as a central processing unit that maintains the state of the sequence and determines the next processing steps.[2]

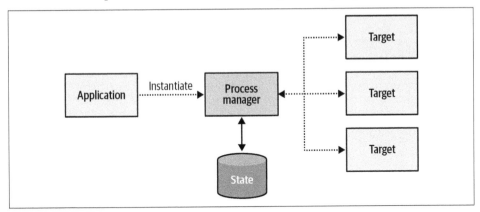

Figure 9-14. Process manager

As a simple rule of thumb, if a saga contains if-else statements to choose the correct course of action, it is probably a process manager.

Another difference between a process manager and a saga is that a saga is instantiated implicitly when a particular event is observed, as in `CampaignActivated` in the preceding examples. A process manager, on the other hand, cannot be bound to a single source event. Instead, it's a coherent business process consisting of multiple steps. Hence, a process manager has to be instantiated explicitly. Consider the following example:

Booking a business trip starts with the routing algorithm choosing the most cost-effective flight route and asking the employee to approve it. In case the employee prefers a different route, their direct manager needs to approve it. After the flight is booked, one of the preapproved hotels has to be booked for the appropriate dates. If no hotels are available, the flight tickets have to be canceled.

In this example, there is no central entity to trigger the trip booking process. The trip booking is the process and it has to be implemented as a process manager (see Figure 9-15).

2 Hohpe, G., & Woolf, B. (2003). *Enterprise Integration Patterns: Designing, Building, and Deploying Messaging Solutions.* Boston: Addison-Wesley.

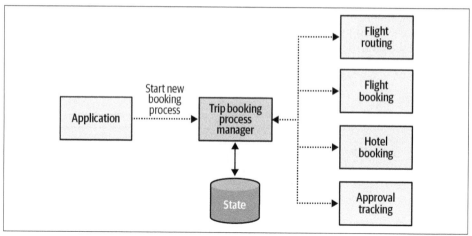

Figure 9-15. Trip booking process manager

From an implementation perspective, process managers are often implemented as aggregates, either state based or event sourced. For example:

```
public class BookingProcessManager
{
    private readonly IList<IDomainEvent> _events;
    private BookingId _id;
    private Destination _destination;
    private TripDefinition _parameters;
    private EmployeeId _traveler;
    private Route _route;
    private IList<Route> _rejectedRoutes;
    private IRoutingService _routing;
    ...

    public void Initialize(Destination destination,
                           TripDefinition parameters,
                           EmployeeId traveler)
    {
        _destination = destination;
        _parameters = parameters;
        _traveler = traveler;
        _route = _routing.Calculate(destination, parameters);

        var routeGenerated = new RouteGeneratedEvent(
            BookingId: _id,
            Route: _route);

        var commandIssuedEvent = new CommandIssuedEvent(
            command: new RequestEmployeeApproval(_traveler, _route)
        );

        _events.Append(routeGenerated);
```

```
        _events.Append(commandIssuedEvent);
}

public void Process(RouteConfirmed confirmed)
{
    var commandIssuedEvent = new CommandIssuedEvent(
        command: new BookFlights(_route, _parameters)
    );

    _events.Append(confirmed);
    _events.Append(commandIssuedEvent);
}

public void Process(RouteRejected rejected)
{
    var commandIssuedEvent = new CommandIssuedEvent(
        command: new RequestRerouting(_traveler, _route)
    );

    _events.Append(rejected);
    _events.Append(commandIssuedEvent);
}

public void Process(ReroutingConfirmed confirmed)
{
    _rejectedRoutes.Append(route);
    _route = _routing.CalculateAltRoute(destination,
                                parameters, rejectedRoutes);
    var routeGenerated = new RouteGeneratedEvent(
        BookingId: _id,
        Route: _route);

    var commandIssuedEvent = new CommandIssuedEvent(
        command: new RequestEmployeeApproval(_traveler, _route)
    );

    _events.Append(confirmed);
    _events.Append(routeGenerated);
    _events.Append(commandIssuedEvent);
}

public void Process(FlightBooked booked)
{
    var commandIssuedEvent = new CommandIssuedEvent(
        command: new BookHotel(_destination, _parameters)
    );

    _events.Append(booked);
    _events.Append(commandIssuedEvent);
}
```

```
    . . .
}
```

In this example, the process manager has its explicit ID and persistent state, describing the trip that has to be booked. As in the earlier example of a saga pattern, the process manager subscribes to events that control the workflow (RouteConfirmed, RouteRejected, ReroutingConfirmed, etc.), and it instantiates events of type Command Issued Event that will be processed by an outbox relay to execute the actual commands.

Conclusion

In this chapter, you learned the different patterns for integrating a system's components. The chapter began by exploring patterns for model translations that can be used to implement anticorruption layers or open-host services. We saw that translations can be handled on the fly or can follow a more complex logic, requiring state tracking.

The outbox pattern is a reliable way to publish aggregates' domain events. It ensures that domain events are always going to be published, even in the face of different process failures.

The saga pattern can be used to implement simple cross-component business processes. More complex business processes can be implemented using the process manager pattern. Both patterns rely on asynchronous reactions to domain events and the issuing of commands.

Exercises

1. Which bounded context integration pattern requires implementation of model transformation logic?

    a. Conformist

    b. Anticorruption layer

    c. Open-host service

    d. B and C

2. What is the goal of the outbox pattern?

    a. Decouple messaging infrastructure from the system's business logic layer

    b. Reliably publish messages

    c. Support implementation of the event-sourced domain model pattern

    d. A and C

3. Apart from publishing messages to a message bus, what are other possible use cases for the outbox pattern?

4. What are the differences between the saga and process manager patterns?

   a. A process manager requires explicit instantiation, while a saga is executed when a relevant domain event is published.

   b. Contrary to a process manager, a saga never requires persistence of its execution state.

   c. A saga requires the components it manipulates to implement the event sourcing pattern, while a process manager doesn't.

   d. The process manager pattern is suitable for complex business workflows.

   e. A and D are correct.

PART III

Applying Domain-Driven Design in Practice

In Parts I and II, we discussed domain-driven design tools for making strategic and tactical design decisions. In this part of the book, we move from theory to practice. You will learn to apply domain-driven design in real-life projects.

- Chapter 10 merges what we discussed about strategic and tactical design into simple rules of thumb that streamline the process of making design decisions. You will learn to quickly identify patterns that match the business domain's complexity and needs.

- In Chapter 11, we will look at domain-driven design from a different perspective. Designing a great solution is important, but not enough. We have to keep it in shape as the project evolves through time. In this chapter, you will learn to apply domain-driven design tools to maintain and evolve software design decisions over time.

- Chapter 12 introduces EventStorming: a hands-on activity that streamlines the process of discovering domain knowledge and building a ubiquitous language.

- Chapter 13 concludes Part III with a selection of tips and tricks for "gently" introducing and incorporating domain-driven design patterns and practices in brownfield projects—the kinds of projects we work on the most.

Design Heuristics

"It depends" is the correct answer to almost any question in software engineering, but not really practical. In this chapter, we will explore what "it" depends on.

In Part I of the book, you learned domain-driven design tools for analyzing business domains and making strategic design decisions. In Part II, we explored tactical design patterns: the different ways to implement business logic, organize system architecture, and establish communication between a system's components. This chapter bridges Parts I and II. You will learn heuristics for applying analysis tools to drive various software design decisions: that is, (business) domain-driven (software) design.

But first, since this chapter is about design heuristics, let's start by defining the term *heuristic*.

Heuristic

A heuristic is not a hard rule that is guaranteed and mathematically proven to be correct in 100% of cases. Rather, it's a rule of thumb: not guaranteed to be perfect, yet sufficient for one's immediate goals. In other words, using heuristics is an effective problem-solving approach that ignores the noise inherent in many cues, focusing instead on the "swamping forces" reflected in the most important cues.[1]

The heuristics presented in this chapter focus on the essential properties of the different business domains and on the essence of the problems addressed by the various design decisions.

---

1 Gigerenzer, G., Todd, P. M., & ABC Research Group (Research Group, Max Planck Institute, Germany). (1999). *Simple Heuristics That Make Us Smart*. New York: Oxford University Press.

Bounded Contexts

As you'll recall from Chapter 3, both wide and narrow boundaries could fit the definition of a valid bounded context encompassing a consistent ubiquitous language. But still, what is the optimal size of a bounded context? This question is especially important in light of the frequent equation of bounded contexts with microservices.[2]

Should we always strive for the smallest possible bounded contexts? As my friend Nick Tune says:

> There are many useful and revealing heuristics for defining the boundaries of a service. Size is one of the least useful.

Rather than making the model a function of the desired size—optimizing for small bounded contexts—it's much more effective to do the opposite: treat the bounded context's size as a function of the model it encompasses.

Software changes affecting multiple bounded contexts are expensive and require lots of coordination, especially if the affected bounded contexts are implemented by different teams. Such changes that are not encapsulated in a single bounded context signal ineffective design of the contexts' boundaries. Unfortunately, refactoring bounded context boundaries is an expensive undertaking, and in many cases, the ineffective boundaries remain unattended and end up accumulating technical debt (see Figure 10-1).

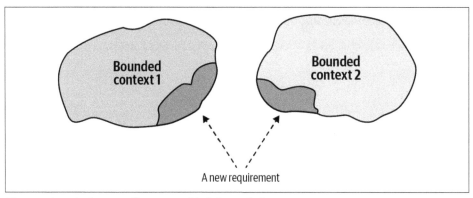

Figure 10-1. A change affecting multiple bounded contexts

Changes that invalidate the bounded contexts' boundaries typically occur when the business domain is not well known or the business requirements change frequently. As you learned in Chapter 1, both volatility and uncertainty are the properties of core

---

2 Chapter 11 is dedicated to the interplay between bounded contexts and microservices.

subdomains, especially at the early stages of implementation. We can use it as a heuristic for designing bounded context boundaries.

Broad bounded context boundaries, or those that encompass multiple subdomains, make it safer to be wrong about the boundaries or the models of the included subdomains. Refactoring logical boundaries is considerably less expensive than refactoring physical boundaries. Hence, when designing bounded contexts, start with wider boundaries. If required, decompose the wide boundaries into smaller ones as you gain domain knowledge.

This heuristic applies mainly to bounded contexts encompassing core subdomains, as both generic and supporting subdomains are more formularized and much less volatile. When creating a bounded context that contains a core subdomain, you can protect yourself against unforeseen changes by including other subdomains that the core subdomain interacts with most often. This can be other core subdomains, or even supporting and generic subdomains, as shown in Figure 10-2.

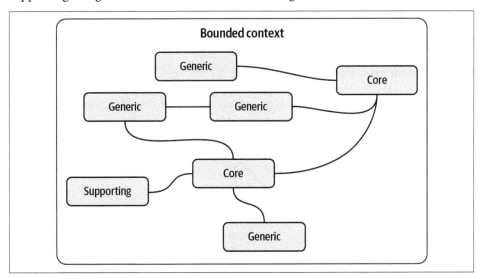

Figure 10-2. Wide bounded context boundaries

Business Logic Implementation Patterns

In Chapters 5–7, where we discussed business logic in detail, you learned four different ways to model business logic: the transaction script, active record, domain model, and event-sourced domain model patterns.

Both the transaction script and active record patterns are better suited for subdomains with simple business logic: supporting subdomains or integrating a third-party solution for a generic subdomain, for example. The difference between the two patterns is the complexity of the data structures. The transaction script pattern can be used for simple data structures, while the active record pattern helps to encapsulate the mapping of complex data structures to the underlying database.

The domain model and its variant, the event-sourced domain model, lend themselves to subdomains that have complex business logic: core subdomains. Core subdomains that deal with monetary transactions, are obligated by law to provide an audit log, or require deep analytics of the system's behavior are better addressed by the event-sourced domain model.

With all of this in mind, an effective heuristic for choosing the appropriate business logic implementation pattern is to ask the following questions:

- Does the subdomain track money or other monetary transactions or have to provide a consistent audit log, or is deep analysis of its behavior required by the business? If so, use the event-sourced domain model. Otherwise...

- Is the subdomain's business logic complex? If so, implement a domain model. Otherwise...

- Does the subdomain include complex data structures? If so, use the active record pattern. Otherwise...

- Implement a transaction script.

Since there is a strong relationship between a subdomain's complexity and its type, we can visualize the heuristics using a domain-driven decision tree, as shown in Figure 10-3.

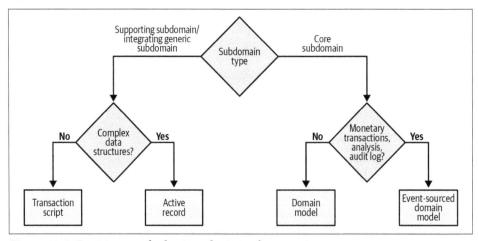

Figure 10-3. Decision tree for business logic implementation pattern

We can use another heuristic to define the difference between complex and simple business logic. The line between these two types of business logic is not terribly sharp, but it's useful. In general, complex business logic includes complicated business rules, invariants, and algorithms. A simple approach mainly revolves around validating the inputs. Another heuristic for evaluating complexity concerns the complexity of the ubiquitous language itself. Is it mainly describing CRUD operations, or is it describing more complicated business processes and rules?

Deciding on the business logic implementation pattern according to the complexity of the business logic and its data structures is a way to validate your assumptions about the subdomain type. Suppose you consider it to be a core subdomain, but the best pattern is active record or transaction script. Or suppose what you believe is a supporting subdomain requires a domain model or an event-sourced domain model; in this case, it's an excellent opportunity to revisit your assumptions about the subdomain and business domain in general. Remember, a core subdomain's competitive advantage is not necessarily technical.

Architectural Patterns

In Chapter 8, you learned about the three architectural patterns: layered architecture, ports & adapters, and CQRS.

Knowing the intended business logic implementation pattern makes choosing an architectural pattern straightforward:

- The event-sourced domain model requires CQRS. Otherwise, the system will be extremely limited in its data querying options, fetching a single instance by its ID only.

- The domain model requires the ports & adapters architecture. Otherwise, the layered architecture makes it hard to make aggregates and value objects ignorant of persistence.

- The Active record pattern is best accompanied by a layered architecture with the additional application (service) layer. This is for the logic controlling the active records.

- The transaction script pattern can be implemented with a minimal layered architecture, consisting of only three layers.

The only exception to the preceding heuristics is the CQRS pattern. CQRS can be beneficial not only for the event-sourced domain model, but also for any other pattern if the subdomain requires representing its data in multiple persistent models.

Figure 10-4 shows a decision tree for choosing an architectural pattern based on these heuristics.

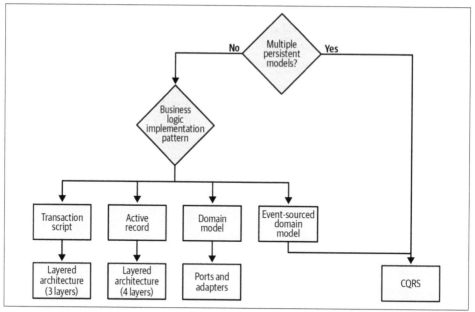

Figure 10-4. Architectural pattern decision tree

Testing Strategy

The knowledge of both the business logic implementation pattern and the architectural pattern can be used as a heuristic for choosing a testing strategy for the codebase. Take a look at the three testing strategies shown in Figure 10-5.

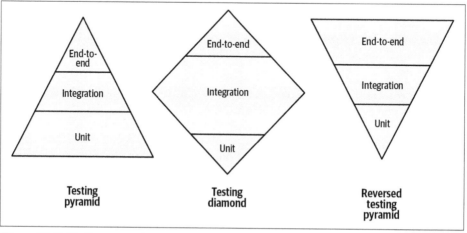

Figure 10-5. Testing strategies

The difference between the testing strategies in the figure is their emphasis on the different types of tests: unit, integration, and end-to-end. Let's analyze each strategy and the context in which each pattern should be used.

Testing Pyramid

The classic testing pyramid emphasizes unit tests, fewer integration tests, and even fewer end-to-end tests. Both variants of the domain model patterns are best addressed with the testing pyramid. Aggregates and value objects make perfect units for effectively testing the business logic.

Testing Diamond

The testing diamond focuses the most on integration tests. When the active record pattern is used, the system's business logic is, by definition, spread across both the service and business logic layers. Therefore, to focus on integrating the two layers, the testing pyramid is the more effective choice.

Reversed Testing Pyramid

The reversed testing pyramid attributes the most attention to end-to-end tests: verifying the application's workflow from beginning to end. Such an approach best fits codebases implementing the transaction script pattern: the business logic is simple and the number of layers is minimal, making it more effective to verify the end-to-end flow of the system.

Figure 10-6 shows the testing strategy decision tree.

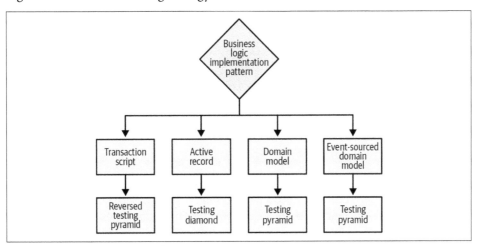

Figure 10-6. Testing strategy decision tree

Tactical Design Decision Tree

The business logic patterns, architectural patterns, and testing strategy heuristics can be unified and summarized with a tactical design decision tree, as depicted in Figure 10-7.

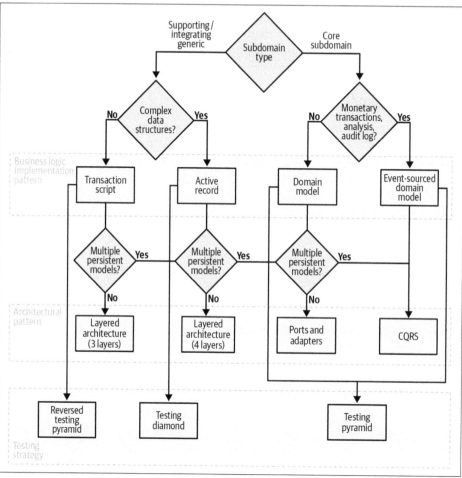

Figure 10-7. Tactical design decision tree

As you can see, identifying subdomains types and following the decision tree gives you a solid starting point for making the essential design decisions. That said, it's important to reiterate that these are heuristics, not hard rules. There is an exception to every rule, let alone heuristics, that by definition are not intended to be correct in 100% of the cases.

The decision tree is based on my preference to use the simple tools, and resort to the advanced patterns—domain model, event-sourced domain model, CQRS, and so on—only when absolutely necessary. On the other hand, I've met teams that have a lot of experience implementing the event-sourced domain model and therefore use it for all their subdomains. For them it's simpler than using different patterns. Can I recommend this approach to everyone? Of course not. In the companies I have worked for or consulted, the heuristics-based approach was more efficient than using the same solution for every problem.

At the end of the day, it depends on your specific context. Use the decision tree illustrated in Figure 10-7, and the design heuristics it is based on, as guiding principles, but not as a replacement for critical thinking. If you find that alternative heuristics fit you better, feel free to alter the guiding principles or build your own decision tree altogether.

Conclusion

This chapter connected Parts I and II of the book to a heuristic-based decision framework. You learned how to apply the knowledge of the business domain and its subdomains to drive technical decisions: choosing safe bounded context boundaries, modeling the application's business logic, and determining the architectural pattern needed to orchestrate the interactions of each bounded context's internal components. Finally, we took a detour into a different topic that is often a subject of passionate arguments—what kind of test is more important—and used the same framework to prioritize the different tests according to the business domain.

Making design decisions is important, but even more so is to verify the decisions' validity over time. In the next chapter, we will shift our discussion to the next phase of the software design lifecycle: the evolution of design decisions.

Exercises

1. Assume you are implementing WolfDesk's (see Preface) ticket lifecycle management system. It's a core subdomain that requires deep analysis of its behavior so that the algorithm can be further optimized over time. What would be your initial strategy implementing the business logic and the component's architecture? What would be your testing strategy?

2. What would be your design decisions for WolfDesk's support agents' shift management module?

3. To ease the process of managing agents' shifts, you want to use an external provider of public holidays for different geographical regions. The process works by periodically calling the external provider and fetching the dates and names of

forthcoming public holidays. What business logic and architectural patterns would you use to implement the integration? How would you test it?

4. Based on your experience, what other aspects of the software development process can be included in the heuristics-based decision tree presented in this chapter?

CHAPTER 11

Evolving Design Decisions

In the modern, fast-paced world we inhabit, companies cannot afford to be lethargic. To keep up with the competition, they have to continually change, evolve, and even reinvent themselves over time. We cannot ignore this fact when designing systems, especially if we intend to design software that's well adapted to the requirements of its business domain. When changes are not managed properly, even the most sophisticated and thoughtful design will eventually become a nightmare to maintain and evolve. This chapter discusses how changes in a software project's environment can affect design decisions and how to evolve the design accordingly. We will examine the four most common vectors of change: business domain, organizational structure, domain knowledge, and growth.

Changes in Domains

In Chapter 2, you've learned the three types of business subdomains and how they are different from one another:

Core
> Activities the company is performing differently from its competitors to gain a competitive advantage

Supporting
> Things the company is doing differently from its competitors, but that do not provide a competitive edge

Generic
> Things all companies do in the same way

In the previous chapters, you saw that the type of subdomain at play affects strategic and tactical design decisions:

- How to design the bounded contexts' boundaries
- How to orchestrate integration between the contexts
- Which design patterns to use to accommodate the complexity of the business logic

To design software that is driven by the business domain's needs, it's crucial to identify the business subdomains and their types. However, that's not the whole story. It's equally important to be alert to the evolution of the subdomains. As an organization grows and evolves, it's not unusual for some of its subdomains to morph from one type to another. Let's look at some examples of such changes.

Core to Generic

Imagine that an online retail company called BuyIT has been implementing its own order delivery solution. It developed an innovative algorithm to optimize its couriers' delivery routes and thus is able to charge lower delivery fees than its competitors.

One day, another company—DeliverIT—disrupts the delivery industry. It claims it has solved the "traveling salesman" problem and provides path optimization as a service. Not only is DeliverIT's optimization more advanced, it is offered at a fraction of the price that it costs BuyIT to perform the same task.

From BuyIT's perspective, once DeliverIT's solution became available as an off-the-shelf product, its core subdomain turned into a generic subdomain. As a result, the optimal solution became available to all of BuyIT's competitors. Without massive investments in research and development, BuyIT can no longer gain a competitive advantage in the path optimization subdomain. What was previously considered a competitive advantage for BuyIT has become a commodity available to all of its competitors.

Generic to Core

Since its inception, BuyIT has been using an off-the-shelf solution to manage its inventory. However, its business intelligence reports are continuously showing inadequate predictions of its customers' demands. Consequently, BuyIT fails to replenish its stock of the most popular products and is wasting warehouse real estate on the unpopular products. After evaluating a few alternative inventory management solutions, BuyIT's management team makes the strategic decision to invest in designing and building an in-house system. This in-house solution will consider the intricacies of the products BuyIT sells and make better predictions of customers' demands.

BuyIT's decision to replace the off-the-shelf solution with its own implementation has turned inventory management from a generic subdomain into a core subdomain: successful implementation of the functionality will provide BuyIT additional competitive advantage over its competitors—the competitors will remain "stuck" with the generic solution and will not be able to use the advanced demand prediction algorithms invented and developed by BuyIT.

A real-life textbook example of a company turning a generic subdomain into a core subdomain is Amazon. Like all service providers, Amazon needed an infrastructure on which to run its services. The company was able to "reinvent" the way it managed its physical infrastructure and later even turned it into a profitable business: Amazon Web Services.

Supporting to Generic

BuyIT's marketing department implements a system for managing the vendors it works with and their contracts. There is nothing special or complex about the system—it's just some CRUD user interfaces for entering data. In other words, it is a typical supporting subdomain.

However, a few years after BuyIT began implementing the in-house solution, an open source contracts management solution came out. The open source project implements the same functionality as the existing solution and has more advanced features, like OCR and full-text search. These additional features had been on BuyIT's backlog for a long time but were never prioritized because of their low business impact. Hence, the company decides to ditch the in-house solution in favor of integrating the open source solution. In doing so, the document management subdomain turns from a supporting into a generic subdomain.

Supporting to Core

A supporting subdomain can also turn into a core subdomain—for example, if a company finds a way to optimize the supporting logic in such a way that it either reduces costs or generates additional profits.

The typical symptom of such a transformation is the increasing complexity of the supporting subdomain's business logic. Supporting subdomains, by definition, are simple, mainly resembling CRUD interfaces or ETL processes. However, if the business logic becomes more complicated over time, there should be a reason for the additional complexity. If it doesn't affect the company's profits, why would it become more complicated? That's accidental business complexity. On the other hand, if it enhances the company's profitability, it's a sign of a supporting subdomain becoming a core subdomain.

Core to Supporting

A core subdomain can, over time, become a supporting subdomain. This can happen when the subdomain's complexity isn't justified. In other words, it's not profitable. In such cases, the organization may decide to cut the extraneous complexity, leaving the minimum logic needed to support implementation of other subdomains.

Generic to Supporting

Finally, for the same reason as a core subdomain, a generic subdomain can turn into a supporting one. Going back to the example of BuyIT's document management system, assume the company has decided that the complexity of integrating the open source solution doesn't justify the benefits and has resorted back to the in-house system. As a result, the generic subdomain has turned into a supporting subdomain.

The changes in subdomains we just discussed are demonstrated in Figure 11-1.

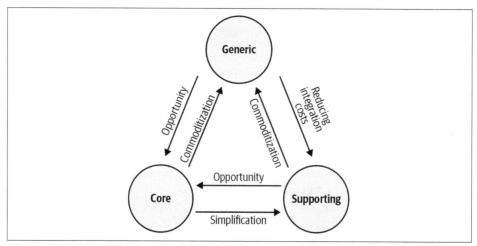

Figure 11-1. Subdomain type change factors

Strategic Design Concerns

A change in a subdomain's type directly affects its bounded context and, consequently, corresponding strategic design decisions. As you learned in Chapter 4, different bounded context integration patterns accommodate the different subdomain types. The core subdomains have to protect their models by using anticorruption layers and have to protect consumers from frequent changes in the implementation models by using published languages (OHS).

Another integration pattern that is affected by such changes is the separate ways pattern. As you saw earlier, teams can use this pattern for supporting and generic subdomains. If the subdomain morphs into a core subdomain, duplicating its functionality by multiple teams is no longer acceptable. Hence, the teams have no choice but to integrate their implementations. The customer–supplier relationship will make the most sense in this case, since the core subdomain will only be implemented by one team.

From an implementation strategy standpoint, core and supporting subdomains differ in how they can be implemented. Supporting subdomains can be outsourced or used as "training wheels" for new hires. Core subdomains must be implemented in-house, as close as possible to the sources of domain knowledge. Therefore, when a supporting subdomain turns into a core subdomain, its implementation should be moved in-house. The same logic works the other way around. If a core subdomain turns into a supporting subdomain, it's possible to outsource the implementation to let the in-house R&D teams concentrate on the core subdomains.

Tactical Design Concerns

The main indicator of a change in a subdomain's type is the inability of the existing technical design to support current business needs.

Let's go back to the example of a supporting subdomain becoming a core subdomain. Supporting subdomains are implemented with relatively simple design patterns for modeling the business logic: namely, the transaction script or active record pattern. As you saw in Chapter 5, these patterns are not a good fit for business logic involving complex rules and invariants.

If complicated rules and invariants are added to the business logic over time, the codebase will become increasingly complex as well. It will be painful to add the new functionality, as the design won't support the new level of complexity. This "pain" is an important signal. Use it as a call to reassess the business domain and design choices.

The need for change in the implementation strategy is nothing to fear. It's normal. We cannot foresee how a business will evolve down the road. We also cannot apply the most elaborate design patterns for all types of subdomains; that would be wasteful and ineffective. We have to choose the most appropriate design and evolve it when needed.

If the decision for how to model the business logic is made consciously, and you are aware of all the possible design choices and the differences between them, migrating from one design pattern to another is not that troublesome. The following subsections highlight a few examples.

Transaction Script to Active Record

At their core, both the transaction script and active record patterns are based on the same principle: the business logic is implemented as a procedural script. The difference between them is how the data structures are modeled: the active record pattern introduces the data structures to encapsulate the complexity of mapping them to the storage mechanism.

As a result, when working with data becomes challenging in a transaction script, refactor it into the active record pattern. Look for complicated data structures and encapsulate them in active record objects. Instead of accessing the database directly, use active records to abstract its model and structure.

Active Record to Domain Model

If the business logic that manipulates active records becomes complex and you notice more and more cases of inconsistencies and duplications, refactor the implementation to the domain model pattern.

Start by identifying value objects. What data structures can be modeled as immutable objects? Look for the related business logic, and make it a part of the value objects as well.

Next, analyze the data structures and look for transactional boundaries. To ensure that all state-modifying logic is explicit, make all of the active records' setters private so that they can only be modified from inside the active record itself. Obviously, expect the compilation to fail; however, the compilation errors will make it clear where the state-modifying logic resides. Refactor it into the active record's boundaries. For example:

```
public class Player
{
    public Guid Id { get; set; }
    public int Points { get; set; }
}

public class ApplyBonus
{
    ...

    public void Execute(Guid playerId, byte percentage)
    {
        var player = _repository.Load(playerId);
        player.Points *= 1 + percentage/100.0;
        _repository.Save(player);
    }
}
```

In the following code, you can see the first steps toward the transformation. The code won't compile yet, but the errors will make it explicit where external components are controlling the object's state:

```
public class Player
{
    public Guid Id { get; private set; }
    public int Points { get; private set; }
}

public class ApplyBonus
{

    ...

    public void Execute(Guid playerId, byte percentage)
    {
        var player = _repository.Load(playerId);
        player.Points *= 1 + percentage/100.0;
        _repository.Save(player);
    }
}
```

In the next iteration, we can move that logic inside the active record's boundary:

```
public class Player
{
    public Guid Id { get; private set; }
    public int Points { get; private set; }

    public void ApplyBonus(int percentage)
    {
        this.Points *= 1 + percentage/100.0;
    }
}
```

When all the state-modifying business logic is moved inside the boundaries of the corresponding objects, examine what hierarchies are needed to ensure strongly consistent checking of business rules and invariants. Those are good candidates for aggregates. Keeping in mind the aggregate design principles we discussed in Chapter 6, look for the smallest transaction boundaries, that is, the smallest amount of data that you need to keep strongly consistent. Decompose the hierarchies along those boundaries. Make sure the external aggregates are only referenced by their IDs.

Finally, for each aggregate, identify its root, or the entry point for its public interface. Make the methods of all the other internal objects in the aggregate private and only callable from within the aggregate.

Domain Model to Event-Sourced Domain Model

Once you have a domain model with properly designed aggregate boundaries, you can transition it to the event-sourced model. Instead of modifying the aggregate's data directly, model the domain events needed to represent the aggregate's lifecycle.

The most challenging aspect of refactoring a domain model into an event-sourced domain model is the history of the existing aggregates: migrating the "timeless" state into the event-based model. Since the fine-grained data representing all the past state changes is not there, you have to either generate past events on a best-effort basis or model migration events.

Generating Past Transitions

This approach entails generating an approximate stream of events for each aggregate so that the stream of events can be projected into the same state representation as in the original implementation. Consider the example you saw in Chapter 7, as represented in Table 11-1.

Table 11-1. A state-based representation of the aggregate's data

lead-in	first-name	last-name	phone_number	status	last-contacted-on	order-placed-on	converted-on	followup-on
12	Shauna	Mercia	555-4753	converted	2020-05-27T 12:02:12.51Z	2020-05-27T 12:02:12.51Z	2020-05-27T 12:02:12.51Z	null

We can assume from the business logic perspective that the instance of the aggregate has been initialized; then the person has been contacted, an order has been placed, and finally, since the status was "converted," the payment for the order has been confirmed. The following set of events can represent all of these assumptions:

```
{
    "lead-id": 12,
    "event-id": 0,
    "event-type": "lead-initialized",
    "first-name": "Shauna",
    "last-name": "Mercia",
    "phone-number": "555-4753"
},
{
    "lead-id": 12,
    "event-id": 1,
    "event-type": "contacted",
    "timestamp": "2020-05-27T12:02:12.51Z"
},
{
    "lead-id": 12,
    "event-id": 2,
```

```json
    "event-type": "order-submitted",
    "payment-deadline": "2020-05-30T12:02:12.51Z",
    "timestamp": "2020-05-27T12:02:12.51Z"
},
{
    "lead-id": 12,
    "event-id": 3,
    "event-type": "payment-confirmed",
    "status": "converted",
    "timestamp": "2020-05-27T12:38:44.12Z"
}
```

When applied one by one, these events can be projected into the exact state representation as in the original system. The "recovered" events can be easily tested by projecting the state and comparing it to the original data.

However, it's important to keep in mind the disadvantage of this approach. The goal of using event sourcing is to have a reliable, strongly consistent history of the aggregates' domain events. When this approach is used, it's impossible to recover the complete history of state transitions. In the preceding example, we don't know how many times the sales agent has contacted the person, and therefore, how many "contacted" events we have missed.

Modeling Migration Events

The alternative approach is to acknowledge the lack of knowledge about past events and explicitly model it as an event. Instead of recovering the events that may have led to the current state, define a migration event and use it to initialize the event streams of existing aggregate instances:

```json
{
    "lead-id": 12,
    "event-id": 0,
    "event-type": "migrated-from-legacy",
    "first-name": "Shauna",
    "last-name": "Mercia",
    "phone-number": "555-4753",
    "status": "converted",
    "last-contacted-on": "2020-05-27T12:02:12.51Z",
    "order-placed-on": "2020-05-27T12:02:12.51Z",
    "converted-on": "2020-05-27T12:38:44.12Z",
    "followup-on": null
}
```

The advantage of this approach is that it makes the lack of past data explicit. At no stage can someone mistakenly assume that the event stream captures all of the domain events that happened during the aggregate instance's lifecycle. The disadvantage is that the traces of the legacy system will remain in the event store forever. For example, if you are using the CQRS pattern (and with the event-sourced domain model you most likely will), the projections will always have to take into account the migration events.

Organizational Changes

Another type of change that can affect a system's design is a change in the organization itself. Chapter 4 looked at different patterns of integrating bounded contexts: partnership, shared kernel, conformist, anticorruption layer, open-host service, and separate ways. Changes in the organization's structure can affect teams' communication and collaboration levels and, as a result, the ways the bounded contexts should be integrated.

A trivial example of such change is growing development centers, as shown in Figure 11-2. Since a bounded context can be implemented by only one team, adding new development teams can cause the existing wider bounded context boundaries to split into smaller ones so that each team can work on its own bounded context.

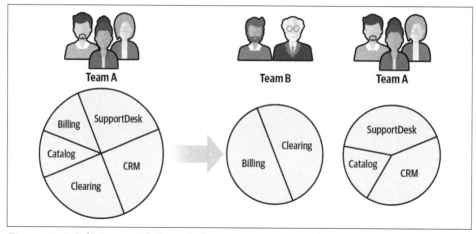

Figure 11-2. Splitting a wide bounded context to accommodate growing engineering teams

Moreover, the organization's development centers are often located in different geographical locations. When the work on the existing bounded contexts is shifted to another location, it may negatively impact the teams' collaboration. As a result, the bounded contexts' integration patterns have to evolve accordingly, as described in the following scenarios.

Partnership to Customer–Supplier

The partnership pattern assumes there is strong communication and collaboration among teams. As time goes by, that might cease to be the case; for example, when work on one of the bounded contexts is moved to a distant development center. Such a change will negatively affect the teams' communication, and it may make sense to move away from the partnership pattern toward a customer–supplier relationship.

Customer–Supplier to Separate Ways

Unfortunately, it's not uncommon for teams to have severe communication problems. The issues might be caused by geographical distance or organizational politics. Such teams may experience more and more integration issues over time. At some point, it may become more cost-effective to duplicate the functionality instead of continuously chasing one another's tails.

Domain Knowledge

As you'll recall, the core tenet of domain-driven design is that domain knowledge is essential for designing a successful software system. Acquiring domain knowledge is one of the most challenging aspects of software engineering, especially for the core subdomains. A core subdomain's logic is not only complicated, but also expected to change often. Moreover, modeling is an ongoing process. Models have to improve as more knowledge of the business domain is acquired.

Many times, the business domain's complexity is implicit. Initially, everything seems simple and straightforward. The initial simplicity is often deceptive and it quickly morphs into complexity. As more functionality is added, more and more edge cases, invariants, and rules are discovered. Such insights are often disruptive, requiring rebuilding the model from the ground up, including the boundaries of the bounded contexts, aggregates, and other implementation details.

From a strategic design standpoint, it's a useful heuristic to design the bounded contexts' boundaries according to the level of domain knowledge. The cost of decomposing a system into bounded contexts that, over time, turn out to be incorrect can be high. Therefore, when the domain logic is unclear and changes often, it makes sense to design the bounded contexts with broader boundaries. Then, as domain knowledge is discovered over time and changes to the business logic stabilize, those broad bounded contexts can be decomposed into contexts with narrower boundaries, or *microservices*. We will discuss the interplay between bounded contexts and microservices in more detail in Chapter 14.

When new domain knowledge is discovered, it should be leveraged to evolve the design and make it more resilient. Unfortunately, changes in domain knowledge are not always positive: domain knowledge can be lost. As time goes by, documentation often becomes stale, people who were working on the original design leave the company, and new functionality is added in an ad hoc manner until, at one point, the codebase gains the dubious status of a legacy system. It's vital to prevent such degradation of domain knowledge proactively. An effective tool for recovering domain knowledge is the EventStorming workshop, which is the topic of the next chapter.

Growth

Growth is a sign of a healthy system. When new functionality is continuously added, it's a sign that the system is successful: it brings value to its users and is expanded to further address users' needs and keep up with competing products. But growth has a dark side. As a software project grows, its codebase can grow into a big ball of mud:

> A big ball of mud is a haphazardly structured, sprawling, sloppy, duct-tape-and-baling-wire, spaghetti-code jungle. These systems show unmistakable signs of unregulated growth, and repeated, expedient repair.
>
> —Brian Foote and Joseph Yoder[1]

The unregulated growth that leads to big balls of mud results from extending a software system's functionality without re-evaluating its design decisions. Growth blows up the components' boundaries, increasingly extending their functionality. It's crucial to examine the effects of growth on design decisions, especially since many domain-driven design tools are all about setting boundaries: business building blocks (subdomains), model (bounded contexts), immutability (value objects), or consistency (aggregates).

The guiding principle for dealing with growth-driven complexity is to identify and eliminate accidental complexity: the complexity caused by outdated design decisions. The essential complexity, or inherent complexity of the business domain, should be managed using domain-driven design tools and practices.

When we discuss DDD in earlier chapters, we follow the process of first analyzing the business domain and its strategic components, designing the relevant models of the business domain, and then designing and implementing the models in code. Let's follow the same script for dealing with growth-driven complexity.

Subdomains

As we discussed in Chapter 1, the subdomains' boundaries can be challenging to identify, and as a result, instead of striving for boundaries that are perfect, we must strive for boundaries that are useful. That is, the subdomains should allow us to

---

1 Brian Foote and Joseph Yoder. Big Ball of Mud. Fourth Conference on Patterns Languages of Programs (PLoP '97/EuroPLoP '97), Monticello, Illinois, September 1997.

identify components of different business value and use the appropriate tools to design and implement the solution.

As the business domain grows, the subdomains' boundaries can become even more blurred, making it harder to identify cases of a subdomain spanning multiple, finer-grained subdomains. Hence, it's important to revisit the identified subdomains and follow the heuristic of coherent use cases (sets of use cases working on the same set of data) to try to identify where to split a subdomain (see Figure 11-3).

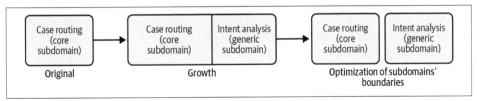

Figure 11-3. Optimizing subdomains' boundaries to accommodate growth

If you are able to identify finer-grained subdomains of different types, this is an important insight that will allow you to manage the business domain's essential complexity. The more precise the information about the subdomains and their types is, the more effective you will be at choosing technical solutions for each subdomain.

Identifying inner subdomains that can be extracted and made explicit is especially important for core subdomains. We should always aim to distill core subdomains as much as possible from all others so that we can invest our effort where it matters most from a business strategy perspective.

Bounded Contexts

In Chapter 3, you learned that the bounded context pattern allows us to use different models of the business domain. Instead of building a "jack of all trades, master of none" model, we can build multiple models, each focused on solving a specific problem.

As a project evolves and grows, it's not uncommon for the bounded contexts to lose their focus and accumulate logic related to different problems. That's accidental complexity. As with subdomains, it's crucial to revisit the bounded contexts' boundaries from time to time. Always look for opportunities to simplify the models by extracting bounded contexts that are laser focused at solving specific problems.

Growth can also make existing implicit design issues explicit. For example, you may notice that a number of bounded contexts become increasingly "chatty" over time, unable to complete any operation without calling another bounded context. That can be a strong signal of an ineffective model and should be addressed by redesigning the bounded contexts' boundaries to increase their autonomy.

Aggregates

When we discussed the domain model pattern in Chapter 6, we used the following guiding principle for designing aggregates' boundaries:

> The rule of thumb is to keep the aggregates as small as possible and include only objects that are required to be in a strongly consistent state by the business domain.

As the system's business requirements grow, it can be "convenient" to distribute the new functionalities among the existing aggregates, without revisiting the principle of keeping aggregates small. If an aggregate grows to include data that is not needed to be strongly consistent by all of its business logic, again, that's accidental complexity that has to be eliminated.

Extracting business functionality into a dedicated aggregate not only simplifies the original aggregate, but potentially can simplify the bounded context it belongs to. Often, such refactoring uncovers an additional hidden model that, once made explicit, should be extracted into a different bounded context.

Conclusion

As Heraclitus famously said, the only constant in life is change. Businesses are no exception. To stay competitive, companies constantly strive to evolve and reinvent themselves. Those changes should be treated as first-class elements of the design process.

As the business domain evolves, changes to its subdomains must be identified and acted on in the system's design. Make sure your past design decisions are aligned with the current state of the business domain and its subdomains. When needed, evolve your design to better match the current business strategy and needs.

It's also important to recognize that changes in the organizational structure can affect communication and cooperation among teams and the ways their bounded contexts can be integrated. Learning about the business domain is an ongoing process. As more domain knowledge is discovered over time, it has to be leveraged to evolve strategic and tactical design decisions.

Finally, software growth is a desired type of change, but when it is not managed correctly, it may have disastrous effects on the system design and architecture. Therefore:

- When a subdomain's functionality is expanded, try to identify more finer-grained subdomain boundaries that will enable you to make better design decisions.
- Don't allow a bounded context to become a "jack of all trades." Make sure the models encompassed by bounded contexts are focused to solve specific problems.

- Make sure your aggregates' boundaries are as small as possible. Use the heuristic of strongly consistent data to detect possibilities to extract business logic into new aggregates.

My final words of wisdom on the topic are to continuously check the different boundaries for signs of growth-driven complexity. Act to eliminate accidental complexities, and use domain-driven design tools to manage the business domain's essential complexity.

Exercises

1. What kind of changes in bounded context integration are often caused by organizational growth?

    a. Partnership to customer–supplier (conformist, anticorruption layer, or open-host service)

    b. Anticorruption layer to open-host service

    c. Conformist to shared kernel

    d. Open-host service to shared kernel

2. Assume that the bounded contexts' integration shifts from a conformist relationship to separate ways. What information can you deduce based on the change?

    a. The development teams struggled to cooperate.

    b. The duplicate functionality is either a supporting or a generic subdomain.

    c. The duplicate functionality is a core subdomain.

    d. A and B.

    e. A and C.

3. What are the symptoms of a supporting subdomain becoming a core subdomain?

    a. It becomes easier to evolve the existing model and implement the new requirements.

    b. It becomes painful to evolve the existing model.

    c. The subdomain changes at a higher frequency.

    d. B and C.

    e. None of the above.

4. What change results from discovering a new business opportunity?

   a. A supporting subdomain turns into a core one.

   b. A supporting subdomain turns into a generic one.

   c. A generic subdomain turns into a core one.

   d. A generic subdomain turns into a supporting one.

   e. A and B.

   f. A and C.

5. What change in the business strategy could turn one of WolfDesk's (the fictitious company described in the Preface) generic subdomains into a core subdomain?

CHAPTER 12

EventStorming

In this chapter, we will take a break from discussing software design patterns and techniques. Instead, we will focus on a low-tech modeling process called *EventStorming*. This process brings together the core aspects of domain-driven design that we covered in the preceding chapters.

You will learn the EventStorming process, how to facilitate an EventStorming workshop, and how to leverage EventStorming to effectively share domain knowledge and build a ubiquitous language.

What Is EventStorming?

EventStorming is a low-tech activity for a group of people to brainstorm and rapidly model a business process. In a sense, EventStorming is a tactical tool for sharing business domain knowledge.

An EventStorming session has a *scope*: the business process that the group is interested in exploring. The participants are exploring the process as a series of domain events, represented by sticky notes, over a timeline. Step by step, the model is enhanced with additional concepts—actors, commands, external systems, and others—until all of its elements tell the story of how the business process works.

Who Should Participate in EventStorming?

> *Just keep in mind that the goal of the workshop is to learn as much as possible in the shortest time possible. We invite key people to the workshop, and we don't want to waste their valuable time.*
>
> —Alberto Brandolini, creator of the *EventStorming* workshop

Ideally, a diverse group of people should participate in the workshop. Indeed, anyone related to the business domain in question can participate: engineers, domain experts, product owners, testers, UI/UX designers, support personnel, and so on. As more people with different backgrounds are involved, more knowledge will be discovered.

Take care not to make the group too big, however. Every participant should be able to contribute to the process, but this can be challenging for groups of more than 10 participants.

What Do You Need for EventStorming?

EventStorming is considered a low-tech workshop because it is done using a pen and paper—a lot of paper, actually. Let's see what you need in order to facilitate an EventStorming session:

Modeling space
> First, you need a large modeling space. A whole wall covered with butcher paper makes the best modeling space, as shown in Figure 12-1. A large whiteboard can fit the purpose as well, but it has to be as big as possible—you will need all the modeling space you can get.

Sticky notes
> Next, you need lots of sticky notes of different colors. The notes will be used to represent different concepts of the business domain, and every participant should be able to add them freely, so make sure you have enough colors and enough for everyone. The colors that are traditionally used for EventStorming are described in the next section. It's best to stick to these conventions, if possible, to be consistent with all of the currently available EventStorming books and trainings.

Markers
> You'll also need markers that you can use to write on the sticky notes. Again, supplies shouldn't be a bottleneck for knowledge sharing—there should be enough markers for all participants.

Snacks
> A typical EventStorming session lasts about two to four hours, so bring some healthy snacks for energy replenishment.

Room

Finally, you need a spacious room. Ensure there isn't a huge table in the middle that will prevent participants from moving freely and observing the modeling space. Also, chairs are a big no-no for EventStorming sessions. You want people to participate and share knowledge, not sit in a corner and zone out. Therefore, if possible, take the chairs out of the room.[1]

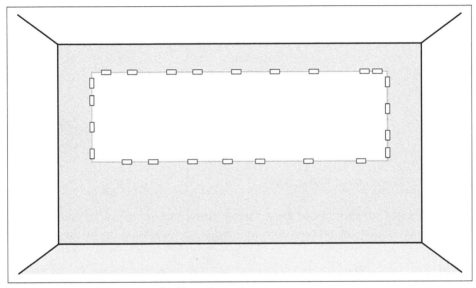

Figure 12-1. Modeling space for EventStorming

The EventStorming Process

An EventStorming workshop is usually conducted in 10 steps. During each step, the model is enriched with additional information and concepts.

Step 1: Unstructured Exploration

EventStorming starts with a brainstorm of the domain events related to the business domain being explored. A *domain event* is something interesting that has happened in the business. It's important to formulate domain events in the past tense (see Figure 12-2)—they are describing things that have already happened.

---

1 Of course, that's not a hard rule. Leave a few chairs if some of the participants find it hard to be on their feet for so long.

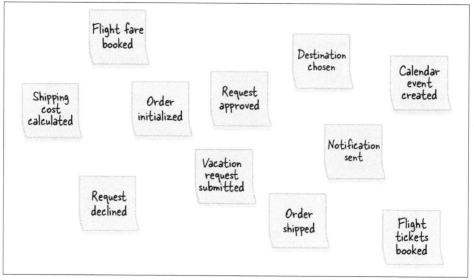

Figure 12-2. Unstructured exploration

During this step, all participants are grabbing a bunch of orange sticky notes, writing down whatever domain events come to mind, and sticking them to the modeling surface.

At this early stage, there is no need to worry about ordering events, or even about redundancy. This step is all about brainstorming the possible things that can happen in the business domain.

The group should continue generating domain events until the rate of adding new ones slows significantly.

Step 2: Timelines

Next, the participants go over the generated domain events and organize them in the order in which they occur in the business domain.

The events should start with the "happy path scenario": the flow that describes a successful business scenario.

Once the "happy path" is done, alternative scenarios can be added—for example, paths where errors are encountered or different business decisions are taken. The flow branching can be expressed as two flows coming from the preceding event or with arrows drawn on the modeling surface, as shown in Figure 12-3.

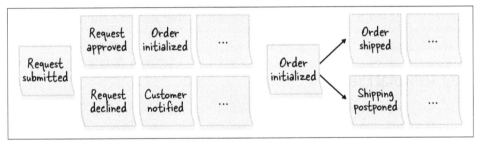

Figure 12-3. Flows of events

This step is also the time to fix incorrect events, remove duplicates, and of course, add missing events if necessary.

Step 3: Pain Points

Once you have the events organized in a timeline, use this broad view to identify points in the process that require attention. These can be bottlenecks, manual steps that require automation, missing documentation, or missing domain knowledge.

It's important to make these inefficiencies explicit so that it will be easy to return to them as the EventStorming session progresses, or to address them afterward. The pain points are marked with rotated (diamond) pink sticky notes, as illustrated in Figure 12-4.

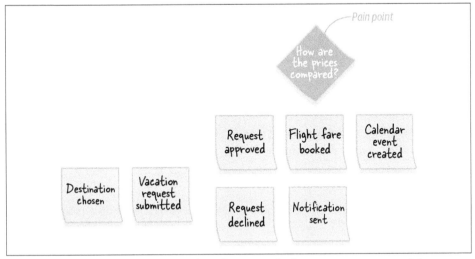

Figure 12-4. A diamond-shaped pink sticky note, which points to an aspect of the process that requires attention: missing domain knowledge about how the airfare prices are compared during the booking process

Of course, this step is not the only opportunity to track pain points. As a facilitator, be aware of the participants' comments throughout the process. When an issue or a concern is raised, document it as a pain point.

Step 4: Pivotal Events

Once you have a timeline of events augmented with pain points, look for significant business events indicating a change in context or phase. These are called *pivotal events* and are marked with a vertical bar dividing the events before and after the pivotal event.

For example, "shopping cart initialized," "order initialized," "order shipped," "order delivered," and "order returned" represent significant changes in the process of making an order, as shown in Figure 12-5.

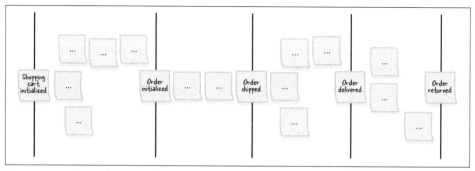

Figure 12-5. Pivotal events denoting context changes in the flow of events

Pivotal events are an indicator of potential bounded context boundaries.

Step 5: Commands

Whereas a domain event describes something that has already happened, a *command* describes what triggered the event or flow of events. Commands describe the system's operations and, contrary to domain events, are formulated in the imperative. For example:

- Publish campaign
- Roll back transaction
- Submit order

Commands are written on light blue sticky notes and placed on the modeling space before the events they can produce. If a particular command is executed by an actor in a specific role, the actor information is added to the command on a small yellow sticky note, as illustrated in Figure 12-6. The actor represents a user persona within the business domain, such as customer, administrator, or editor.

Naturally, not all commands will have an associated actor. Therefore, add the actor information only where it's obvious. In the next step we will augment the model with additional entities that can trigger commands.

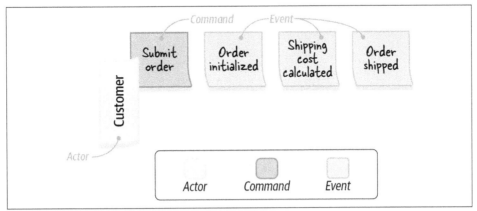

Figure 12-6. The "Submit Order" command, executed by the customer (actor) and followed by the "Order initialized," "Shipping cost calculated," and "Order shipped" events

Step 6: Policies

Almost always, some commands are added to the model but have no specific actor associated with them. During this step, you look for automation policies that might execute those commands.

An *automation policy* is a scenario in which an event triggers the execution of a command. In other words, a command is automatically executed when a specific domain event occurs.

On the modeling surface, policies are represented as purple sticky notes connecting events to commands, as shown by the "Policy" sticky note in Figure 12-7.

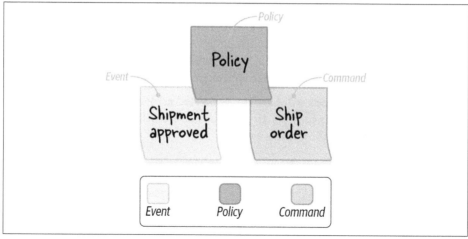

Figure 12-7. An automation policy that triggers the "Ship Order" command when the "Shipment Approved" event is observed

If the command in question should be triggered only if some decision criteria is met, you can specify the decision criteria explicitly on the policy sticky note. For example, if you need to trigger the escalate command after the "complaint received" event, but only if the complaint was received from a VIP customer, you can explicitly state the "only for VIP customers" condition on the policy sticky.

If the events and commands are far apart, you can draw an arrow on the modeling surface to connect them.

Step 7: Read Models

A read model is the view of data within the domain that the actor uses to make a decision to execute a command. This can be one of the system's screens, a report, a notification, and so on.

The read models are represented by green sticky notes (see the "Shopping cart" note in Figure 12-8) with a short description of the source of information needed to support the actor's decision. Since a command is executed after the actor has viewed the read model, on the modeling surface the read models are positioned before the commands.

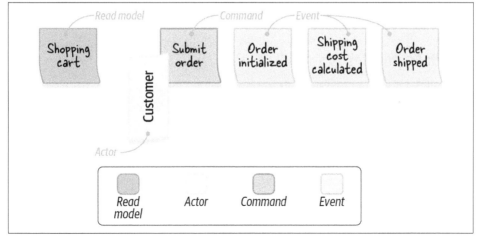

Figure 12-8. The view of the "Shopping cart" (read model) needed for the customer (actor) to make their decision to submit the order (command)

Step 8: External Systems

This step is about augmenting the model with external systems. An *external system* is defined as any system that is not a part of the domain being explored. It can execute commands (input) or can be notified about events (output).

The external systems are represented by pink sticky notes. In Figure 12-9, the CRM (external system) triggers execution of the "Ship Order" command. When the shipment is approved (event), it is communicated to the CRM (external system) through a policy.

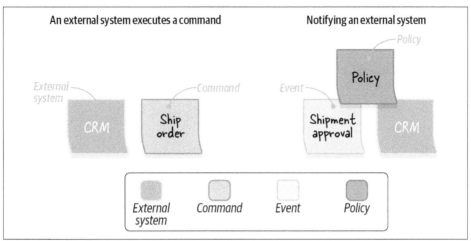

Figure 12-9. External system triggering execution of a command (left) and approval of the event being communicated to the external system (right)

By the end of this step, all commands should either be executed by actors, triggered by policies, or called by external systems.

Step 9: Aggregates

Once all the events and commands are represented, the participants can start thinking about organizing related concepts in aggregates. An *aggregate* receives commands and produces events.

Aggregates are represented as large yellow sticky notes, with commands on the left and events on the right, as depicted in Figure 12-10.

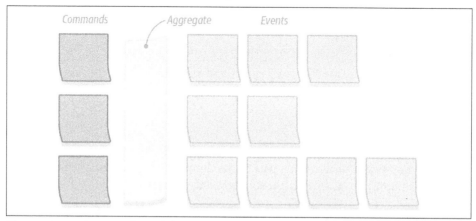

Figure 12-10. Commands and domain events organized in an aggregate

Step 10: Bounded Contexts

The last step of an EventStorming session is to look for aggregates that are related to each other, either because they represent closely related functionality or because they're coupled through policies. The groups of aggregates form natural candidates for bounded contexts' boundaries, as shown in Figure 12-11.

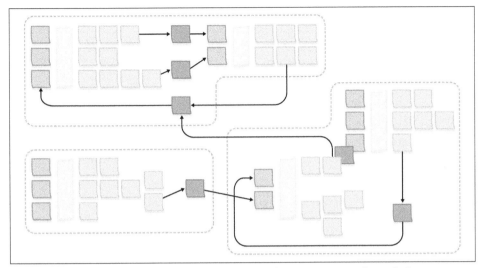

Figure 12-11. A possible decomposition of the resultant system into bounded contexts

Variants

Alberto Brandolini, the creator of the EventStorming workshop, defines the Event-Storming process as *guidance, not hard rules*. You are free to experiment with the process to find the "recipe" that works best for you.

In my experience, when introducing EventStorming in an organization I prefer to start by exploring the big picture of the business domain by following steps 1 (chaotic exploration) through 4 (pivotal events). The resultant model covers a wide range of the company's business domain, builds a strong foundation for ubiquitous languages, and outlines possible boundaries for bounded contexts.

After gaining the big picture and identifying the different business processes, we continue to facilitate a dedicated EventStorming session for each relevant business process—this time, following all the steps to model the complete process.

At the end of a full EventStorming session, you will have a model describing the business domain's events, commands, aggregates, and even possible bounded contexts. However, all of these are just nice bonuses. The real value of an EventStorming session is the process itself—the sharing of knowledge among different stakeholders, alignment of their mental models of the business, discovery of conflicting models, and, last but not least, formulation of the ubiquitous language.

The resultant model can be adopted as a basis for implementing an event-sourced domain model. The decision of whether to go that route or not depends on your business domain. If you decide to implement the event-sourced domain model, you have the bounded context boundaries, the aggregates, and of course, the blueprint of the required domain events.

When to Use EventStorming

The workshop can be facilitated for many reasons:

Build a ubiquitous language
　　As the group cooperates in building the model of the business process, they instinctively synchronize the terminology and start using the same language.

Model the business process
　　An EventStorming session is an effective way to build a model of the business process. Since it is based on DDD-oriented building blocks, it is also an effective way to discover the boundaries of aggregates and bounded contexts.

Explore new business requirements
　　You can use EventStorming to ensure that all the participants are on the same page regarding the new functionality and reveal edge cases not covered by the business requirements.

Recover domain knowledge
　　Over time, domain knowledge can get lost. This is especially acute in legacy systems that require modernization. EventStorming is an effective way to merge the knowledge held by each participant into a single coherent picture.

Explore ways to improve an existing business process
　　Having an end-to-end view of a business process provides the perspective needed to notice inefficiencies and opportunities to improve the process.

Onboard new team members
　　Facilitating an EventStorming session together with new team members is a great way to expand their domain knowledge.

In addition to when to use EventStorming, it's important to mention when not to use it. EventStorming will be less successful when the business process you're exploring is simple or obvious, such as following a series of sequential steps without any interesting business logic or complexity.

Facilitation Tips

When facilitating an EventStorming session with a group of people who have never done EventStorming before, I prefer to start with a quick overview of the process. I explain what we are about to do, the business process we are about to explore, and the modeling elements we will use in the workshop. As we go through the elements—domain events, commands, actors, and so on—I build a legend, depicted in

Figure 12-12, using the sticky notes we will use and labels to help the participants remember the color code. The legend should be visible to all participants during the workshop.

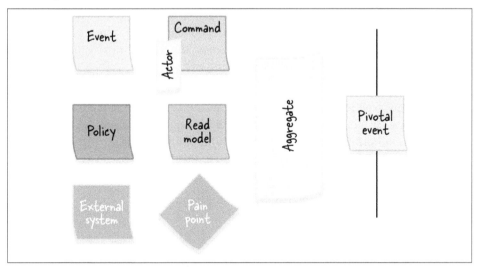

Figure 12-12. Legend depicting the various elements of the EventStorming process written on the corresponding sticky notes

Watch the Dynamics

As the workshop progresses, it's important to track the energy of the group. If the dynamics are slowing down, see whether you can reignite the process by asking questions or whether it's time to advance to the next stage of the workshop.

Remember that EventStorming is a group activity, so ensure that it is handled as such. Make sure everyone has a chance to participate in the modeling and the discussion. If you notice that some participants are shying away from the group, try to involve them in the process by asking questions about the current state of the model.

EventStorming is an intense activity, and at some point, the group will need a break. Don't resume the session until all the participants are back in the room. Resume the process by going through the current state of the model to return the group to a collaborative modeling mood.

Remote EventStorming

EventStorming was invented as a low-tech activity in which people interact and learn together in the same room. The creator of the workshop, Alberto Brandolini, has often objected to conducting EventStorming remotely because it's impossible to achieve the same levels of participation, and hence, collaboration and knowledge sharing, when the group is not colocated.

However, with the onset of the COVID-19 pandemic in 2020, it became impossible to have in-person meetings and do EventStorming as it was meant to be done. A number of tools attempted to enable collaboration and facilitation of remote EventStorming sessions. At the time of this writing, the most notable of them is miro.com. Be more patient when doing online EventStorming and take into account the less effective communication that results.

In addition, my experience shows that remote EventStorming sessions are more effective with a smaller number of participants. While as many as 10 people can attend an in-person EventStorming session, I prefer to limit online sessions to five participants. When you need more participants to contribute their knowledge, you can facilitate multiple sessions, and afterward compare and merge the resultant models.

When the situation allows, return to in-person EventStorming.

Conclusion

EventStorming is a collaboration-based workshop for modeling business processes. Apart from the resultant models, its primary benefit is knowledge sharing. By the end of the session, all the participants will synchronize their mental models of the business process and take the first steps toward using a ubiquitous language.

EventStorming is like riding a bicycle. It's much easier to learn by doing it than to read about it in a book. Nevertheless, the workshop is fun and easy to facilitate. You don't need to be an EventStorming black belt to get started. Just facilitate the session, follow the steps, and learn during the process.

Exercises

1. Who should be invited to an EventStorming session?

    a. Software engineers

    b. Domain experts

    c. QA engineers

    d. All stakeholders having knowledge of the business domain that you want to explore

2. When is it a good opportunity to facilitate an EventStorming session?

    a. To build a ubiquitous language.

    b. To explore a new business domain.

    c. To recover lost knowledge of a brownfield project.

    d. To introduce new team members.

    e. To discover ways to optimize the business process.

    f. All of the above answers are correct.

3. What outcomes can you expect from an EventStorming session?

    a. A better shared understanding of the business domain

    b. A strong foundation for a ubiquitous language

    c. Uncovered white spots in the understanding of the business domain

    d. An event-based model that can be used to implement a domain model

    e. All of the above, but depending on the session's purpose

CHAPTER 13

Domain-Driven Design in the Real World

We have covered domain-driven design tools for analyzing business domains, sharing knowledge, and making strategic and tactical design decisions. Just imagine how fun it will be to apply this knowledge in practice. Let's consider a scenario in which you are working on a greenfield project. All of your coworkers have a strong grasp of domain-driven design, and right from the get-go all are doing their best to design effective models and, of course, are devotedly using the ubiquitous language. As the project advances, the bounded contexts' boundaries are explicit and effective in protecting the business domain models. Finally, since all tactical design decisions are aligned with the business strategy, the codebase is always in great shape: it speaks the ubiquitous language and implements the design patterns that accommodate the model's complexity. Now wake up.

Your chances of experiencing the laboratory conditions I just described are about as good as winning the lottery. Of course, it's possible, but not likely. Unfortunately, many people mistakenly believe that domain-driven design can only be applied in greenfield projects and in ideal conditions in which everybody on the team is a DDD black belt. Ironically, the projects that can benefit from DDD the most are the brownfield projects: those that already proved their business viability and need a shake-up to fight accumulated technical debt and design entropy. Coincidentally, working on such brownfield, legacy, big-balls-of-mud codebases is where we spend most of our software engineering careers.

Another common misconception about DDD is that it's an all-or-nothing proposition—either you apply every tool the methodology has to offer, or it's not domain-driven design. That's not true. It might seem overwhelming to come to grips with all of these concepts, let alone implement them in practice. Luckily, you don't have to apply all of the patterns and practices to gain value from domain-driven design. This is especially true for brownfield projects, where it's practically impossible to introduce all the patterns and practices in a reasonable time frame.

In this chapter, you will learn strategies for applying domain-driven design tools and patterns in the real world, including on brownfield projects and in less-than-ideal environments.

Strategic Analysis

Following the order of our exploration of domain-driven design patterns and practices, the best starting point for introducing DDD in an organization is to invest time in understanding the organization's business strategy and the current state of its systems' architecture.

Understand the Business Domain

First, identify the company's business domain:

- What is the organization's business domain(s)?
- Who are its customers?
- What service, or value, does the organization provide to customers?
- What companies or products is the organization competing with?

Answering these questions will give you a bird's-eye view of the company's high-level goals. Next, "zoom in" to the domain and look for the business building blocks the organization employs to achieve its high-level goals: the subdomains.

A good initial heuristic is the company's org chart: its departments and other organizational units. Examine how these units cooperate to allow the company to compete in its business domain.

Furthermore, look for the signs of specific types of subdomains.

Core subdomains

To identify the company's core subdomains, look for what differentiates it from its competitors:

- Does the company have a "secret sauce" that its competitors lack? For example, intellectual property, such as patents and algorithms designed in-house?
- Keep in mind that the competitive advantage, and thus the core subdomains, are not necessarily technical. Does the company possess a nontechnical competitive

advantage? For example, the ability to hire top-level personnel, produce a unique artistic design, and so on?

Another powerful yet unfortunate heuristic for core subdomains is identifying the worst-designed software components—those big balls of mud that all engineers hate but the business is unwilling to rewrite from scratch because of the accompanying business risk. The key here is that the legacy system cannot be replaced with a ready-made system—it would be a generic subdomain—and any modification to it entails business risks.

Generic subdomains

To identify generic subdomains, look for off-the-shelf solutions, subscription services, or integration of open source software. As you learned in Chapter 1, the same ready-made solutions should be available to the competing companies, and those companies leveraging the same solution should have no business impact on your company.

Supporting subdomains

For supporting subdomains, look for the remaining software components that cannot be replaced with ready-made solutions yet do not directly provide a competitive advantage. If the code is in rough shape, it triggers less emotional response from software engineers since it changes infrequently. Thus, the effects of the suboptimal software design are not as severe as for the core subdomains.

You don't have to identify all of the core subdomains. It won't be practical or even possible to do so, even for a medium-sized company. Instead, identify the overall structure, but pay closer attention to the subdomains that are most relevant to the software systems you are working on.

Explore the Current Design

Once you are familiar with the problem domain, you can continue to investigate the solution and its design decisions. First, start with the high-level components. These are not necessarily bounded contexts in the DDD sense, but rather boundaries used to decompose the business domain into subsystems.

The characteristic property to look for is the components' decoupled lifecycles. Even if the subsystems are managed in the same source control repository (mono-repo) or if all the components reside in a single monolithic codebase, check which can be evolved, tested, and deployed independently from the others.

Evaluate the tactical design

For each high-level component, check which business subdomains it contains and what technical design decisions were taken: what patterns are used to implement the business logic and define the component's architecture?

Does the solution fit the complexity of the problem? Are there areas where more elaborate design patterns are needed? Conversely, are there any subdomains where it's possible to cut corners or use existing, off-the-shelf solutions? Use this information to make smarter strategic and tactical decisions.

Evaluate the strategic design

Use the knowledge of the high-level components to chart the current design's context map, as though these high-level components were bounded contexts. Identify and track the relationships between the components in terms of bounded context integration patterns.

Finally, analyze the resultant context map and evaluate the architecture from a domain-driven design perspective. Are there suboptimal strategic design decisions? For example:

- Multiple teams working on the same high-level component
- Duplicate implementations of core subdomains
- Implementation of a core subdomain by an outsourced company
- Friction because of frequently failing integration
- Awkward models spreading from external services and legacy systems

These insights are a good starting point for planning the design modernization strategy. But first, given this more in-depth knowledge of both the problem (business domain) and the solution (current design) spaces, look for lost domain knowledge. As we discussed in Chapter 11, knowledge of the business domain can get lost for various reasons. The problem is widespread and acute in core subdomains, where the business logic is both complex and business critical. If you encounter such cases, facilitate EventStorming sessions to try to recover the knowledge. Also, use the EventStorming session as the foundation for cultivating a ubiquitous language.

Modernization Strategy

The "big rewrite" endeavors, in which the engineers are trying to rewrite the system from scratch, this time designing and implementing the whole system correctly, are rarely successful. Even more rarely does management support such architectural makeovers.

A safer approach to improving the design of existing systems is to think big but start small. As Eric Evans says, not all of a large system will be well designed. That's a fact we have to accept, and therefore we must strategically decide where to invest in terms of modernization efforts. A prerequisite for making this decision is to have boundaries dividing the system's subdomains. The boundaries don't have to be physical, making each subdomain a full-fledged bounded context. Instead, start by ensuring that at least the logical boundaries (namespace, modules, and packages, depending on the technology stack) are aligned with the subdomains' boundaries, as shown in Figure 13-1.

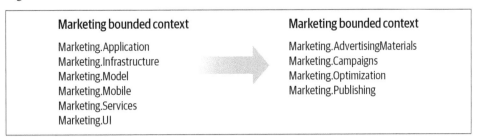

Figure 13-1. Reorganizing the bounded context's modules to reflect the business subdomains' boundaries rather than technical implementation patterns

Adjusting the system's modules is a relatively safe form of refactoring. You are not modifying the business logic, just repositioning the types in a more well-organized structure. That said, ensure that references by full type names, such as the dynamic loading of libraries, reflection, and so on, are not breaking.

In addition, keep track of the subdomains' business logic implemented in different codebases; stored procedures in a database, serverless functions, and so on. Make sure to introduce the new boundaries in those platforms as well. For instance, if some of the logic is handled in the database's stored procedures, either rename the procedures to reflect the module they belong to or introduce a dedicated database schema and relocate the stored procedures.

Strategic Modernization

As we discussed in Chapter 10, it can be risky to prematurely decompose the system into the smallest bounded contexts possible. We will discuss bounded contexts and microservices in more detail in the next chapter. For now, look for where the most value can be gained by turning the logical boundaries into physical boundaries. The process of extracting a bounded context(s) by turning a logical boundary into a physical one is shown in Figure 13-2.

Questions to ask yourself:

- Are multiple teams working on the same codebase? If so, decouple the development lifecycles by defining bounded contexts for each team.
- Are conflicting models being used by the different components? If so, relocate the conflicting models into separate bounded contexts.

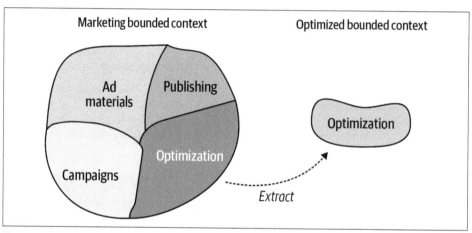

Figure 13-2. Extracting a bounded context by turning a logical boundary into a physical boundary

When the minimum required bounded contexts are in place, examine the relationships and integration patterns between them. See how the teams working on different bounded contexts communicate and collaborate. Especially when they are communicating through ad hoc or shared-kernel–like integration, do the teams have shared goals and adequate collaboration levels?

Pay attention to problems that the context integration patterns can address:

Customer–supplier relationships
    As we discussed in Chapter 11, organizational growth can invalidate prior communication and collaboration patterns. Look for components designed for a *partnership* relationship of multiple engineering teams, but where the partnership is no longer sustainable. Refactor to the appropriate type of customer–supplier relationship (conformist, anticorruption layer, or open-host service).

Anticorruption layer
    Anticorruption layers can be useful for protecting bounded contexts from legacy systems, especially, when legacy systems are using inefficient models that tend to spread into downstream components.

Another common use case for implementing an anticorruption layer is to protect a bounded context from frequent changes in the public interfaces of an upstream service it uses.

Open-host service

If changes in the implementation details of one component often ripple through the system and affect its consumers, consider making it an open-host service: decouple its implementation model from the public API it exposes.

Separate ways

Especially in large organizations, you may encounter friction among engineering teams resulting from having to collaborate and co-evolve a shared functionality. If the "apple of discord" functionality is not business critical—that is, it's not a core subdomain—the teams can go their *separate ways* and implement their own solutions, eliminating the source of friction.

Tactical Modernization

First and foremost, from a tactical standpoint, look for the most "painful" mismatches in business value and implementation strategies, such as core subdomains implementing patterns that don't match the complexity of the model—transaction script or active record. These system components that directly impact the success of the business have to change the most often, yet are painful to maintain and evolve due to poor design.

Cultivate a Ubiquitous Language

A prerequisite to the successful modernization of a design is the domain knowledge and effective model of the business domain. As I have mentioned several times throughout this book, domain-driven design's ubiquitous language is essential for achieving knowledge and building an effective solution model.

Don't forget domain-driven design's shortcut for gathering domain knowledge: EventStorming. Use EventStorming to build a ubiquitous language with the domain experts and explore the legacy codebase, especially if the codebase is an undocumented mess that no one truly understands. Gather everyone related to its functionality and explore the business domain. EventStorming is a fantastic tool for recovering domain knowledge.

Once you are equipped with the domain knowledge and its model(s), decide which business logic implementation patterns best suit the business functionality in question. As a starting point, use the design heuristics described in Chapter 10. The next decision you have to make concerns the modernization strategy: gradually replacing whole components of the system (the strangler pattern), or gradually refactoring the existing solution.

Strangler pattern

Strangler fig, shown in Figure 13-3, is a family of tropical trees that share a peculiar growth pattern: stranglers grow over other trees—host trees. A strangler begins its life as a seed in the upper branches of the host tree. As the strangler grows, it makes its way down until it roots in the soil. Eventually, the strangler grows foliage that overshadows the host tree, leading to the host tree's death.

Figure 13-3. A strangler fig growing on top of its host tree (source: https://unsplash.com/photos/y_l5tep9wxI)

The strangler migration pattern is based on the same growth dynamic as the tree the pattern is named after. The idea is to create a new bounded context—the strangler—use it to implement new requirements, and gradually migrate the legacy context's functionality into it. At the same time, except for hotfixes and other emergencies, the evolution and development of the legacy bounded context stops. Eventually, all functionality is migrated to the new bounded context—the strangler— and following the analogy, leading to the death of the host—the legacy codebase.

Usually, the strangler pattern is used in tandem with the façade pattern: a thin abstraction layer that acts as the public interface and is in charge of forwarding the requests to processing either by the legacy or the modernized bounded context. When migration completes—that is, when the host dies—the façade is removed as it is no longer necessary (see Figure 13-4).

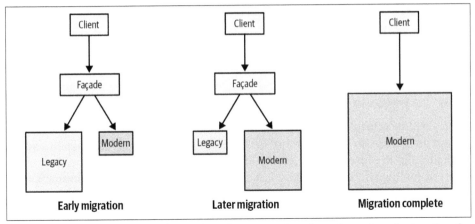

Figure 13-4. The façade layer forwarding the request based on the status of migrating the functionality from the legacy to the modernized system; once the migration is complete, both the façade and the legacy system are removed

Contrary to the principle that each bounded context is a separate subsystem, and thus cannot share its database with other bounded contexts, the rule can be relaxed when implementing the strangler pattern. Both the modernized and the legacy contexts can use the same database for the sake of avoiding complex integration between the contexts, which in many cases can entail distributed transactions—both contexts have to work with the same data, as shown in Figure 13-5.

The condition for bending the one-database-per-bounded-context rule is that eventually, and better sooner than later, the legacy context will be retired, and the database will be used exclusively by the new implementation.

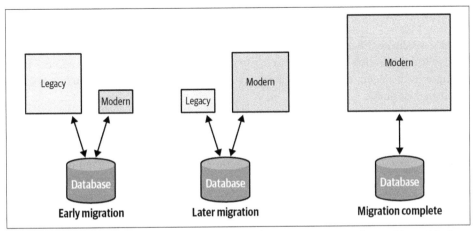

Figure 13-5. Both the legacy and the modernized systems temporarily working with the same database

An alternative to strangler-based migration is modernizing the legacy codebase in place, also called *refactoring*.

Refactoring tactical design decisions

In Chapter 11, you learned the various aspects of migrating tactical design decisions. However, there are two nuances to be aware of when modernizing a legacy codebase.

First, small incremental steps are safer than a big rewrite. Therefore, don't refactor a transaction script or active record straight to an event-sourced domain model. Instead, take the intermediate step of designing state-based aggregates. Invest the effort in finding effective aggregate boundaries. Ensure that all related business logic resides within those boundaries. Going from state-based to event-sourced aggregates will be orders of magnitude safer than discovering wrong transactional boundaries in an event-sourced aggregate.

Second, following the same reasoning of taking small incremental steps, refactoring to a domain model doesn't have to be an atomic change. Instead, you can gradually introduce the elements of the domain model pattern.

Start by looking for possible value objects. Immutable objects can significantly reduce the solution's complexity, even if you are not using a full-blown domain model.

As we discussed in Chapter 11, refactoring active records into aggregates doesn't have to be done overnight. It can be done in gradual steps. Start by gathering the related business logic. Next, analyze the transactional boundaries. Are there decisions that require strong consistency but operate on eventually consistent data? Or conversely, does the solution enforce strong consistency where eventual consistency would suffice? When analyzing the codebase, don't forget that these decisions are driven by business, not technology, concerns. Only after a thorough analysis of the transactional requirements should you design the aggregate's boundaries.

Finally, when necessary as you're refactoring legacy systems, protect the new codebase from old models using an anticorruption layer, and protect the consumers from changes in the legacy codebase by implementing an open-host service and exposing a published language.

Pragmatic Domain-Driven Design

As we discussed in this chapter's introduction, applying domain-driven design is not an all-or-nothing endeavor. You don't have to apply every tool DDD has to offer. For example, for some reason, the tactical patterns might not work for you. Maybe you prefer to use other design patterns because they work better in your specific domain, or just because you find other patterns more effective. That's totally fine!

As long as you analyze your business domain and its strategy, look for effective models to solve particular problems, and most importantly, make design decisions based on the business domain's needs: that's domain-driven design!

It's worth reiterating that domain-driven design is not about aggregates or value objects. Domain-driven design is about letting your business *domain drive* software *design* decisions.

Selling Domain-Driven Design

When I present on this topic at technology conferences, there is one question that I'm asked almost every time: "That all sounds great, but how do I 'sell' domain-driven design to my team and management?" That's an extremely important question.

Selling is hard, and personally, I hate selling. That said, if you think about it, designing software is selling. We are selling our ideas to the team, to management, or to customers. However, a methodology that covers such a wide range of design decision aspects, and even reaches outside the engineering zone to involve other stakeholders, can be extremely hard to sell.

Management support is essential for making any considerable changes in an organization. However, unless the top-level managers are already familiar with domain-driven design or are willing to invest time to learn the business value of the methodology, it's not top of mind for them, especially because of a seemingly large shift in the engineering process that DDD entails. Fortunately, however, it doesn't mean you can't use domain-driven design.

Undercover Domain-Driven Design

Make domain-driven design a part of your professional toolbox, not an organizational strategy. DDD's patterns and practices are engineering techniques, and since software engineering is your job, use them!

Let's see how to incorporate DDD into your day-to-day job without making much ado about it.

Ubiquitous language

The use of a ubiquitous language is the cornerstone practice of domain-driven design. It is essential for domain knowledge discovery, communication, and effective solution modeling.

Luckily, this practice is so trivial that it's borderline common sense. Listen carefully to the language the stakeholders use when they speak about the business domain. Gently steer the terminology away from technical jargon and toward its business meaning.

Look for inconsistent terms and ask for clarifications. For example, if there are multiple names for the same thing, look for the reason. Are those different models intertwined in the same solution? Look for contexts and make them explicit. If the meaning is the same, follow common sense and ask for one term to be used.

Also, communicate with domain experts as much as possible. These efforts shouldn't necessarily require formal meetings. Watercoolers and coffee breaks are great communication facilitators. Speak with the domain experts about the business domain. Try using their language. Look for difficulties in understanding and ask for clarifications. Don't worry—domain experts are usually happy to collaborate with engineers who are sincerely interested in learning about the problem domain!

Most importantly, use the ubiquitous language in your code and all project-related communication. Be patient. Changing the terminology that has been used in an organization for a while will take time, but eventually, it will catch on.

Bounded contexts

When exploring possible decomposition options, resolve to the principles behind what the bounded context pattern is based on:

- Why is it better to design problem-oriented models instead of a single model for all use cases? Because "all-in-one" solutions are rarely effective for anything.
- Why can't a bounded context host conflicting models? Because of the increased cognitive load and solution complexity.
- Why is it a bad idea for multiple teams to work on the same codebase? Because of friction and hindered collaboration between the teams.

Use the same reasoning for bounded context integration patterns: make sure you understand the problem each pattern is supposed to solve.

Tactical design decisions

When discussing tactical design patterns, don't appeal to authority: "Let's use an aggregate here because the DDD book says so!" Instead, appeal to logic. For example:

- Why are explicit transactional boundaries important? To protect the consistency of the data.
- Why can't a database transaction modify more than one instance of an aggregate? To ensure that the consistency boundaries are correct.
- Why can't an aggregate's state be modified directly by an external component? To ensure that all the related business logic is colocated and not duplicated.
- Why can't we offload some of the aggregate's functionality to a stored procedure? To make sure that no logic is duplicated. Duplicated logic, especially in logically

and physically distant components of a system, tends to go out of sync and lead to data corruption.

- Why should we strive for small aggregate boundaries? Because wide transactional scope will both increase the complexity of the aggregate and negatively impact the performance.
- Why, instead of event sourcing, can't we just write events to a logfile? Because there are no long-term data consistency guarantees.

Speaking of event sourcing, when the solution calls for an event-sourced domain model, implementation of this pattern might be hard to sell. Let's take a look at a Jedi mind trick that can help with this.

Event-sourced domain model

Despite its many advantages, event sourcing sounds too radical for many people. As with everything we've discussed in this book, the solution is to let the business domain drive this decision.

Talk to domain experts. Show them the state- and event-based models. Explain the differences and the advantages offered by event sourcing, especially with regard to the dimension of time. More often than not, they will be ecstatic with the level of insight it provides and will advocate event sourcing themselves.

And while interacting with the domain experts, don't forget to work on the ubiquitous language!

Conclusion

In this chapter, you learned various techniques for leveraging domain-driven design tools in real-life scenarios: when working on brownfield projects and legacy codebases, and not necessarily with a team of DDD experts.

As in greenfield projects, always start by analyzing the business domain. What are the company's goals and its strategy for achieving them? Use the organizational structure and existing software design decisions to identify the organization's subdomains and their types. With this knowledge, plan the modernization strategy. Look for pain points. Look to gain the most business value. Modernize legacy code either by refactoring or by replacing the relevant components. Either way, do it gradually. Big rewrites entail more risk than business value!

Finally, you can use domain-driven design tools even if DDD is not widely adopted in your organization. Use the right tools, and when discussing them with colleagues, always use the logic and principles behind each pattern.

This chapter concludes our discussion of domain-driven design on its own. In Part IV, you will learn about the interplay of DDD with other methodologies and patterns.

Exercises

1. Assume you want to introduce domain-driven design tools and practices to a brownfield project. What is going to be your first step?

   a. Refactor all business logic to the event-sourced domain model.

   b. Analyze the organization's business domain and its strategy.

   c. Improve the system's components by ensuring that they follow the principles of proper bounded contexts.

   d. It's impossible to use domain-driven design in a brownfield project.

2. In what ways does the strangler pattern contradict some of the core principles of domain-driven design during the migration process?

   a. Multiple bounded contexts are using a shared database.

   b. If the modernized bounded context is a core subdomain, its implementation gets duplicated in the old and the new implementations.

   c. Multiple teams are working on the same bounded context.

   d. A and B.

3. Why is it generally not a good idea to refactor active-record-based business logic straight into the event-sourced domain model?

   a. A state-based model makes it easier to refactor aggregates' boundaries during the learning process.

   b. It's safer to introduce big changes gradually.

   c. A and B.

   d. None of the above. It's reasonable to refactor even a transaction script straight into an event-sourced domain model.

4. When you're introducing the aggregate pattern, your team asks why the aggregate can't just reference all the possible entities and thus make it possible to traverse the whole business domain from one place. How do you answer them?

Relationships to Other Methodologies and Patterns

So far in this book you've learned how to use domain-driven design to design software solutions according to an organization's business strategy and needs. We saw how to apply DDD tools and practices to make sense of the business domain, design the boundaries of the system's components, and implement the business logic.

Domain-driven design covers a lot of the software development lifecycle, but it can't cover all of software engineering. Other methodologies and tools have their roles. In Part IV, we will discuss DDD in relation to other methodologies and patterns:

- It's no secret that domain-driven design gained most of its traction due to the popularity of the microservices-based architectural style. In Chapter 14, we will explore the interplay between microservices and domain-driven design and how the two approaches complement each other.

- The event-driven architecture is a popular method of architecting scalable, performant, and resilient distributed systems. In Chapter 15, you will learn the principles of event-driven architecture and how to leverage DDD to design effective asynchronous communication.

- Chapter 16 concludes the book with effective modeling in the context of data analytics. You will learn about the predominant data management architectures, data warehouses and data lakes, and how their shortcomings are addressed by the data mesh architecture. We will also analyze and discuss how DDD and the data mesh architecture are based on the same design principles and goals.

CHAPTER 14

Microservices

In the mid-2010s, microservices took the software engineering industry by storm. The intent was to address modern systems' need to change quickly, scale, and fit the distributed nature of cloud computing naturally. Many companies made the strategic decision to decompose their monolithic codebases in favor of the flexibility provided by the microservices-based architecture. Unfortunately, many such endeavors didn't end well. Instead of flexible architectures, these companies ended up with distributed big balls of mud—designs that are much more fragile, clumpy, and expensive than the monoliths the companies wanted to break apart.

Historically, microservices are often associated with DDD, especially with the bounded context pattern. Many people even use the terms *bounded context* and *microservices* interchangeably. But are they really the same thing? This chapter explores the relationship between domain-driven design methodology and the microservices architectural pattern. You will learn the interplay between the patterns, and more importantly, how you can leverage DDD to design effective microservices-based systems.

Let's start with the basics and define what exactly are services and microservices.

What Is a Service?

According to OASIS, a service is a mechanism that enables access to one or more capabilities, where the access is provided using a prescribed interface.[1] The *prescribed interface* is any mechanism for getting data in or out of a service. It can be synchronous, such as a request/response model, or asynchronous, such as a model that is

---

1 Reference model for service-oriented architecture v1.0. (n.d.). Retrieved June 14, 2021, from OASIS (*https://oreil.ly/IXhpG*).

producing and consuming events. This is the service public interface, as shown in Figure 14-1, which provides a means for communicating and integrating with other system components.

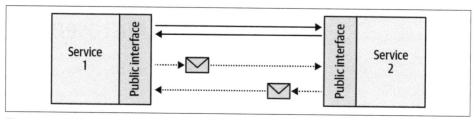

Figure 14-1. Communication between services

Randy Shoup (*https://oreil.ly/IU6xJ*) likens a service's interface to a front door. All data going into or out of the service has to pass through the front door. Furthermore, a service's public interface defines the service itself: the functionality exposed by the service. A well-expressed interface is enough to describe the functionality implemented by a service. For example, the public interface illustrated in Figure 14-2 explicitly describes the functionality of the service.

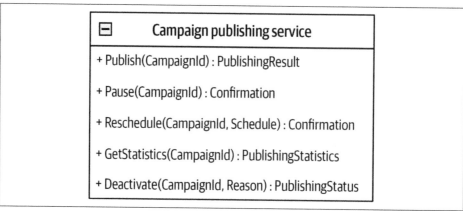

Figure 14-2. A service's public interface

This takes us to the definition of microservice.

What Is a Microservice?

The definition of a microservice is surprisingly simple. Since a service is defined by its public interface, a microservice is a service with a micro-public interface: a micro-front door.

Having a micro-public interface makes it easier to understand both the function of a single service and its integration with other system components. Reducing a service's functionality also limits its reasons for change and makes the service more autonomous for development, management, and scale.

In addition, it explains the practice of microservices not exposing their databases. Exposing a database, making it a part of the service's front door, would make its public interface huge. For example, how many different SQL queries can you execute on a relational database? Since SQL is quite a flexible language, the likely estimate would be infinity. Hence, microservices encapsulate their databases. The data can only be accessed through a much more compact, integration-oriented public interface.

Method as a Service: Perfect Microservices?

Saying that a microservice is a micro-public interface is deceptively simple. It may sound as though limiting service interfaces to a single method would result in perfect microservices. Let's see what will happen if we apply this naïve decomposition in practice.

Consider the backlog management service in Figure 14-3. Its public interface consists of eight public methods, and we want to apply the "one method per service" rule.

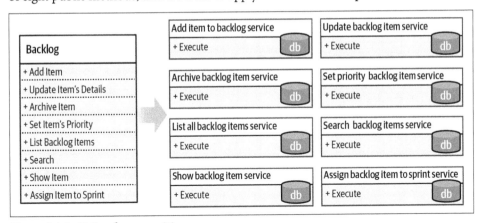

Figure 14-3. Naïve decomposition

Since these are well-behaved microservices, each encapsulates its database. No one service is allowed to access another service's database directly; only through its public interface. But currently, there is no public interface for that. The services have to work together and synchronize the changes each service is applying. As a result, we need to expand the services' interfaces to account for these integration-related concerns. Furthermore, when visualized, the integrations and data flow between the resultant services resemble a typical distributed big ball of mud, as shown in Figure 14-4.

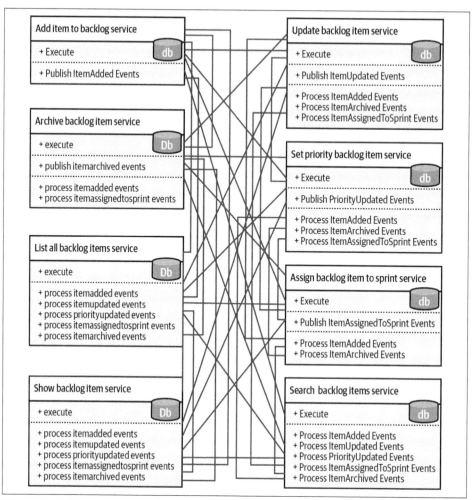

Figure 14-4. Integration complexity

Paraphrasing Randy Shoup's metaphor, by decomposing the system to such fine-grained services, we definitely minimized the services' front doors. However, to implement the overarching system's functionality, we had to add enormous "staff only" entrances to each service. Let's see what we can learn from this example.

Design Goal

Following the simplistic decomposition heuristic of having each service expose only a single method proved to be suboptimal for many reasons. First, it's simply not possible. Since the services have to work together, we were forced to expand their public interfaces with integration-related public methods. Second, we won the battle but lost the war. Each service ended up being much simpler than the original design, however the resultant system became orders of magnitude more complex.

The goal of the microservices architecture is to produce a flexible system. Concentrating the design efforts on a single component, but ignoring its interactions with the rest of the system, goes against the very definition of a system:

- A set of connected things or devices that operate together
- A set of computer equipment and programs used together for a particular purpose

Hence, a system cannot be built out of independent components. In a proper microservices-based system, however decoupled, the services still have to be integrated and communicate with each other. Let's take a look at the interplay between the complexity of individual microservices and the complexity of the overarching system.

System Complexity

Forty years ago, there was no cloud computing, there were no global-scale requirements, and there was no need to deploy a system every 11.7 seconds. But engineers still had to tame systems' complexity. Even though the tools in those days were different, the challenges—and more importantly, the solution—are relevant nowadays and can be applied to the design of microservices-based systems.

In his book, *Composite/Structured Design*, Glenford J. Myers discusses how to structure procedural code to reduce its complexity. On the first page of the book, he writes:

> There is much more to the subject of complexity than simply attempting to minimize the local complexity of each part of a program. A much more important type of complexity is global complexity: the complexity of the overall structure of a program or system (i.e., the degree of association or interdependence among the major pieces of a program).

In our context, *local complexity* is the complexity of each individual microservice, whereas *global complexity* is the complexity of the whole system. Local complexity depends on the implementation of a service; global complexity is defined by the interactions and dependencies between the services. Which of the complexities is more important to optimize when designing a microservices-based system? Let's analyze both extremes.

It's surprisingly easy to reduce global complexity to a minimum. All we have to do is eliminate any interactions between the system's components—that is, implement all functionality in one monolithic service. As we've seen earlier, this strategy may work in certain scenarios. In others, it may lead to the dreaded big ball of mud: probably the highest possible level of local complexity.

On the other hand, we know what happens when we optimize only the local complexity but neglect the system's global complexity—the even more dreaded distributed big ball of mud. This relationship is shown in Figure 14-5.

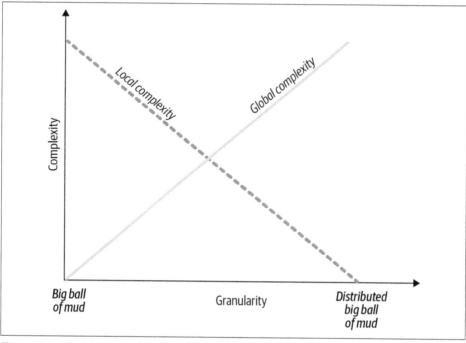

Figure 14-5. Service granularity and system complexities

To design a proper microservices-based system, we have to optimize both global and local complexities. Setting the design goal of optimizing either one individually is a local optima. The global optima balances both complexities. Let's see how the notion of micro-public interfaces lends itself to balancing global and local complexities.

Microservices as Deep Services

A module in a software system, or any system, for that matter, is defined by its function and logic. A *function* is what the module is supposed to do—its business functionality. The *logic* is the module's business logic—how the module implements its business functionality.

In his book, *The Philosophy of Software Design*, John Ousterhout discusses the notion of modularity and proposes a simple yet powerful visual heuristic for evaluating a module's design: depth.

Ousterhout proposes to visualize a module as a rectangle, as shown in Figure 14-6. The rectangle's top edge represents the module's function, or the complexity of its public interface. A wider rectangle represents broader functionality, while a narrower one has a more restricted function and thus a simpler public interface. The area of the rectangle represents the module's logic, or the implementation of its functionality.

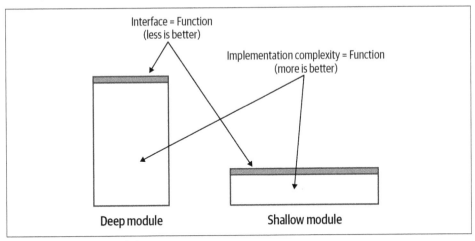

Figure 14-6. Deep modules

According to this model, effective modules are deep: a simple public interface encapsulates complex logic. Ineffective modules are shallow: a shallow module's public interface encapsulates much less complexity than a deep module. Consider the method in the following listing:

```
int AddTwoNumbers(int a, int b)
{
   return a + b;
}
```

This is the extreme case of a shallow module: the public interface (the method's signature) and its logic (the methods) are exactly the same. Having such a module introduces extraneous "moving parts," and thus, instead of encapsulating complexity, it adds accidental complexity to the overarching system.

Microservices as Deep Modules

Apart from different terminology, the notion of deep modules differs from the microservices pattern in that the modules can denote both logical and physical boundaries, while microservices are strictly physical. Otherwise, both concepts and their underlying design principles are the same.

The services implementing a single business method, shown in Figure 14-3, are shallow modules. Because we had to introduce integration-related public methods, the resultant interfaces are "wider" than they should have been.

From a system complexity standpoint, a deep module reduces the system's global complexity, while a shallow module increases it by introducing a component that doesn't encapsulate its local complexity.

Shallow services are also the reason why so many microservices-oriented projects fail. The mistaken definitions of a microservice as a service having no more than X lines of code, or as a service that should be easier to rewrite than to modify, concentrate on the individual service while missing the most important aspect of the architecture: the system.

The threshold upon which a system can be decomposed into microservices is defined by the use cases of the system that the microservices are a part of. If we decompose a monolith into services, the cost of introducing a change goes down. It is minimized when the system is decomposed into microservices. However, if you keep decomposing past the microservices threshold, the deep services will become more and more shallow. Their interfaces will grow back up. This time, due to integration needs, the cost of introducing a change will go up as well, and the overall system's architecture will turn into the dreaded distributed big ball of mud. This is depicted in Figure 14-7.

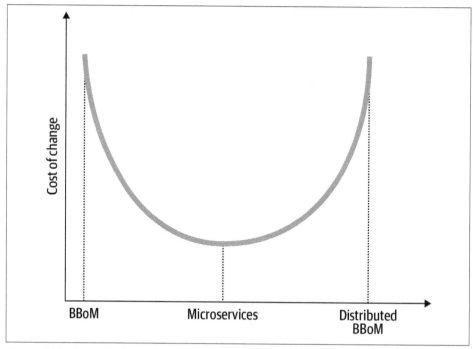

Figure 14-7. Granularity and cost of change

Now that we've learned what microservices are, let's take a look at how domain-driven design can help us find the boundaries of deep services.

Domain-Driven Design and Microservices' Boundaries

As microservices, many of the domain-driven design patterns discussed in the previous chapters are about boundaries: the bounded context is the boundary of a model, a subdomain bounds a business capability, while aggregate and value objects are transactional boundaries. Let's see which of these boundaries lends itself to the notion of microservices.

Bounded Contexts

The microservices and bounded context patterns have a lot in common, so much so that the patterns are often used interchangeably. Let's see whether that's really the case: do bounded contexts' boundaries correlate with the boundaries of effective microservices?

Both microservices and bounded contexts are physical boundaries. Microservices, as bounded contexts, are owned by a single team. As in bounded contexts, conflicting models cannot be implemented in a microservice, resulting in complex interfaces. Microservices are indeed bounded contexts. But does this relationship work the other way around? Can we say that bounded contexts are microservices?

As you learned in Chapter 3, bounded contexts protect the consistency of ubiquitous languages and models. No conflicting models can be implemented in the same bounded context. Say you are working on an advertising management system. In the system's business domain, the business entity Lead is represented by different models in the Promotions and Sales contexts. Hence, Promotions and Sales are bounded contexts, each defining one and only one model of the Campaign entity, which is valid in its boundary, as shown in Figure 14-8.

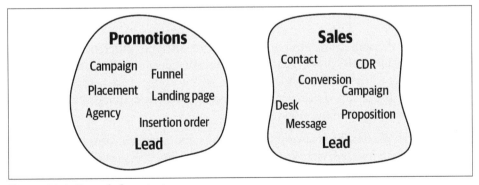

Figure 14-8. Bounded contexts

For simplicity's sake, let's assume there are no other conflicting models in the system besides Lead. This makes the resultant bounded contexts naturally wide—each bounded context can contain multiple subdomains. The subdomains can be moved from one bounded context to another one. As long as the subdomains do not imply conflicting models, all the alternative decompositions in Figure 14-9 are perfectly valid bounded contexts.

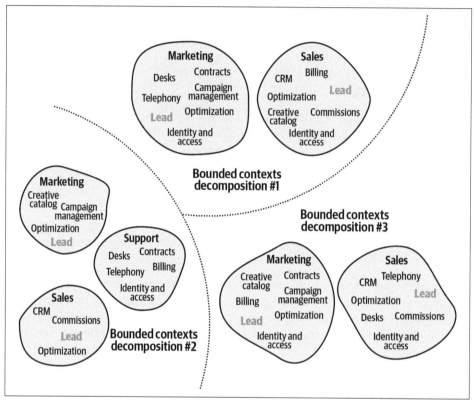

Figure 14-9. Alternative decompositions to bounded contexts

The different decompositions to bounded contexts attribute different requirements, such as different teams' sizes and structures, lifecycle dependencies, and so on. But can we say that all the valid bounded contexts in this example are necessarily microservices? No. Especially considering the relatively wide functionalities of the two bounded contexts in decomposition 1.

Therefore, the relationship between microservices and bounded contexts is not symmetric. Although microservices are bounded contexts, not every bounded context is a microservice. Bounded contexts, on the other hand, denote the boundaries of the largest valid monolith. Such a monolith should not be confused with a big ball of mud; it's a viable design option that protects the consistency of its ubiquitous language, or its model of the business domain. As we will discuss in Chapter 15, such broad boundaries are more effective than microservices in certain cases.

Figure 14-10 visually demonstrates the relationship between bounded contexts and microservices. The area between the bounded contexts and microservices is safe. These are valid design options. However, if the system is not decomposed into proper bounded contexts or is decomposed past the microservices threshold, it will result in a big ball of mud or a distributed big ball of mud, respectively.

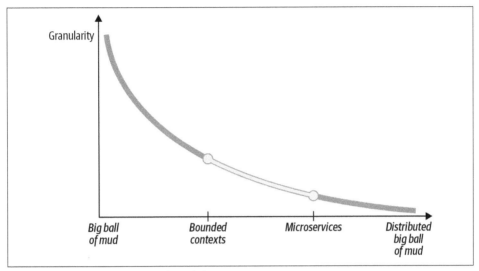

Figure 14-10. Granularity and modularity

Next, let's examine the other extreme: whether aggregates can help find the microservices' boundaries.

Aggregates

While bounded contexts impose limits on the widest valid boundaries, the aggregate pattern does the opposite. The aggregate's boundary is the narrowest boundary possible. Decomposing an aggregate into multiple physical services, or bounded contexts, is not only suboptimal but, as you will learn in Appendix A, leads to undesired consequences, to say the least.

As bounded contexts, aggregates' boundaries are also often considered to drive the boundaries of microservices. An aggregate is an indivisible business functionality unit that encapsulates the complexities of its internal business rules, invariants, and logic. That said, as you learned earlier in this chapter, microservices are not about individual services. An individual service has to be considered in the context of its interactions with other components of the system:

Does the aggregate in question communicate with other aggregates in its subdomain?

- Does it share value objects with other aggregates?
- How likely will the aggregate's business logic changes affect other components of the subdomain and vice versa?

The stronger the aggregate's relationship is with the other business entities of its subdomain, the shallower it will be as an individual service.

There will be cases in which having an aggregate as a service will produce a modular design. However, much more often such fine-grained services will increase the overarching system's global complexity.

Subdomains

A more balanced heuristic for designing microservices is to align the services with the boundaries of business subdomains. As you learned in Chapter 1, subdomains are correlated with fine-grained business capabilities. These are the business building blocks required for the company to compete in its business domain(s). From a business domain perspective, subdomains describe the capabilities—what the business does—without explaining how the capabilities are implemented. From a technical standpoint, subdomains represent sets of coherent use cases: using the same model of the business domain, working on the same or closely related data, and having a strong functional relationship. A change in the business requirements of one of the use cases is likely to affect the other use cases, as shown in Figure 14-11.

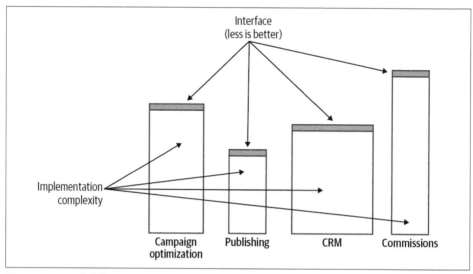

Figure 14-11. Subdomains

The subdomains' granularity and the focus on the functionality—the "what" rather than the "how"—makes subdomains naturally deep modules. A subdomain's description—the function—encapsulates the more complex implementation details—the logic. The coherent nature of the use cases contained in a subdomain also ensures the resultant module's depth. Splitting them apart in many cases would result in a more complex public interface and thus shallower modules. All of these things make subdomains a safe boundary for designing microservices.

Aligning microservices with subdomains is a safe heuristic that produces optimal solutions for the majority of microservices. That said, there will be cases where other boundaries will be more efficient; for example, staying in the wider, linguistic boundaries of the bounded context or, due to nonfunctional requirements, resorting to an aggregate as a microservice. The solution depends not only on the business domain but also on the organization's structure, business strategy, and nonfunctional requirements. As we discussed in Chapter 11, it's crucial to continuously adapt the software architecture and design to changes in the environment.

Compressing Microservices' Public Interfaces

In addition to finding service boundaries, domain-driven design can help make services deeper. This section demonstrates how the open-host service and anticorruption layer patterns can simplify the microservices' public interfaces.

Open-Host Service

The open-host service decouples the bounded context's model of the business domain from the model used for integration with other components of the system, as shown in Figure 14-12.

Introducing the integration-oriented model, the published language, reduces the system's global complexity. First, it allows us to evolve the service's implementation without impacting its consumers: the new implementation model can be translated to the existing published language. Second, the published language exposes a more restrained model. It is designed around integration needs. It encapsulates the complexity of the implementation that is not relevant to the service's consumers. For example, it can expose less data and in a more convenient model for consumers.

Having a simpler public interface (function) over the same implementation (logic) makes the service "deeper" and contributes to a more effective microservice design.

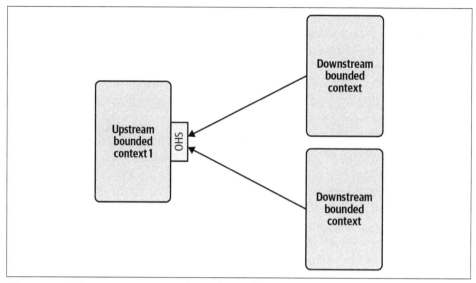

Figure 14-12. Integrating services through a published language

Anticorruption Layer

The anticorruption layer (ACL) pattern works the other way around. It reduces the complexity of integrating the service with other bounded contexts. Traditionally, the anticorruption layer belongs to the bounded context it protects. However, as we discussed in Chapter 9, this notion can be taken a step further and implemented as a standalone service.

The ACL service in Figure 14-13 reduces both the local complexity of the consuming bounded context and the system's global complexity. The consuming bounded context's business complexity is separated from the integration complexity. The latter is offloaded to the ACL service. Because the consuming bounded context is working with a more convenient, integration-oriented model, its public interface is compressed—it doesn't reflect the integration complexity exposed by the producing service.

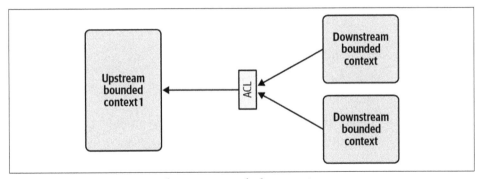

Figure 14-13. Anticorruption layer as a stand-alone service

Conclusion

Historically, the microservice-based architectural style is deeply interconnected with domain-driven design, so much so that the terms *microservice* and *bounded context* are often used interchangeably. In this chapter, we analyzed the connection between the two and saw that they are not the same thing.

All microservices are bounded contexts, but not all bounded contexts are necessarily microservices. In its essence, a microservice defines the smallest valid boundary of a service, while a bounded context protects the consistency of the encompassed model and represents the widest valid boundaries. Defining boundaries to be wider than their bounded contexts will result in a big ball of mud, while boundaries that are smaller than microservices will lead to a distributed big ball of mud.

Nevertheless, the connection between microservices and domain-driven design is tight. We saw how domain-driven design tools can be used to design effective microservice boundaries.

In Chapter 15, we will continue discussing high-level system architecture but from a different perspective: asynchronous integration through event-driven architecture. You will learn how to leverage the different kinds of event messages to further optimize microservices' boundaries.

Exercises

1. What is the relationship between bounded contexts and microservices?

    a. All microservices are bounded contexts.

    b. All bounded contexts are microservices.

    c. Microservices and bounded contexts are different terms for the same concept.

    d. Microservices and bounded contexts are completely different concepts and cannot be compared.

2. What part of a microservice should be "micro"?

    a. The number of pizzas required to feed the team implementing the microservices. The metric has to take into account the team members' different dietary preferences and average daily calorie intakes.

    b. The number of lines of code it takes to implement the service's functionality. Since the metric is agnostic of the lines' widths, it's preferable to implement microservices on ultrawide monitors.

    c. The most important aspect of designing microservices-based systems is to get microservices-friendly middleware and other infrastructural components, preferably from microservices-certified vendors.

    d. The knowledge of the business domain and its intricacies exposed across the service's boundary and reflected by its public interface.

3. What are the safe component boundaries?

    a. Boundaries wider than bounded contexts.

    b. Boundaries narrower than microservices.

    c. Boundaries between bounded contexts (widest) and microservices (narrowest).

    d. All boundaries are safe.

4. Is it a good design decision to align microservices with the boundaries of aggregates?

    a. Yes, aggregates always make for proper microservices.

    b. No, aggregates should never be exposed as individual microservices.

    c. It's impossible to make a microservice out of a single aggregate.

    d. The decision depends on the business domain.

CHAPTER 15

Event-Driven Architecture

As microservices, event-driven architecture (EDA) is ubiquitous in modern distributed systems. Many advise using event-driven communication as the default integration mechanism when designing loosely coupled, scalable, fault-tolerant distributed systems.

Event-driven architecture is often linked to domain-driven design. After all, EDA is based on events, and events are prominent in DDD—we have domain events, and when needed, we even use events as the system's source of truth. It may be tempting to leverage DDD's events as the basis for using event-driven architecture. But is this a good idea?

Events are not a kind of secret sauce that you can just pour over a legacy system and turn it into a loosely coupled distributed system. Quite the opposite: careless application of EDA can turn a modular monolith into a distributed big ball of mud.

In this chapter, we will explore the interplay between EDA and DDD. You will learn the essential building blocks of event-driven architecture, common causes for failed EDA projects, and how you can leverage DDD's tools to design effective, asynchronously integrated systems.

Event-Driven Architecture

Stated simply, *event-driven architecture* is an architectural style in which a system's components communicate with one another asynchronously by exchanging event messages (see Figure 15-1). Instead of calling the services' endpoints synchronously, the components publish events to notify other system elements of changes in the system's domain. The components can subscribe to events raised in the system and react accordingly. A typical example of an event-driven execution flow is the saga pattern that was described in Chapter 9.

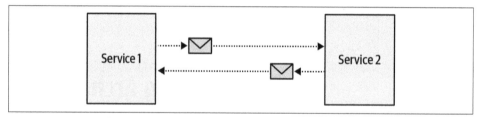

Figure 15-1. Asynchronous communication

It's important to highlight the difference between event-driven architecture and event sourcing. As we discussed in Chapter 7, event sourcing is a method for capturing changes in state as a series of events.

Although both event-driven architecture and event sourcing are based on events, the two patterns are conceptually different. EDA refers to the communication between services, while event sourcing happens inside a service. The events designed for event sourcing represent state transitions (of aggregates in an event-sourced domain model) implemented in the service. They are aimed at capturing the intricacies of the business domain and are not intended to integrate the service with other system components.

As you will see later in this chapter, there are three types of events, and some are more suited for integration than others.

Events

In an EDA system, the exchange of events is the key communication mechanism for integrating the components and making them a system. Let's take a look at events in more detail and see how they differ from messages.

Events, Commands, and Messages

So far, the definition of an event is similar to the definition of the message pattern.[1] However, the two are different. An event is a message, but a message is not necessarily an event. There are two types of messages:

---

1 Hohpe, G., & Woolf, B. (2003). *Enterprise Integration Patterns: Designing, Building, and Deploying Messaging Solutions.* Boston: Addison-Wesley.

Event

A message describing a change that has already happened

Command

A message describing an operation that has to be carried out

An event is something that has already happened, whereas a command is an instruction to do something. Both events and commands can be communicated asynchronously as messages. However, a command can be rejected: the command's target can refuse to execute the command, for example, if the command is invalid or if it contradicts the system's business rules. A recipient of an event, on the other hand, cannot cancel the event. The event describes something that has already happened. The only thing that can be done to overturn an event is to issue a compensating action—a command, as it's carried out in the saga pattern.

Since an event describes something that has already happened, an event's name should be formulated in the past tense: for example, DeliveryScheduled, ShipmentCompleted, or DeliveryConfirmed.

Structure

An event is a data record that can be serialized and transmitted using the messaging platform of choice. A typical event schema includes the event's metadata and its payload—the information communicated by the event:

```
{
    "type": "delivery-confirmed",
    "event-id": "14101928-4d79-4da6-9486-dbc4837bc612",
    "correlation-id": "08011958-6066-4815-8dbe-dee6d9e5ebac",
    "delivery-id": "05011927-a328-4860-a106-737b2929db4e",
    "timestamp": 1615718833,
    "payload": {
        "confirmed-by": "17bc9223-bdd6-4382-954d-f1410fd286bd",
        "delivery-time": 1615701406
    }
}
```

An event's payload not only describes the information conveyed by the event, but also defines the event's type. Let's discuss the three types of events in detail and how they differ from one another.

Types of Events

Events can be categorized into one of three types:[2] event notification, event-carried state transfer, or domain events.

Event notification

An event notification is a message regarding a change in the business domain that other components will react to. Examples include PaycheckGenerated and CampaignPublished, among others.

The event notification should not be verbose: the goal is to notify the interested parties about the event, but the notification shouldn't carry all the information needed for the subscribers to react to the event. For example:

```
{
    "type": "paycheck-generated",
    "event-id": "537ec7c2-d1a1-2005-8654-96aee1116b72",
    "delivery-id": "05011927-a328-4860-a106-737b2929db4e",
    "timestamp": 1615726445,
    "payload": {
        "employee-id": "456123",
        "link": "/paychecks/456123/2021/01"
    }
}
```

In the preceding code, the event notifies the external components of a paycheck that was generated. It doesn't carry all the information related to the paycheck. Instead, the receiver can use the link to fetch more detailed information. This notification flow is depicted in Figure 15-2.

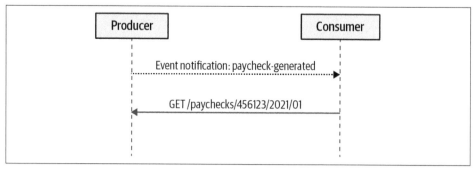

Figure 15-2. Event notification flow

---

2 Fowler, M. (n.d.). *What do you mean by "Event-Driven"?* Retrieved August 12, 2021, from Martin Fowler (blog) (*https://oreil.ly/aSK5l*).

In a sense, integration through event notification messages is similar to the Wireless Emergency Alert (WEA) system in the United States and EU-Alert in Europe (see Figure 15-3). The systems use cell towers to broadcast short messages, notifying citizens about public health concerns, safety threats, and other emergencies. The systems are limited to sending messages with a maximum length of 360 characters. This short message is enough to notify you about the emergency, but you have to proactively use other information sources to get more details.

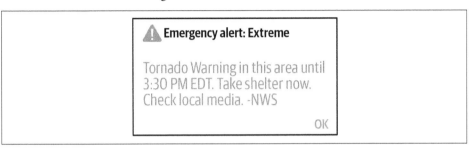

Figure 15-3. Emergency alert system

Succinct event notifications can be preferable in multiple scenarios. Let's take a closer look at two: security and concurrency.

Security. Enforcing the recipient to explicitly query for the detailed information prevents sharing sensitive information over the messaging infrastructure and requires additional authorization of the subscribers to access the data.

Concurrency. Due to the asynchronous nature of event-driven integration, the information can already be rendered stale when it reaches the subscribers. If the information's nature is sensitive to race conditions, querying it explicitly allows getting the up-to-date state.

Furthermore, in the case of concurrent consumers, where only one subscriber should process an event, the querying process can be integrated with pessimistic locking. This ensures the producer's side that no other consumer will be able to process the message.

Event-carried state transfer

Event-carried state transfer (ECST) messages notify subscribers about changes in the producer's internal state. Contrary to event notification messages, ECST messages include all the data reflecting the change in the state.

ECST messages can come in two forms. The first is a complete snapshot of the modified entity's state:

```
{
    "type": "customer-updated",
    "event-id": "6b7ce6c6-8587-4e4f-924a-cec028000ce6",
    "customer-id": "01b18d56-b79a-4873-ac99-3d9f767dbe61",
    "timestamp": 1615728520,
    "payload": {
        "first-name": "Carolyn",
        "last-name": "Hayes",
        "phone": "555-1022",
        "status": "follow-up-set",
        "follow-up-date": "2021/05/08",
        "birthday": "1982/04/05",
        "version": 7
    }
}
```

The ECST message in the preceding example includes a complete snapshot of a customer's updated state. When operating large data structures, it may be reasonable to include in the ECST message only the fields that were actually modified:

```
{
    "type": "customer-updated",
    "event-id": "6b7ce6c6-8587-4e4f-924a-cec028000ce6",
    "customer-id": "01b18d56-b79a-4873-ac99-3d9f767dbe61",
    "timestamp": 1615728520,
    "payload": {
        "status": "follow-up-set",
        "follow-up-date": "2021/05/10",
        "version": 8
    }
}
```

Whether ECST messages include complete snapshots or only the updated fields, a stream of such events allows consumers to hold a local cache of the entities' states and work with it. Conceptually, using event-carried state transfer messages is an asynchronous data replication mechanism. This approach makes the system more fault tolerant, meaning that the consumers can continue functioning even if the producer is not available. It is also a way to improve the performance of components that have to process data from multiple sources. Instead of querying the data sources each time the data is needed, all the data can be cached locally, as shown in Figure 15-4.

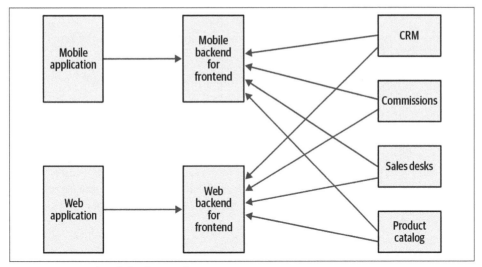

Figure 15-4. Backend for frontend

Domain event

The third type of event message is the domain event that we described in Chapter 6. In a way, domain events are somewhere between event notification and ECST messages: they both describe a significant event in the business domain, and they contain all the data describing the event. Despite the similarities, these types of messages are conceptually different.

Domain events versus event notification

Both domain events and event notifications describe changes in the producer's business domain. That said, there are two conceptual differences.

First, domain events include all the information describing the event. The consumer does not need to take any further action to get the complete picture.

Second, the modeling intent is different. Event notifications are designed with the intent to alleviate integration with other components. Domain events, on the other hand, are intended to model and describe the business domain. Domain events can be useful even if no external consumer is interested in them. That's especially true in event-sourced systems, where domain events are used to model all possible state transitions. Having external consumers interested in all the available domain events would result in suboptimal design. We will discuss this in greater detail later in this chapter.

Domain events versus event-carried state transfer

The data contained in domain events is conceptually different from the schema of a typical ECST message.

An ECST message provides sufficient information to hold a local cache of the producer's data. No single domain event is supposed to expose such a rich model. Even the data included in a specific domain event is not sufficient for caching the aggregate's state, as other domain events that the consumer is not subscribed to may affect the same fields.

Furthermore, as in the case of notification events, the modeling intent is different for the two types of messages. The data included in domain events is not intended to describe the aggregate's state. Instead, it describes a business event that happened during its lifecycle.

Event types: Example

Here is an example that demonstrates the differences between the three types of events. Consider the following three ways to represent the event of marriage:

```
eventNotification = {
    "type": "marriage-recorded",
    "person-id": "01b9a761",
    "payload": {
        "person-id": "126a7b61",
        "details": "/01b9a761/marriage-data"
    }
};

ecst = {
    "type": "personal-details-changed",
    "person-id": "01b9a761",
    "payload": {
        "new-last-name": "Williams"
    }
};

domainEvent = {
    "type": "married",
    "person-id": "01b9a761",
    "payload": {
        "person-id": "126a7b61",
        "assumed-partner-last-name": true
    }
};
```

`marriage-recorded` is an event notification message. It contains no information except the fact that the person with the specified ID got married. It contains minimal information about the event, and the consumers interested in more details will have to follow the link in the `details` field.

`personal-details-changed` is an event-carried state transfer message. It describes the changes in the person's personal details, namely that their last name has been changed. The message doesn't explain the reason why it has changed. Did the person get married or divorced?

Finally, `married` is a domain event. It is modeled as close as possible to the nature of the event in the business domain. It includes the person's ID and a flag indicating whether the person assumed their partner's name.

Designing Event-Driven Integration

As we discussed in Chapter 3, software design is predominantly about boundaries. Boundaries define what belongs inside, what remains outside, and most importantly, what goes across the boundaries—essentially, how the components are integrated with one another. The events in an EDA-based system are first-class design elements, affecting both how the components are integrated and the components' boundaries themselves. Choosing the correct type of event message is what makes (decouples) or breaks (couples) a distributed system.

In this section, you will learn heuristics for applying different event types. But first, let's see how to use events to design a strongly coupled, distributed big ball of mud.

Distributed Big Ball of Mud

Consider the system shown in Figure 15-5.

The CRM bounded context is implemented as an event-sourced domain model. When the CRM system had to be integrated with the Marketing bounded context, the teams decided to leverage the event-sourced data model's flexibility and let the consumer—in this case, Marketing—subscribe to the CRM's domain events and use them to project the model that fits their needs.

When the AdsOptimization bounded context was introduced, it also had to process the information produced by the CRM bounded context. Again, the teams decided to let AdsOptimization subscribe to all domain events produced in the CRM and project the model that fits AdsOptimization's needs.

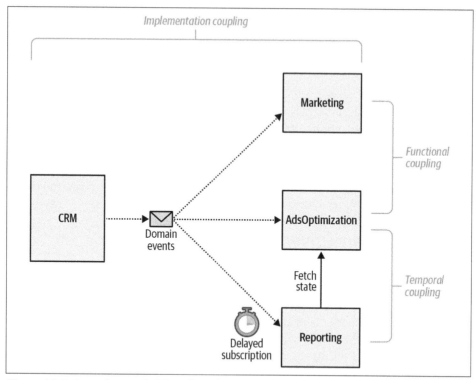

Figure 15-5. Strongly coupled distributed system

Interestingly, both the Marketing and AdsOptimization bounded contexts had to present the customers' information in the same format, and hence ended up projecting the same model out of the CRM's domain events: a flattened snapshot of each customer's state.

The Reporting bounded context subscribed only to a subset of domain events published by the CRM and used as event notification messages to fetch the calculations performed in the AdsOptimization context. However, since both AdsOptimization bounded contexts use the same events to trigger their calculations, to ensure that the Reporting model is updated the AdsOptimization context introduced a delay. It processed messages five minutes after receiving them.

This design is terrible. Let's analyze the types of coupling in this system.

Temporal Coupling

The AdsOptimization and Reporting bounded contexts are temporally coupled: they depend on a strict order of execution. The AdsOptimization component has to finish its processing before the Reporting module is triggered. If the order is reversed, inconsistent data will be produced in the Reporting system.

To enforce the required execution order, the engineers introduced the processing delay in the Reporting system. This delay of five minutes lets the AdsOptimization component finish the required calculations. Obviously, this doesn't prevent incorrect order of execution:

- AdsOptimization may be overloaded and unable to finish the processing in five minutes.
- A network issue may delay the delivery of incoming messages to the AdsOptimization service.
- The AdsOptimization component can experience an outage and stop processing incoming messages.

Functional Coupling

The Marketing and AdsOptimization bounded contexts both subscribed to the CRM's domain events and ended up implementing the same projection of the customers' data. In other words, the business logic that transforms incoming domain events into a state-based representation was duplicated in both bounded contexts, and it had the same reasons for change: they had to present the customers' data in the same format. Therefore, if the projection was changed in one of the components, the change had to be replicated in the second bounded context.

That's an example of functional coupling: multiple components implementing the same business functionality, and if it changes, both components have to change simultaneously.

Implementation Coupling

This type of coupling is more subtle. The Marketing and AdsOptimization bounded contexts are subscribed to all the domain events generated by the CRM's event-sourced model. Consequently, a change in the CRM's implementation, such as adding a new domain event or changing the schema of an existing one, has to be reflected in both subscribing bounded contexts! Failing to do so can lead to inconsistent data. For example, if an event's schema changes, the subscribers' projection logic will fail. On the other hand, if a new domain event is added to the CRM's model, it can potentially affect the projected models, and thus, ignoring it will lead to projecting an inconsistent state.

Refactoring the Event-Driven Integration

As you can see, blindly pouring events on a system makes it neither decoupled nor resilient. You may assume that this is an unrealistic example, but unfortunately, this example is based on a true story. Let's see how the events can be adjusted to improve the design dramatically.

Exposing all the domain events constituting the CRM's data model couples the subscribers to the producer's implementation details. The implementation coupling can be addressed by exposing either a much more restrained set of events or a different type of events.

The Marketing and AdsOptimization subscribers are functionally coupled to each other by implementing the same business functionality.

Both implementation and functional coupling can be tackled by encapsulating the projection logic in the producer: the CRM bounded contexts. Instead of exposing its implementation details, the CRM can follow the consumer-driven contract pattern: project the model needed by the consumers and make it a part of the bounded context's published language—an integration-specific model, decoupled from the internal implementation model. As a result, the consumers get all the data they need and are not aware of the CRM's implementation model.

To tackle the temporal coupling between the AdsOptimization and Reporting bounded contexts, the AdsOptimization component can publish an event notification message, triggering the Reporting component to fetch the data it needs. This refactored system is shown in Figure 15-6.

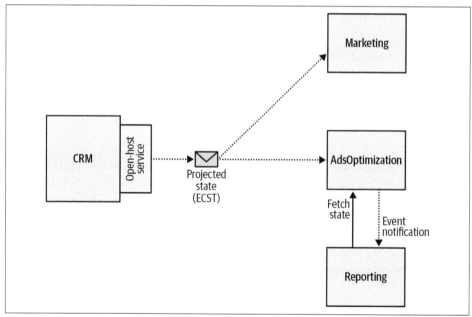

Figure 15-6. Refactored system

Event-Driven Design Heuristics

Matching types of events to the tasks at hand makes the resultant design orders of magnitude less coupled, more flexible, and fault tolerant. Let's formulate the design heuristics behind the applied changes.

Assume the worst

As Andrew Grove put it, only the paranoid survive.[3] Use this as a guiding principle when designing event-driven systems:

- The network is going to be slow.
- Servers will fail at the most inconvenient moment.
- Events will arrive out of order.
- Events will be duplicated.

Most importantly, these events will occur most frequently on weekends and public holidays.

The word *driven* in event-driven architecture means your whole system depends on successful delivery of the messages. Hence, avoid the "things will be okay" mindset like the plague. Ensure that the events are always delivered consistently, no matter what:

- Use the outbox pattern to publish messages reliably.
- When publishing messages, ensure that the subscribers will be able to deduplicate the messages and identify and reorder out-of-order messages.
- Leverage the saga and process manager patterns when orchestrating cross-bounded context processes that require issuing compensating actions.

Use public and private events

Be wary of exposing implementation details when publishing domain events, especially in event-sourced aggregates. Treat events as an inherent part of the bounded context's public interface. Therefore, when implementing the open-host service pattern, ensure that the events are reflected in the bounded context's published language. Patterns for transforming event-based models are discussed in Chapter 9.

When designing bounded contexts' public interfaces, leverage the different types of events. Event-carried state transfer messages compress the implementation model

---

3 Grove, A. S. (1998). *Only the Paranoid Survive*. London: HarperCollins Business.

into a more compact model that communicates only the information the consumers need.

Event notification messages can be used to further minimize the public interface.

Finally, sparingly use domain events for communication with external bounded contexts. Consider designing a set of dedicated public domain events.

Evaluate consistency requirements

When designing event-driven communication, evaluate the bounded contexts' consistency requirements as an additional heuristic for choosing the event type:

- If the components can settle for eventually consistent data, use the event-carried state transfer message.
- If the consumer needs to read the last write in the producer's state, issue an event notification message, with a subsequent query to fetch the producer's up-to-date state.

Conclusion

This chapter presented event-driven architecture as an inherent aspect of designing a bounded context's public interface. You learned the three types of events that can be used for cross-bounded context communication:

Event notification
  A notification that something important has happened, but requiring the consumer to query the producer for additional information explicitly.

Event-carried state transfer
  A message-based data replication mechanism. Each event contains a snapshot of a state that can be used to maintain a local cache of the producer's data.

Domain event
  A message describing an event in the producer's business domain.

Using inappropriate types of events will derail an EDA-based system, inadvertently turning it into a big ball of mud. To choose the correct type of events for integration, evaluate the bounded contexts' consistency requirements and be wary of exposing implementation details. Design an explicit set of public and private events. Finally, ensure that the system delivers the messages, even in the face of technical issues and outages.

Exercises

1. Which of the following statements is/are correct?

   a. Event-driven architecture defines the events intended to travel across components' boundaries.

   b. Event sourcing defines the events that are intended to stay within the bounded context's boundary.

   c. Event-driven architecture and event sourcing are different terms for the same pattern.

   d. A and B are correct.

2. What type of event is best suited for communicating changes in state?

   a. Event notification.

   b. Event-carried state transfer.

   c. Domain event.

   d. All event types are equally good for communicating changes in state.

3. Which bounded context integration pattern calls for explicitly defining public events?

   a. Open-host service

   b. Anticorruption layer

   c. Shared kernel

   d. Conformist

4. The services S1 and S2 are integrated asynchronously. S1 has to communicate data and S2 needs to be able to read the last written data in S1. Which type of event fits this integration scenario?

   a. S2 should publish event-carried state transfer events.

   b. S2 should publish public event notifications, which will signal S1 to issue a synchronous request to get the most up-to-date information.

   c. S2 should publish domain events.

   d. A and B.

CHAPTER 16

Data Mesh

So far in this book, we have discussed models used to build operational systems. Operational systems implement real-time transactions that manipulate the system's data and orchestrate its day-to-day interactions with its environment. These models are the online transactional processing (OLTP) data. Another type of data that deserves attention and proper modeling is online analytical processing (OLAP) data.

In this chapter, you will learn about the analytical data management architecture called data mesh. You will see how the data mesh–based architecture works and how it differs from the more traditional OLAP data management approaches. Ultimately, you will see how domain-driven design and data mesh accommodate each other. But first, let's see what these analytical data models are and why we can't just reuse the operational models for analytical use cases.

Analytical Data Model Versus Transactional Data Model

They say knowledge is power. Analytical data is the knowledge that gives companies the power to leverage accumulated data to gain insights into how to optimize the business, better understand customers' needs, and even make automated decisions by training machine learning (ML) models.

The analytical models (OLAP) and operational models (OLTP) serve different types of consumers, enable the implementation of different kinds of use cases, and are therefore designed following other design principles.

Operational models are built around the various entities from the system's business domain, implementing their lifecycles and orchestrating their interactions with one another. These models, depicted in Figure 16-1, are serving operational systems and hence have to be optimized to support real-time business transactions.

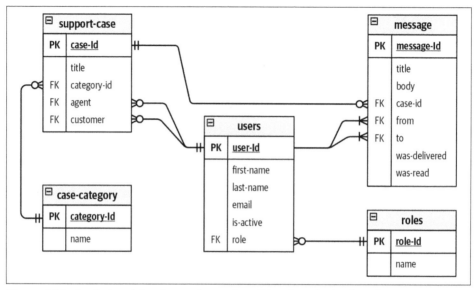

Figure 16-1. A relational database schema describing the relationships between entities in an operational model

Analytical models are designed to provide different insights into the operational systems. Instead of implementing real-time transactions, an analytical model aims to provide insights into the performance of business activities and, more importantly, how the business can optimize its operations to achieve greater value.

From a data structure perspective, OLAP models ignore the individual business entities and instead focus on business activities by modeling fact tables and dimension tables. We'll take a closer look at each of these tables next.

Fact Table

Facts represent business activities that have already happened. Facts are similar to the notion of domain events in the sense that both describe things that happened in the past. However, contrary to domain events, there is no stylistic requirement to name facts as verbs in the past tense. Still, facts represent activities of business processes. For example, a fact table `Fact_CustomerOnboardings` would contain a record for each new onboarded customer and `Fact_Sales` a record for each committed sale. Figure 16-2 shows an example of a fact table.

	Fact_SolvedCases
PK	**CaseId**
FK	AgentKey
FK	CategoryKey
FK	OpenedOnDateKey
FK	ClosedOnDateKey
FK	CustomerKey

Figure 16-2. A fact table containing records for cases solved by a company's support desk

Also, similar to domain events, fact records are never deleted or modified: analytical data is append-only data: the only way to express that current data is outdated is to append a new record with the current state. Consider the fact table Fact_CaseStatus in Figure 16-3. It contains the measurements of the statuses of support requests through time. There is no explicit verb in the fact name, but the business process captured by the fact is the process of taking care of support cases.

Fact_CaseStatus					
CaseId	**Timestamp**	**AgentKey**	**CategoryKey**	**CustomerKey**	**StatusKey**
case-141408202228	2021-06-15 10:30:00		12	10060512	1
case-141408202228	15/06/2021 11:00:00	285889	12	10060512	2
case-141408202228	15/06/2021 11:30:00	285889	12	10060512	2
case-141408202228	15/06/2021 12:00:00	285889	12	10060512	3
case-141408202228	15/06/2021 12:30:00	285889	12	10060512	2
case-141408202228	15/06/2021 13:00:00	285889	12	10060512	4

Figure 16-3. A fact table describing state changes during the lifecycle of a support case

Another significant difference between the OLAP and OLTP models is the granularity of the data. Operational systems require the most precise data to handle business transactions. For analytical models, aggregated data is more efficient in many use cases. For example, in the Fact_CaseStatus table shown in Figure 16-3, you can see that the snapshots are taken every 30 minutes. The data analysts working with the model decide what level of granularity will best suit their needs. Creating a fact record for each change of the measurement—for example, each change of a case's data—would be wasteful in some cases and even technically impossible in others.

Dimension Table

Another essential building block of an analytical model is a dimension. If a fact represents a business process or action (a verb), a dimension describes the fact (an adjective).

The dimensions are designed to describe the facts' attributes and are referenced as a foreign key from a fact table to a dimension table. The attributes modeled as dimensions are any measurements or data that is repeated across different fact records and cannot fit in a single column. For example, the schema in Figure 16-4 augments the SolvedCases fact with its dimensions.

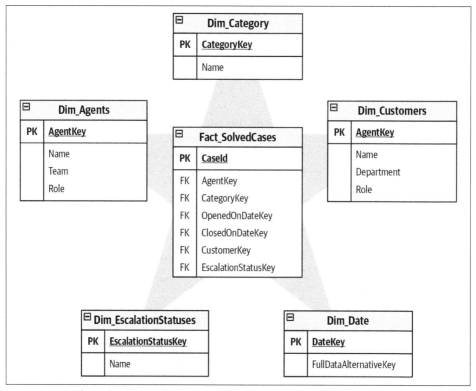

Figure 16-4. The SolvedCases fact surrounded by its dimensions

The reason for the high normalization of the dimensions is the analytical system's need to support flexible querying. That's another difference between operational and analytical models. It's possible to predict how an operational model will be queried to support the business requirements. The querying patterns of the analytical models are not predictable. The data analysts need flexible ways of looking at the data, and it's hard to predict what queries will be executed in the future. As a result, the normalization supports dynamic querying and filtering, and grouping the facts data across the different dimensions.

Analytical Models

The table structure depicted in Figure 16-5 is called the *star schema*. It is based on the many-to-one relationships between the facts and their dimensions: each dimension record is used by many facts; a fact's foreign key points to a single dimension record.

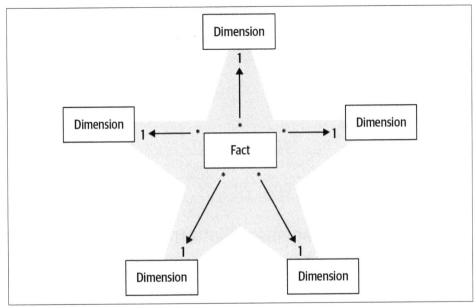

Figure 16-5. The many-to-one relationship between facts and their dimensions

Another predominant analytical model is the snowflake schema. The snowflake schema is based on the same building blocks: facts and dimensions. However, in the snowflake schema, the dimensions are multilevel: each dimension is further normalized into more fine-grained dimensions, as shown in Figure 16-6.

As a result of the additional normalization, the snowflake schema will use less space to store the dimension data and is easier to maintain. However, querying the facts' data will require joining more tables, and therefore, more computational resources are needed.

Both the star and snowflake schemas allow data analysts to analyze business performance, gaining insights into what can be optimized and built into business intelligence (BI) reports.

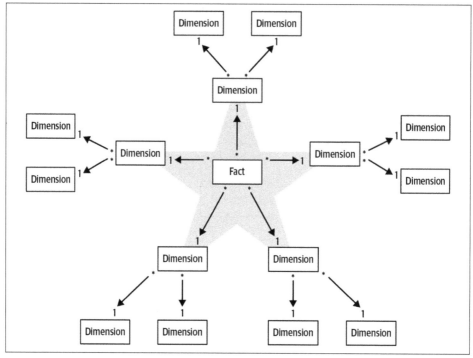

Figure 16-6. Multilevel dimensions in the snowflake schema

Analytical Data Management Platforms

Let's shift the discussion from analytical modeling to data management architectures that support generating and serving analytical data. In this section, we will discuss two common analytical data architectures: data warehouse and data lake. You will learn the basic working principles of each architecture, how they differ from each other, and the challenges of each approach. Knowledge of how the two architectures work will build the foundation for discussing the main topic of this chapter: the data mesh paradigm and its interplay with domain-driven design.

Data Warehouse

The data warehouse (DWH) architecture is relatively straightforward. Extract data from all of the enterprise's operational systems, transform the source data into an analytical model, and load the resultant data into a data analysis–oriented database. This database is the data warehouse.

This data management architecture is based primarily on the extract-transform-load (ETL) scripts. The data can come from various sources: operational databases, streaming events, logs, and so on. In addition to translating the source data into a facts/dimensions-based model, the transformation step may include additional operations such as removing sensitive data, deduplicating records, reordering events, aggregating fine-grained events, and more. In some cases, the transformation may require temporary storage for the incoming data. This is known as the staging area.

The resultant data warehouse, shown in Figure 16-7, contains analytical data covering all of the enterprise's business processes. The data is exposed using the SQL language (or one of its dialects) and is used by data analysts and BI engineers.

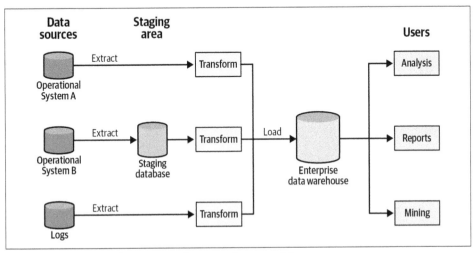

Figure 16-7. A typical enterprise data warehouse architecture

The careful reader will notice that the data warehouse architecture shares some of the challenges discussed in Chapters 2 and 3.

First, at the heart of the data warehouse architecture is the goal of building an enterprise-wide model. The model should describe the data produced by all of the enterprise's systems and address all of the different use cases for analytical data. The analytical model enables, for example, optimizing the business, reducing operational costs, making intelligent business decisions, reporting, and even training ML models. As you learned in Chapter 3, such an approach is impractical for anything by the smallest organizations. Designing a model for the task at hand, such as building reports or training ML models, is a much more effective and scalable approach.

The challenge of building an all-encompassing model can be partly addressed by the use of data marts. A data mart is a database that holds data relevant for well-defined analytical needs, such as analysis of a single business department. In the data mart model shown in Figure 16-8, one mart is populated directly by an ETL process from an operational system, while another mart extracts its data from the data warehouse.

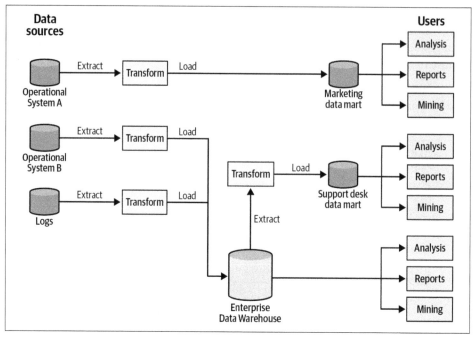

Figure 16-8. The enterprise data warehouse architecture augmented with data marts

When the data is ingested into a data mart from the enterprise data warehouse, the enterprise-wide model still needs to be defined in the data warehouse. Alternatively, data marts can implement dedicated ETL processes to ingest data directly from the operational systems. In this case, the resultant model makes it challenging to query data across different marts—for example, across different departments—as it requires a cross-database query and significantly impacts performance.

Another challenging aspect of the data warehouse architecture is that the ETL processes create a strong coupling between the analytical (OLAP) and the operational (OLTP) systems. The data consumed by the ETL scripts is not necessarily exposed through the system's public interfaces. Often, DWH systems simply fetch all the data residing in the operational systems' databases. The schema used in the operational database is not a public interface, but rather an internal implementation detail. As a result, a slight change in the schema is destined to break the data warehouse's ETL scripts. Since the operational and analytical systems are implemented and maintained by somewhat distant organizational units, the communication between the two is challenging and leads to lots of friction between the teams. This communication pattern is shown in Figure 16-9.

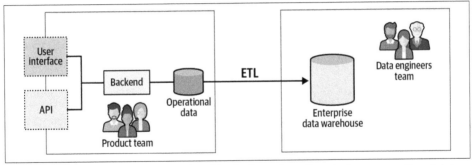

Figure 16-9. Data warehouse populated by fetching data directly from operational databases, ignoring the integration-oriented public interfaces

The data lake architecture addresses some of the shortcomings of the data warehouse architecture.

Data Lake

As a data warehouse, the data lake architecture is based on the same notion of ingesting the operational systems' data and transforming it into an analytical model. However, there is a conceptual difference between the two approaches.

A data lake–based system ingests the operational systems' data. However, instead of being transformed right away into an analytical model, the data is persisted in its raw form, that is, in the original operational model.

Eventually, the raw data cannot fit the needs of data analysts. As a result, it is the job of the data engineers and the BI engineers to make sense of the data in the lake and implement the ETL scripts that will generate analytical models and feed them into a data warehouse. Figure 16-10 depicts a data lake architecture.

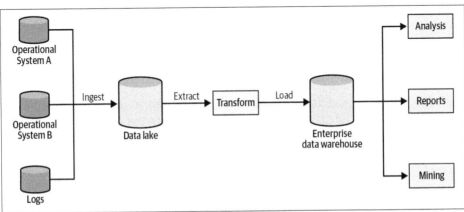

Figure 16-10. Data lake architecture

Since the operational systems' data is persisted in its original, raw form and is transformed only afterward, the data lake allows working with multiple, task-oriented analytical models. One model can be used for reporting, another for training ML models, and so on. Furthermore, new models can be added in the future and initialized with the existing raw data.

That said, the delayed generation of analytical models increases the complexity of the overall system. It's not uncommon for data engineers to implement and support multiple versions of the same ETL script to accommodate different versions of the operational model, as shown in Figure 16-11.

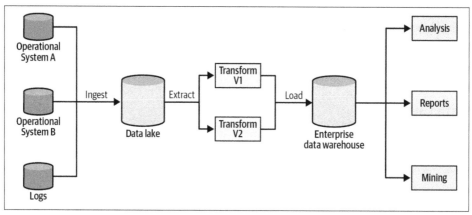

Figure 16-11. Multiple versions of the same ETL script accommodating different versions of the operational model

Furthermore, since data lakes are schema-less—there is no schema imposed on the incoming data—and there is no control over the quality of the incoming data, the data lake's data becomes chaotic at certain levels of scale. Data lakes make it easy to ingest data but much more challenging to make use of it. Or, as is often said, a data lake becomes a data swamp. The data scientist's job becomes orders of magnitude more complex to make sense of the chaos and to extract useful analytical data.

Challenges of Data Warehouse and Data Lake Architectures

Both data warehouse and data lake architectures are based on the assumption that the more data that is ingested for analytics, the more insight the organization will gain. Both approaches, however, tend to break under the weight of "big" data. The transformation of operational to analytical models converges to thousands of unmaintainable, ad hoc ETL scripts at scale.

From a modeling perspective, both architectures trespass the boundaries of the operational systems and create dependencies on their implementation details. The resultant coupling to the implementation models creates friction between the operational and analytical systems teams, often to the point of preventing changes to the operational models for the sake of not breaking the analysis system's ETL jobs.

To make matters worse, since the data analysts and data engineers belong to a separate organizational unit, they often lack the deep knowledge of the business domain possessed by the operational systems' development teams. Instead of the knowledge of the business domain, they are specialized mainly in big data tooling.

Last but not least, the coupling to the implementation models is especially acute in domain-driven design–based projects, in which the emphasis is on continuously evolving and improving the business domain's models. As a result, a change in the operational model can have unforeseen consequences in the analytical model. Such changes are frequent in DDD projects and often result in friction between R&D and data teams.

These limitations of data warehouses and data lakes inspired a new analytical data management architecture: data mesh.

Data Mesh

The data mesh architecture is, in a sense, domain-driven design for analytical data. As the different patterns of DDD draw boundaries and protect their contents, the data mesh architecture defines and protects model and ownership boundaries for analytical data.

The data mesh architecture is based on four core principles: decompose data around domains, data as a product, enable autonomy, and build an ecosystem. Let's discuss each principle in detail.

Decompose Data Around Domains

Both the data warehouse and data lake approaches aim to unify all of the enterprise's data into one big model. The resultant analytical model is ineffective for all the same reasons as an enterprise-wide operational model is. Furthermore, gathering data from all systems into one location blurs the ownership boundaries of the various data elements.

Instead of building a monolithic analytical model, the data mesh architecture calls for leveraging the same solution we discussed in Chapter 3 for operational data: use multiple analytical models and align them with the origin of the data. This naturally aligns the ownership boundaries of the analytical models with the bounded contexts' boundaries, as shown in Figure 16-12. When the analysis model is decomposed according to the system's bounded contexts, the generation of the analysis data becomes the responsibility of the corresponding product teams.

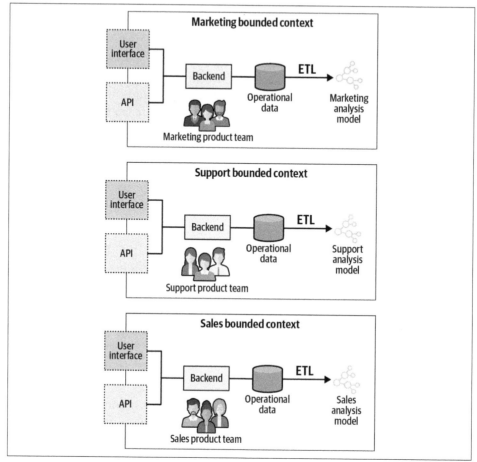

Figure 16-12. Aligning the ownership boundaries of the analytical models with the bounded contexts' boundaries

Each bounded context now owns its operational (OLTP) and analytical (OLAP) models. Consequently, the same team owns the operational model, now in charge of transforming it into the analytical model.

Data as a Product

The classic data management architectures make it difficult to discover, understand, and fetch quality analytical data. This is especially acute in the case of data lakes.

The data as a product principle calls for treating the analytical data as a first-class citizen. Instead of the analytical systems having to get the operational data from dubious sources (internal database, logfiles, etc.), in a data mesh–based system the bounded contexts serve the analytical data through well-defined output ports, as shown in Figure 16-13.

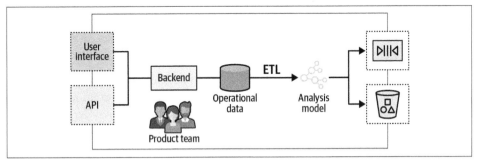

Figure 16-13. Polyglot data endpoints exposing the analytical data to the consumers

Analytical data should be treated the same as any public API:

- It should be easy to discover the necessary endpoints: the data output ports.
- The analytical endpoints should have a well-defined schema describing the served data and its format.
- The analytical data should be trustworthy, and as with any API, it should have defined and monitored service-level agreements (SLAs).
- The analytical model should be versioned as a regular API and correspondingly manage integration-breaking changes in the model.

Furthermore, since the analytical data is treated as a product, it has to address the needs of its consumers. The bounded context's team is in charge of ensuring that the resultant model addresses the needs of its consumers. Contrary to the data warehouse and data lake architectures, with data mesh, accountability for data quality is a top-level concern.

The goal of the distributed data management architecture is to allow the fine-grained analytical models to be combined to address the organization's data analysis needs. For example, if a BI report should reflect data from multiple bounded contexts, it should be able to easily fetch their analytical data if needed, apply local transformations, and produce the report.

Finally, different consumers may require the analytical data in different forms. Some may prefer to execute SQL queries, others to fetch analytical data from an object storage service, and so on. As a result, the data products have to be polyglot, serving the data in formats that suit different consumers' needs.

To implement the data as a product principle, product teams require adding data-oriented specialists. That's the missing piece in the cross-functional teams puzzle, which traditionally includes only specialists related to the operational systems.

Enable Autonomy

The product teams should be able to both create their own data products and consume data products served by other bounded contexts. Just as in the case of bounded contexts, the data products should be interoperable.

It would be wasteful, inefficient, and hard to integrate if each team builds their own solution for serving analytical data. To prevent this from happening, a platform is needed to abstract the complexity of building, executing, and maintaining interoperable data products. Designing and building such a platform is a considerable undertaking and requires a dedicated data infrastructure platform team.

The data infrastructure platform team should be in charge of defining the data product blueprints, unified access patterns, access control, and polyglot storage that can be leveraged by product teams, as well as monitoring the platform and ensuring that the SLAs and objectives are met.

Build an Ecosystem

The final step to creating a data mesh system is to appoint a federated governance body to enable interoperability and ecosystem thinking in the domain of the analytical data. Typically, that would be a group consisting of the bounded contexts' data and product owners and representatives of the data infrastructure platform team, as shown in Figure 16-14.

The governance group is in charge of defining the rules to ensure a healthy and interoperable ecosystem. The rules have to be applied to all data products and their interfaces, and it's the group's responsibility to ensure adherence to the rules throughout the enterprise.

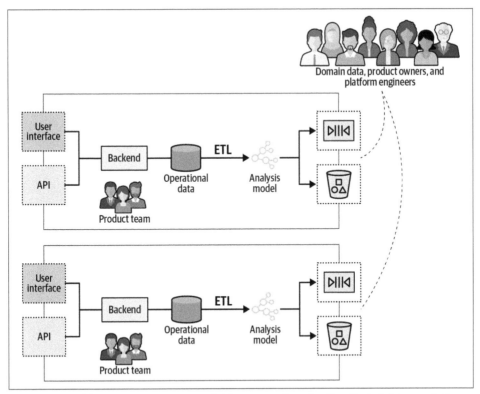

Figure 16-14. The governance group, which ensures that the distributed data analytics ecosystem is interoperable, healthy, and serves the organization's needs

Combining Data Mesh and Domain-Driven Design

These are the four principles that the data mesh architecture is based on. The emphasis on defining boundaries, and encapsulating the implementation details behind well-defined output ports, makes it evident that the data mesh architecture is based on the same reasoning as domain-driven design. Furthermore, some of the domain-driven design patterns can greatly support implementing the data mesh architecture.

First and foremost, the ubiquitous language and the resultant domain knowledge are essential for designing analytical models. As we discussed in the data warehouse and data lake sections, domain knowledge is lacking in traditional architectures.

Second, exposing a bounded context's data in a model that is different from its operational model is the open-host pattern. In this case, the analytical model is an additional published language.

The CQRS pattern makes it easy to generate multiple models of the same data. It can be leveraged to transform the operational model into an analytical model. The CQRS pattern's ability to generate models from scratch makes it easy to generate and serve multiple versions of the analytical model simultaneously, as shown in Figure 16-15.

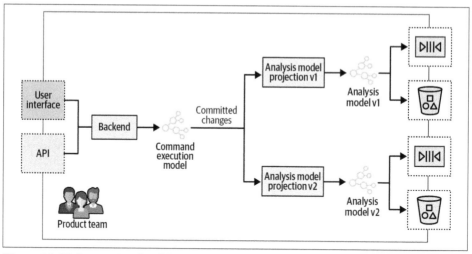

Figure 16-15. Leveraging the CQRS pattern to simultaneously serve the analytical data in two different schema versions

Finally, since the data mesh architecture combines the different bounded contexts' models to implement analytical use cases, the bounded context integration patterns for operational models apply for analytical models as well. Two product teams can evolve their analytical models in partnership. Another can implement an anticorruption layer to protect itself from an ineffective analytical model. Or, on the other hand, the teams can go their separate ways and produce duplicate implementations of analytical models.

Conclusion

In this chapter, you learned the different aspects of designing software systems, in particular, defining and managing analytical data. We discussed the predominant models for analytical data, including the star and snowflake schemas, and how the data is traditionally managed in data warehouses and data lakes.

The data mesh architecture aims to address the challenges of the traditional data management architectures. At its core, it applies the same principles as domain-driven design but to analytical data: decomposing the analytical model into manageable units and ensuring that the analytical data can be reliably accessed and used through its public interfaces. Ultimately, the CQRS and bounded context integration patterns can support implementing the data mesh architecture.

Exercises

1. Which of the following statements is/are correct regarding the differences between transactional (OLTP) and analytical (OLAP) models?

   a. OLAP models should expose more flexible querying options than OLTP models.

   b. OLAP models are expected to undergo more updates than OLTP models, and thus have to be optimized for writes.

   c. OLTP data is optimized for real-time operations, whereas it's acceptable to wait seconds or even minutes for an OLAP query's response.

   d. A and C are correct.

2. Which bounded context integration pattern is essential for implementation of the data mesh architecture?

   a. Shared kernel

   b. Open-host service

   c. Anticorruption layer

   d. Partnership

3. Which architectural pattern is essential for implementation of the data mesh architecture?

   a. Layered architecture.

   b. Ports & adapters.

   c. CQRS.

   d. Architectural patterns cannot support implementation of an OLAP model.

4. The definition of data mesh architecture calls for decomposing data around "domains." What is DDD's term for denoting the data mesh's domains?

   a. Bounded contexts.

   b. Business domains.

   c. Subdomains.

   d. There is no synonym for a data mesh's domains in DDD.

Closing Words

To complete our exploration of domain-driven design I want to get back to the quote we started with:

> There is no sense in talking about the solution before we agree on the problem, and no sense talking about the implementation steps before we agree on the solution.
>
> —Efrat Goldratt-Ashlag

This quote neatly summarizes our DDD journey.

Problem

To provide a software solution, we first have to understand the problem: what is the *business domain* that we are working in, what are the business goals, and what is the strategy for achieving them.

We used the *ubiquitous language* to gain a deep understanding of the business domain and its logic that we have to implement in software.

You learned to manage the complexity of the business problem by breaking it apart into *bounded contexts*. Each bounded context implements a single model of the business domain, aimed at solving a specific problem.

We discussed how to identify and categorize the building blocks of business domains: *core*, *supporting*, and *generic subdomains*. Table E-1 compares these three types of subdomains.

Table E-1. The three types of subdomains

Subdomain type	Competitive advantage	Complexity	Volatility	Implementation	Problem
Core	Yes	High	High	In-house	Interesting
Generic	No	High	Low	Buy/adopt	Solved
Supporting	No	Low	Low	In-house/outsource	Obvious

Solution

You learned to leverage this knowledge to design solutions optimized for each type of subdomain. We discussed four business logic implementation patterns—*transaction script, active record, domain model*, and *event sourced domain model*—and the scenarios in which each pattern shines. You also saw three architectural patterns that provide the required scaffolding for the implementation of business logic: *layered architecture, ports & adapters*, and *CQRS*. Figure E-1 summarizes the heuristics for tactical decision-making using these patterns.

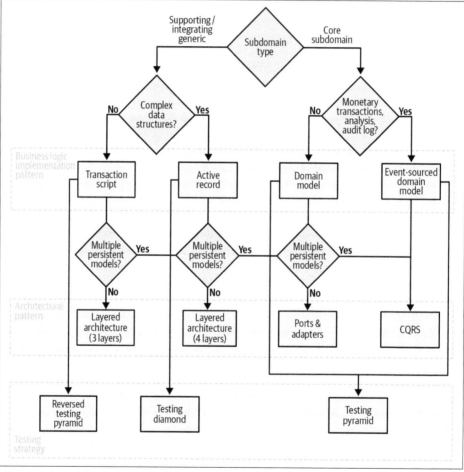

Figure E-1. Decision tree summarizing heuristics for tactical decision-making

Implementation

In Part III, we discussed how to turn theory into practice. You learned how to effectively build a ubiquitous language by facilitating an EventStorming session, how to keep the design in shape as the business domain evolves, and how to introduce and start using domain-driven design in brownfield projects.

In Part IV, we discussed the interplay between domain-driven design and other methodologies and patterns: microservices, event-driven architecture, and data mesh. We saw that not only can DDD be used in tandem with these techniques, but they in fact complement each other.

Further Reading

I hope this book got you interested in domain-driven design. If you want to keep learning, here are some books that I wholeheartedly recommend.

Advanced Domain-Driven Design

- Evans, E. (2003). *Domain-Driven Design: Tackling Complexity in the Heart of Software*. Boston: Addison-Wesley.

  Eric Evans's original book that introduced the domain-driven design methodology. Although it doesn't reflect newer aspects of DDD such as domain events and event sourcing, it's still essential reading for becoming a DDD black belt.

- Martraire, C. (2019). *Living Documentation: Continuous Knowledge Sharing by Design*. Boston: Addison-Wesley.

  In this book, Cyrille Martraire proposes a domain-driven design–based approach to knowledge sharing, documentation, and testing.

- Vernon, V. (2013). *Implementing Domain-Driven Design*. Boston: Addison-Wesley.

  Another timeless DDD classic. Vaughn Vernon provides in-depth discussion and detailed examples of domain-driven design thinking and the use of its strategic and tactical toolset. As a learning foundation, Vaughn uses a real-world example of failing initiatives with DDD and the teams' rejuvenated journey afforded by applying essential course corrections.

- Young, G. (2017). *Versioning in an Event Sourced System* (*https://leanpub.com/esversioning/read*). Leanpub.

  In Chapter 7, we discussed that it can be challenging to evolve an event-sourced system. This book is dedicated to this topic.

Architectural and Integration Patterns

- Dehghani, Z. (Expected to be published in 2022). *Data Mesh: Delivering Data-Driven Value at Scale*. Boston: O'Reilly.

  Zhamak Dehghani is the author of the data mesh pattern that we discussed in Chapter 16. In this book, Dehghani explains the principles behind the data management architecture, as well as how to implement the data mesh architecture in practice.

- Fowler, M. (2002). *Patterns of Enterprise Application Architecture*. Boston: Addison-Wesley.

  The classic application architecture patterns book that I quoted multiple times in Chapter 5 and Chapter 6. This is the book in which the transaction script, active record, and domain model patterns were originally defined.

- Hohpe, G., & Woolf, B. (2003). *Enterprise Integration Patterns: Designing, Building, and Deploying Messaging Solutions*. Boston: Addison-Wesley.

  Many of the patterns discussed in Chapter 9 were originally introduced in this book. Read this book for more component integration patterns.

- Richardson, C. (2019). *Microservice Patterns: With Examples in Java*. New York: Manning Publications.

  In this book, Chris Richardson provides many detailed examples of patterns often used when architecting microservices-based solutions. Among the discussed patterns are saga, process manager, and outbox, which we discussed in Chapter 9.

Modernization of Legacy Systems

- Kaiser, S. (Expected to be published in 2022). *Adaptive Systems with Domain-Driven Design, Wardley Mapping, and Team Topologies*. Boston: Addison-Wesley.

  Susanne Kaiser shares her experience of modernizing legacy systems by leveraging domain-driven design, Wardley mapping, and team topologies.

- Tune, N. (Expected to be published in 2022). *Architecture Modernization: Product, Domain, & Team Oriented* (*https://leanpub.com/arch-modernization-ddd*). Leanpub.

  In this book, Nick Tune discusses in depth how to leverage domain-driven design and other techniques to modernize brownfield projects' architecture.

- Vernon, V., & Jaskula, T. (2021). *Implementing Strategic Monoliths and Microservices*. Boston: Addison-Wesley.

A hands-on book in which the authors demonstrate ageless software engineering tools, including rapid discovery and learning, domain-driven approaches, and handling the intricacies of properly implementing monolith- and microservices-based solutions, all while focusing on the most important aspect: delivering innovative business strategy.

- Vernon, V., & Jaskula, T. (2021). *Strategic Monoliths and Microservices*. Boston: Addison-Wesley.

In this book Vaughn and Tomasz promote software strategic thinking by exploring how to achieve all-important innovations using discovery-based learning along with a domain-driven approach, and how to select the most purposeful architecture and tools for the job: microservices, monoliths, or a blend, and how to make them work together.

EventStorming

- Brandolini, A. (Not yet published). *Introducing EventStorming* (*https://lean pub.com/introducing_eventstorming*). Leanpub.

Alberto Brandolini is the creator of the EventStorming workshop, and in this book, he explains in detail the process and rationale behind EventStorming.

- Rayner, P. (Not yet published). *The EventStorming Handbook* (*https://lean pub.com/eventstorming_handbook*). Leanpub.

Paul Rayner explains how he uses EventStorming in practice, including numerous tips and tricks for facilitating a successful session.

Conclusion

That's it! Thank you so much for reading this book. I hope you enjoyed it and that you will use what you've learned from it.

What I hope you take away from this book are the logic and the principles behind domain-driven design tools. Don't follow domain-driven design blindly as a dogma, but rather understand the reasoning it is based on. This understanding will significantly increase your opportunities to apply DDD and gain value from it. Understanding the philosophy of domain-driven design is also the key to leveraging value by incorporating the methodology's concepts individually, especially in brownfield projects.

Finally, always watch your ubiquitous language, and when in doubt, do EventStorming. Good luck!

Applying DDD: A Case Study

In this appendix, I will share how my domain-driven design journey started: the story of a start-up company that, for the purposes of this example, we'll refer to as "Marketnovus." At Marketnovus, we had been employing DDD methodology since the day the company was founded. Over the years, not only had we committed every possible DDD mistake, but we also had the opportunity to learn from those mistakes and fix them. I will use this story and the mistakes we made to demonstrate the role that DDD patterns and practices play in the success of a software project.

This case study consists of two parts. In the Part I, I'll walk you through the stories of five of Marketnovus's bounded contexts, what design decisions were made, and what the outcomes were. In the second part, I will discuss how these stories reflect the material you learned in this book.

Before we begin, I need to stress that Marketnovus doesn't exist anymore. As a result, this appendix is in no way promotional. Furthermore, since this is a defunct company, I'm free to speak honestly about our experiences.

Five Bounded Contexts

Before we delve into the bounded contexts and how they were designed, as well-behaved DDD practitioners we have to start by defining Marketnovus's business domain.

Business Domain

Imagine you are producing a product or a service. Marketnovus allowed you to outsource all of your marketing-related chores. Marketnovus's experts would come up with a marketing strategy for your product. Its copywriters and graphic designers would produce tons of creative material, such as banners and landing pages, that would be used to run advertising campaigns promoting your product. All the leads generated by these campaigns would be handled by Marketnovus's sales agents, who would make the calls and sell your product. This process is depicted in Figure A-1.

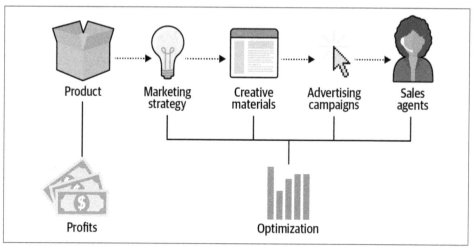

Figure A-1. Marketing process

Most importantly, this marketing process provided many opportunities for optimization, and that's exactly what the analysis department was in charge of. They analyzed all the data to make sure Marketnovus and its clients were getting the biggest bang for their buck, whether by pinpointing the most successful campaigns, celebrating the most effective creatives, or ensuring that the sales agents were working on the most promising leads.

Since we were a self-funded company, we had to get rolling as fast as possible. As a result, right after the company was founded, the first version of our software system had to implement the first one-third of our value chain:

- A system for managing contracts and integrations with external publishers
- A catalog for our designers to manage creative materials
- A campaign management solution to run advertising campaigns

I was overwhelmed and had to find a way to wrap my head around all the complexities of the business domain. Fortunately, not long before we started working, I read a book that promised just that. Of course, I'm talking about Eric Evans's seminal work, *Domain-Driven Design: Tackling Complexity at the Heart of Software*.

If you have read this book's Preface, you know Evans's book provided the answers I'd been seeking for quite a while: how to design and implement business logic. That said, for me it wasn't an easy book to comprehend on the first read. Nevertheless, I felt like I'd already gotten a strong grasp of DDD just by reading the tactical design chapters.

Guess how the system was initially designed? It would definitely make a certain prominent individual[1] from the DDD community very proud.

Bounded Context #1: Marketing

The architectural style of our first solution could be neatly summarized as "aggregates everywhere." Agency, campaign, placement, funnel, publisher: each and every noun in the requirements was proclaimed as an aggregate.

All of those so-called aggregates resided in a huge, lone, bounded context. Yes, a big, scary monolith, the kind everyone warns you about nowadays.

And of course, those were no aggregates. They didn't provide any transactional boundaries, and they had almost no behavior in them. All the business logic was implemented in an enormous service layer.

When you aim to implement a domain model but end up with the active record pattern, it is often termed an "anemic domain model" antipattern. In hindsight, this design was a by-the-book example of how not to implement a domain model. However, things looked quite different from a business standpoint.

From the business's point of view, this project was considered a huge success! Despite the flawed architecture, we were able to deliver working software in a very aggressive time to market. How did we do it?

A kind of magic

We somehow managed to come up with a robust ubiquitous language. None of us had any prior experience in online marketing, but we could still hold a conversation with domain experts. We understood them, they understood us, and to our astonishment, domain experts turned out to be very nice people! They genuinely appreciated the fact that we were willing to learn from them and their experience.

The smooth communication with the domain experts allowed us to grasp the business domain in no time and implement its business logic. Yes, it was a pretty big monolith, but for two developers in a garage, it was just good enough. Again, we produced working software in a very aggressive time to market.

---

1 @DDDBorat is a parody Twitter account known for sharing bad advice on domain-driven design.

Our early understanding of domain-driven design

Our understanding of domain-driven design at this stage could be represented with the simple diagram shown in Figure A-2.

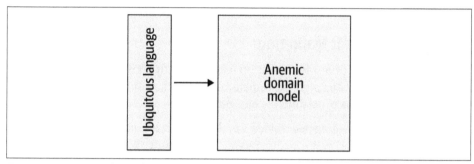

Figure A-2. Our early understanding of domain-driven design

Bounded Context #2: CRM

Soon after we deployed the campaign management solution, leads started flowing in, and we were in a rush. Our sales agents needed a robust customer relationship management (CRM) system to manage the leads and their lifecycles.

The CRM had to aggregate all incoming leads, group them based on different parameters, and distribute them across multiple sales desks around the globe. It also had to integrate with our clients' internal systems, both to notify the clients about changes in the leads' lifecycles and to complement our leads with additional information. And, of course, the CRM had to provide as many optimization opportunities as possible. For example, we needed to be able to make sure the agents were working on the most promising leads, assign leads to agents based on their qualifications and past performance, and allow a very flexible solution for calculating agents' commissions.

Since no off-the-shelf product fit our requirements, we decided to roll out our own CRM system.

More "aggregates"!

The initial implementation approach was to continue focusing on the tactical patterns. Again, we pronounced every noun as an aggregate and shoehorned them into the same monolith. This time, however, something felt wrong right from the start.

We noticed that, all too often, we were adding awkward prefixes to those "aggregates" names: for example, CRMLead and MarketingLead, MarketingCampaign and CRMCampaign. Interestingly, we never used those prefixes in our conversations with the domain experts. Somehow, they always understood the meaning from the context.

Then I recalled that domain-driven design has a notion of bounded contexts that we had been ignoring so far. After revisiting the relevant chapters of Evans's book, I learned that bounded contexts solve exactly the same issue we were experiencing: they protect the consistency of the ubiquitous language. Furthermore, by that time, Vaughn Vernon had published his "Effective Aggregate Design" paper (*https://oreil.ly/ tJ0pb*). The paper made explicit all the mistakes we were making when designing the aggregates. We were treating aggregates as data structures, but they play a much larger role by protecting the consistency of the system's data.

We took a step back and redesigned the CRM solution to reflect these revelations.

Solution design: Take two

We started by dividing our monolith into two distinct bounded contexts: marketing and CRM. Of course, we didn't go all the way to microservices here; we just did the bare minimum to protect the ubiquitous language.

However, in the new bounded context, the CRM, we were not going to repeat the same mistakes we made in the marketing system. No more anemic domain models! Here we would implement a real domain model with real, by-the-book aggregates. In particular, we vowed that:

- Each transaction would affect only one instance of an aggregate.
- Instead of an ORM, each aggregate itself would define the transactional scope.
- The service layer would go on a very strict diet, and all the business logic would be refactored into the corresponding aggregates.

We were so enthusiastic about doing things the right way. But, soon enough, it became apparent that modeling a proper domain model is hard!

Relative to the marketing system, everything took much more time! It was almost impossible to get the transactional boundaries right the first time. We had to evaluate at least a few models and test them, only to figure out later that the one we hadn't thought about was the correct one. The price of doing things the "right" way was very high: lots of time.

Soon it became obvious to everyone that there was no chance in hell we would meet the deadlines! To help us out, management decided to offload implementation of some of the features to…the database administrators team.

Yes, to implement the business logic in stored procedures.

This one decision resulted in much damage down the line. Not because SQL is not the best language for describing business logic. No, the real issue was a bit more subtle and fundamental.

Tower of Babel 2.0

This situation produced an implicit bounded context whose boundary dissected one of our most complex business entities: the Lead.

The result was two teams working on the same business component and implementing closely related features, but with minimal interaction between them. Ubiquitous language? Give me a break! Literally, each team had its own vocabulary to describe the business domain and its rules.

The models were inconsistent. There was no shared understanding. Knowledge was duplicated, and the same rules were implemented twice. Rest assured, when the logic had to change, the implementations went out of sync immediately.

Needless to say, the project wasn't delivered anywhere near on time, and it was full of bugs. Nasty production issues that had flown under the radar for years corrupted our most precious asset: our data.

The only way out of this mess was to completely rewrite the Lead aggregate, this time with proper boundaries, which we did a couple of years later. It wasn't easy, but the mess was so bad there was no other way around it.

A broader understanding of domain-driven design

Even though this project failed pretty miserably by business standards, our understanding of domain-driven design evolved a bit: build a ubiquitous language, protect its integrity using bounded contexts, and instead of implementing an anemic domain model everywhere, implement a proper domain model everywhere. This model is shown in Figure A-3.

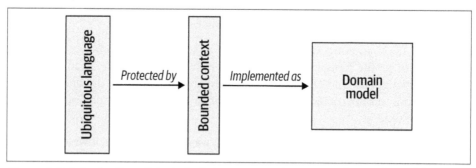

Figure A-3. Introduction of strategic design concepts into our understanding of domain-driven design

Of course, a crucial part of domain-driven design was missing here: subdomains, their types, and how they affect a system's design.

Initially we wanted to do the best job possible, but we ended up wasting time and effort on building domain models for supporting subdomains. As Eric Evans put it, not all of a large system will be well designed. We learned that the hard way, and we wanted to use the acquired knowledge in our next project.

Bounded Context #3: Event Crunchers

After the CRM system was rolled out, we suspected that an implicit subdomain was spread across marketing and CRM. Whenever the process of handling incoming customer events had to be modified, we had to introduce changes both in the marketing and CRM bounded contexts.

Since conceptually this process didn't belong to any of them, we decided to extract this logic into a dedicated bounded context called "event crunchers," shown in Figure A-4.

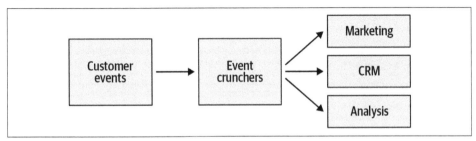

Figure A-4. The event crunchers bounded context handling the incoming customer events

Since we didn't make any money out of the way we move data around, and there weren't any off-the-shelf solutions that could have been used, event crunchers resembled a supporting subdomain. We designed it as such.

Nothing fancy this time: just layered architecture and some simple transaction scripts. This solution worked great, but only for a while.

As our business evolved, we implemented more and more features in the event crunchers. It started with business intelligence (BI) people asking for some flags: a flag to mark a new contact, another one to mark various first-time events, some more flags to indicate some business invariants, and so on.

Eventually, those simple flags evolved into a real business logic, with complex rules and invariants. What started out as transaction scripts evolved into a full-fledged core business subdomain.

Unfortunately, nothing good happens when you implement complex business logic as transaction scripts. Since we didn't adapt our design to cope with the complex business logic, we ended up with a very big ball of mud. Each modification to the codebase became more and more expensive, quality went downhill, and we were forced to rethink the event crunchers design. We did that a year later. By that time, the business logic had become so complex that it could only be tackled with event sourcing. We refactored the event crunchers' logic into an event-sourced domain model, with other bounded contexts subscribing to its events.

Bounded Context #4: Bonuses

One day, the sales desk managers asked us to automate a simple yet tedious procedure they had been doing manually: calculate the commissions for the sales agents.

Again, it started out simple: once a month, just calculate a percentage of each agent's sales and send the report to the managers. As before, we contemplated whether this was a core subdomain. The answer was no. We weren't inventing anything new, weren't making money out of this process, and if it was possible to buy an existing implementation, we definitely would. Not core, not generic, but another supporting subdomain.

We designed the solution accordingly: active record objects, orchestrated by a "smart" service layer, as shown in Figure A-5.

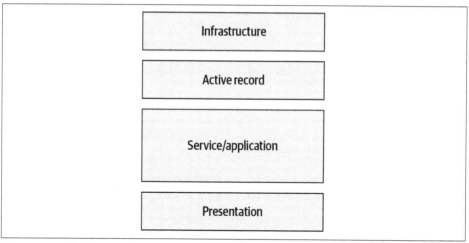

Figure A-5. The bonuses bounded context implemented using the active record and layered architecture patterns

Once the process became automated, boy, did everyone in the company become creative about it. Our analysts wanted to optimize the heck out of this process. They wanted to try out different percentages, tie percentages to sales amounts and prices, unlock additional commissions for achieving different goals, and on and on. Guess when the initial design broke down?

Again, the codebase started turning into an unmanageable ball of mud. Adding new features became more and more expensive, bugs started to appear—and when you're dealing with money, even the smallest bug can have BIG consequences.

Design: Take two

As with the event crunchers project, at some point we couldn't bear it anymore. We had to throw away the old code and rewrite the solution from the ground up, this time as an event-sourced domain model.

And just as in the event crunchers project, the business domain was initially categorized as a supporting one. As the system evolved, it gradually mutated into a core subdomain: we found ways to make money out of these processes. However, there is a striking difference between these two bounded contexts.

Ubiquitous language

For the bonuses project, we had a ubiquitous language. Even though the initial implementation was based on active records, we could still have a ubiquitous language.

As the domain's complexity grew, the language used by the domain experts got more and more complicated as well. At some point, it could no longer be modeled using active records! This realization allowed us to notice the need for a change in the design much earlier than we did in the event crunchers project. We saved a lot of time and effort by not trying to fit a square peg into a round hole, thanks to the ubiquitous language.

A classic understanding of domain-driven design

At this point, our understanding of domain-driven design had finally evolved into a classic one: ubiquitous language, bounded contexts, and different types of subdomains, each designed according to its needs, as shown in Figure A-6.

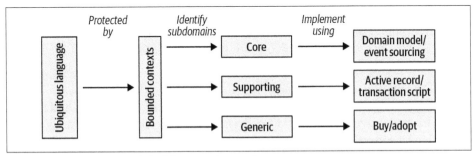

Figure A-6. A classic model of domain-driven design

However, things took quite an unexpected turn for our next project.

Bounded Context #5: The Marketing Hub

Our management was looking for a profitable new vertical. They decided to try using our ability to generate a massive number of leads and sell them to smaller clients, ones we hadn't worked with before. This project was called "marketing hub."

Since management had defined this business domain as a new profit opportunity, it was clearly a core business domain. Hence, designwise, we pulled out the heavy artillery: event-sourced domain model and CQRS. Also, back then, a new buzzword, *microservices*, started gaining lots of traction. We decided to give it a try.

Our solution looked like the implementation shown in Figure A-7.

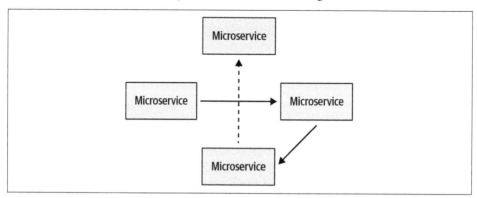

Figure A-7. A microservices-based implementation of the marketing hub bounded context

Small services, each having its own database, with both synchronous and asynchronous communication between them: on paper, it looked like a perfect solution design. In practice, not so much.

Micro what?

We näively approached microservices thinking that the smaller the service was, the better. So we drew service boundaries around the aggregates. In DDD lingo, each aggregate became a bounded context on its own.

Again, initially this design looked great. It allowed us to implement each service according to its specific needs. Only one would be using event sourcing, and the rest would be state-based aggregates. Moreover, all of them could be maintained and evolved independently.

However, as the system grew, those services became more and more chatty. Eventually, almost each service required data from all the other services to complete some of its operations. The result? What was intended to be a decoupled system ended up being a distributed monolith: an absolute nightmare to maintain.

Unfortunately, there was another, much more fundamental issue we had with this architecture. To implement the marketing hub, we used the most complex patterns for modeling the business domain: domain model and event-sourced domain model. We carefully crafted those services. But it all was in vain.

The real problem

Despite the fact that the business considered the marketing hub to be a core subdomain, it had no technical complexity. Behind that complex architecture stood a very simple business logic, one so simple that it could have been implemented using plain active records.

As it turned out, the businesspeople were looking to profit by leveraging our existing relationships with other companies, and not through the use of clever algorithms.

The technical complexity ended up being much higher than the business complexity. To describe such discrepancies in complexities, we use the term *accidental complexity*, and our initial design ended up being exactly that. The system was overengineered.

Discussion

Those were the five bounded contexts I wanted to tell you about: marketing, CRM, event crunchers, bonuses, and marketing hub. Of course, such a wide business domain as Marketnovus entailed many more bounded contexts, but I wanted to share the bounded contexts we learned from the most.

Now that we've walked through the five bounded contexts, let's look at this from a different perspective. How did application or misapplication of core elements of domain-driven design influence our outcomes? Let's take a look.

Ubiquitous Language

In my experience, ubiquitous language is the "core subdomain" of domain-driven design. The ability to speak the same language with our domain experts has been indispensable to us. It turned out to be a much more effective way to share knowledge than tests or documents.

Moreover, the presence of a ubiquitous language has been a major predictor of a project's success for us:

- When we started, our implementation of the marketing system was far from perfect. However, the robust ubiquitous language compensated for the architectural shortcomings and allowed us to deliver the project's goals.

- In the CRM context, we screwed it up. Unintentionally, we had two languages describing the same business domain. We strived to have a proper design, but because of the communication issues we ended up with a huge mess.

- The event crunchers project started as a simple supporting subdomain, and we didn't invest in the ubiquitous language. We regretted this decision big time when the complexity started growing. It would have taken us much less time if we initially started with a ubiquitous language.

- In the bonuses project, the business logic became more complex by orders of magnitude, but the ubiquitous language allowed us to notice the need for a change in the implementation strategy much earlier.

Hence, ubiquitous language is not optional, regardless of whether you're working on a core, supporting, or generic subdomain.

We learned the importance of investing in the ubiquitous language as early as possible. It requires immense effort and patience to "fix" a language if it has been spoken for a while in a company (as was the case with our CRM system). We were able to fix the implementation. It wasn't easy, but eventually we did it. That's not the case, however, for the language. For years, some people were still using the conflicting terms defined in the initial implementation.

Subdomains

As you learned in Chapter 1, there are three types of subdomains— core, supporting, and generic—and it's important to identify the subdomains at play when designing the solution.

It can be challenging to identify a subdomain's type. As we discussed in Chapter 1, it's important to identify the subdomains at the granularity level that is relevant to the software system you are building. For example, our marketing hub initiative was intended to be the company's additional profit source. However, the software aspect of this functionality was a supporting subdomain, while leveraging the relationships and contracts with other companies was the actual competitive advantage, the real core subdomain.

Furthermore, as you learned in Chapter 11, it's not enough to identify a subdomain's type. You also have to be aware of the possible evolutions of the subdomain into another type. At Marketnovus, we witnessed almost all the possible combinations of changes in subdomain types:

- Both the event crunchers and bonuses started as supporting subdomains, but once we discovered ways to monetize these processes, they became our core subdomains.

- In the marketing context, we implemented our own creative catalog. There was nothing really special or complex about it. However, a few years later, an open source project came out that offered even more features than we originally had. Once we replaced our implementation with this product, the supporting subdomain became a generic one.

- In the CRM context, we had an algorithm that identified the most promising leads. We refined it over time and tried different implementations, but eventually it was replaced with a machine learning model running in a cloud vendor's managed service. Technically, a core subdomain became generic.

- As we've seen, our marketing hub system started as a core, but ended up being a supporting subdomain, since the competitive edge resided in a completely different dimension.

As you've learned throughout this book, the subdomain types affect a wide range of design decisions. Failing to properly identify a subdomain can be a costly mistake as, for example, in the case of the event crunchers and the marketing hub.

Mapping design decisions to subdomains

Here is a trick I came up with at Marketnovus to foolproof the identification of subdomains: reverse the relationship between subdomains and tactical design decisions. Choose the business logic implementation pattern. No speculation or gold plating; simply choose the pattern that fits the requirements at hand. Next, map the chosen pattern to a suitable subdomain type. Finally, verify the identified subdomain type with the business vision.

Reversing the relationship between subdomains and tactical design decisions creates an additional dialogue between you and the business. Sometimes businesspeople need us as much as we need them.

If they think something is a core business, but you can hack it in a day, then it is either a sign that you need to look for finer-grained subdomains or that questions should be raised about the viability of that business.

On the other hand, things get interesting if a subdomain is considered a supporting one by the business but can only be implemented using the advanced modeling techniques: domain model or event-sourced domain model.

First, the businesspeople may have gotten overly creative with their requirements and ended up with accidental business complexity. It happens. In such a case, the requirements can, and probably should, be simplified.

Second, it might be that the businesspeople don't yet realize they employ this subdomain to gain an additional competitive edge. This happened in the case of the bonuses project. By uncovering this mismatch, you're helping the business identify new profit sources faster.

Don't ignore pain

Most importantly, never ignore "pain" when implementing the system's business logic. It is a crucial signal to evolve and improve either the model of the business domain or the tactical design decisions. In the latter case, it means the subdomain has evolved, and it's time to go back and rethink its type and implementation strategy. If the type has changed, talk with the domain experts to understand the business context. If you need to redesign the implementation to meet new business realities, don't be afraid of this kind of change. Once the decision of how to model the business logic is made consciously and you're aware of all the possible options, it becomes much easier to react to such a change and refactor the implementation to a more elaborate pattern.

Boundaries of Bounded Contexts

At Marketnovus, we tried quite a few strategies for setting the boundaries of bounded contexts:

- Linguistic boundaries: We split our initial monolith into marketing and CRM contexts to protect their ubiquitous languages.
- Subdomain-based boundaries: Many of our subdomains were implemented in their own bounded contexts; for example, event crunchers and bonuses.
- Entity-based boundaries: As we discussed earlier, this approach had limited success in the marketing hub project, but it worked in others.
- Suicidal boundaries: As you may remember, in the initial implementation of the CRM we dissected an aggregate into two different bounded contexts. Never try this at home, okay?

Which of these strategies is the recommended one? None of them fits in all cases. In our experience, it was much safer to extract a service out of a bigger one than to start with services that are too small. Hence, we preferred to start with bigger boundaries and decompose them later, as more knowledge was acquired about the business. How wide are those initial boundaries? As we discussed in Chapter 11, it all goes back to the business domain: the less you know about the business domain, the wider the initial boundaries.

This heuristic served us well. For example, in the cases of the marketing and CRM bounded contexts, each encompassed multiple subdomains. As time passed, we gradually decomposed the initially wide boundaries into microservices. As we defined in Chapter 14, throughout the evolution of the bounded contexts, we stayed in the range of the safe boundaries. We were able to avoid going past the safe boundaries by doing the refactoring only after gaining enough knowledge of the business domain.

Conclusion

In the stories of Marketnovus's bounded contexts I showed how our understanding of domain-driven design evolved through time (refer to Figure A-6 for a refresher):

- We always started by building a ubiquitous language with the domain experts to learn as much as possible about the business domain.
- In the case of conflicting models, we decomposed the solution into bounded contexts, following the linguistic boundaries of the ubiquitous language.
- We identified the subdomains' boundaries and their types in each bounded context.
- For each subdomain we chose an implementation strategy by using tactical design heuristics.
- We verified the initial subdomain types with those resulting from the tactical design. In cases of mismatching types, we discussed them with the business. Sometimes this dialogue led to changes in the requirements, because we were able to provide a new perspective on the project to the product owners.
- As more domain knowledge was acquired, and if it was needed, we decomposed the bounded contexts further into contexts with narrower boundaries.

If we compare this vision of domain-driven design with the one we started with, I'd say the main difference is that we went from "aggregates everywhere" to "ubiquitous language everywhere."

In parting, since I've told you the story of how Marketnovus started, I want to share how it ended.

The company became profitable very quickly, and eventually it was acquired by its biggest client. Of course, I cannot attribute its success solely to domain-driven design. However, during all those years, we were constantly in "start-up mode."

What we term "start-up mode" in Israel is called "chaos" in the rest of the world: constantly changing business requirements and priorities, aggressive time frames, and a tiny R&D team. DDD allowed us to tackle all of these complexities and keep delivering working software. Hence, when I look back, the bet we placed on domain-driven design paid off in full.

Answers to Exercise Questions

Chapter 1

1. D: B and C. Only core subdomains provide competitive advantages that differentiate the company from other players in its industry.

2. B: Generic. Generic subdomains are complex but do not entail any competitive advantage. Hence, it's preferable to use an existing, battle-proven solution.

3. A: Core. Core subdomains are expected to be the most volatile since these are areas in which the company aims to provide new solutions and it often requires quite a few interactions to find the most optimized solution.

4. WolfDesk's business domain is Help Desk management systems.

5. We can identify the following core subdomains that allow WolfDesk to differentiate itself from its competitors and support its business model:

   a. Ticket lifecycle management algorithm that is intended to close tickets and thus encourage users to open new ones

   b. Fraud detection system to prevent abuse of its business model

   c. Support autopilot that both eases the tenants' support agents' work and further reduces the tickets' lifespan

6. The following supporting subdomains can be identified in the description of the company:

   a. Management of a tenant's ticket categories

   b. Management of a tenant's products, regarding which the customers can open support tickets

   c. Entry of a tenant's support agents' work schedules

7. The following generic subdomains can be identified in the description of the company:

    a. "Industry standard" ways of authenticating and authorizing users

    b. Using external providers for authentication and authorization (SSO)

    c. The serverless compute infrastructure the company leverages to ensure elastic scalability and minimize the compute costs of onboarding new tenants

Chapter 2

1. D: All of the project's stakeholders should contribute their knowledge and understanding of the business domain.

2. D: A ubiquitous language should be used in all project-related communication. The software's source code should also "speak" its ubiquitous language.

3. WolfDesk's customers are *tenants*. To start using the system, tenants go through a quick *onboarding* process. The company's charging model is based on the number of *tickets* that were opened during a *charging period*. The *ticket lifecycle* management algorithm ensures that *inactive tickets* are automatically closed. WolfDesk's *fraud detection* algorithm prevents tenants from abusing its business model. The *support autopilot* functionality tries to find solutions for new tickets automatically. A *ticket* belongs to a support *category* and is associated with a *product* for which the tenant provides support. A *support agent* can only process tickets during their *work time, which* is defined by their *shift schedules*.

Chapter 3

1. B: Bounded contexts are designed, while subdomains are discovered.

2. D: All of the above. A bounded context is a boundary of a model, and a model is only applicable in its bounded context. Bounded contexts are implemented in independent projects/solutions, thus allowing each bounded context to have its own development lifecycle. Finally, a bounded context should be implemented by a single development team, and therefore, it is also an ownership boundary.

3. D: It depends. There is no perfect size of a bounded context for all projects and cases. Different factors, such as models, organizational constraints, and nonfunctional requirements, affect the optimum scope of a bounded context.

4. D: B and C are correct. A bounded context should be owned by one team only. At the same time, the same team can own multiple bounded contexts.

5. It's safe to assume that the operation model, implementing the *tickets'* lifecycle, will be different from the one used for fraud detection and the support autopilot feature. Fraud detection algorithms usually require more analytics-oriented

modeling, whereas, the autopilot feature is likely to use a model optimized for use with machine learning algorithms.

Chapter 4

1. D: Separate ways. The pattern entails duplicate implementation of a functionality in multiple bounded contexts. Duplicating complex, volatile, and business-critical business logic should be avoided at all costs.

2. A: Core subdomain. A core subdomain is most likely to leverage an anticorruption layer to protect itself from ineffective models exposed by upstream services, or to contain frequent changes in the upstream's public interfaces.

3. A: Core subdomain. A core subdomain is most likely to implement the open-host service. Decoupling its implementation model from the public interface (published language) makes it more convenient to evolve the core subdomain's model without affecting its downstream consumers.

4. B: Shared kernel. The shared kernel pattern is an exception to the bounded contexts' single team ownership rule. It defines a small portion of the model that is shared and can be evolved simultaneously by multiple bounded contexts. The shared part of the model should be always kept as small as possible.

Chapter 5

1. C: Neither of these patterns can be used to implement a core subdomain. Both transaction script and active record lend themselves to the case of simple business logic, whereas core subdomains involve more complex business logic.

2. D: All of the above issues are possible:

    a. If the execution fails after line 6, the caller retries the operation, and the same agent is chosen by the FindLeastBusyAgent method, the agent's ActiveTickets counter will be increased by more than 1.

    b. If the execution fails after line 6 but the caller *doesn't* retry the operation, the counter will be increased, while the ticket itself won't be created.

    c. If the execution fails after line 12, the ticket is created and assigned, but the notification on line 14 won't be sent.

3. If the execution fails after line 12 and the caller retries the operation and it succeeds, the same ticket will be persisted and assigned twice.

4. All of WolfDesk's supporting subdomains are good candidates for implementation as transaction script or active record as their business logic is relatively straightforward:

a. Management of a tenant's ticket categories

b. Management of a tenant's products, regarding which the customers can open support tickets

c. Entry of a tenant's support agents' work schedules

Chapter 6

1. C: Value objects are immutable. (Also, they can contain both data and behavior.)
2. B: Aggregates should be designed to be as small as possible, as long as the business domain's data consistency requirements are intact.
3. B: To ensure correct transactional boundaries.
4. D: A and C.
5. B: An aggregate encapsulates all of its business logic, but business logic manipulating an active record can be located outside of its boundary.

Chapter 7

1. A: Domain events use value objects to describe what has happened in the business domain.
2. C: Multiple state representations can be projected and you can always add additional projections in the future.
3. D: Both B and C are correct.
4. The ticket lifecycle algorithm is a good candidate to be implemented as an event-sourced domain model. Generating domain events for all state transitions can make it more convenient to project additional state representations optimized for the fraud detection algorithm and the support autopilot functionality.

Chapter 8

1. D: A and C.
2. D: B and C.
3. C: Infrastructure layer.
4. E: A and D.
5. Working with multiple models projected by the CQRS pattern doesn't contradict the bounded context's requirement of being a model boundary, since only one of the models is defined as the source of truth and is used for making changes in the aggregates' states.

Chapter 9

1. D: B and C.

2. B: Reliably publish messages.

3. The outbox pattern can be used to implement asynchronous execution of external components. For example, it can be used for sending email messages.

4. E: A and D are correct.

Chapter 10

1. Event-sourced domain model, CQRS architecture, and testing strategy that focuses on unit tests.

2. The shifts can be modeled as active records, working in the layered architectural pattern. The testing strategy should primarily focus on integration tests.

3. The business logic can be implemented as a transaction script, organized in a layered architecture. From a testing perspective, it's worth concentrating on end-to-end tests, verifying the full integration flow.

Chapter 11

1. A: Partnership to customer–supplier (conformist, anticorruption layer, or open-host service). As an organization grows, it can become more challenging for teams to integrate their bounded contexts in an ad hoc fashion. As a result, they switch to a more formal integration pattern.

2. D: A and B. A is correct because bounded contexts go separate ways when the cost of duplication is lower than the overhead of collaboration. C is incorrect because it's a terrible idea to duplicate implementation of a core subdomain. Consequently, B is correct because the separate ways pattern can be used for supporting and generic subdomains.

3. D: B and C.

4. F: A and C.

5. Upon reaching a certain level of growth, WolfDesk could follow the footsteps of Amazon and implement its own compute platform to further optimize its ability to scale elastically and optimize its infrastructure costs.

Chapter 12

1. D: All stakeholders having knowledge of the business domain that you want to explore.

2. F: All the answers are sound reasons to facilitate an EventStorming session.

3. E: All the answers are possible outcomes of an EventStorming session. The outcome you should expect to get depends on your initial purpose for facilitating the session.

Chapter 13

1. B: Analyze the organization's business domain and its strategy.

2. D: A and B.

3. C: A and B.

4. An aggregate with a bounded context-wide boundary may make all of the bounded context's data a part of one big transaction. It's also likely that performance issues with this approach will be evident from the get go. Once that happens, the transactional boundary will be removed. As a result, it will no longer be possible to assume that the information residing in the aggregate is strongly consistent.

Chapter 14

1. A: All microservices are bounded contexts. (But not all bounded contexts are microservices.)

2. D: The knowledge of the business domain and its intricacies exposed across the service's boundary and reflected by its public interface.

3. C: Boundaries between bounded contexts (widest) and microservices (narrowest).

4. D: The decision depends on the business domain.

Chapter 15

1. D: A and B are correct.

2. B: Event-carried state transfer.

3. A: Open-host service.

4. B: S2 should publish public event notifications, which will signal S1 to issue a synchronous request to get the most up-to-date information.

Chapter 16

1. D: A and C are correct.

2. B: Open-host service. One of the published languages exposed by the open-host service can be OLAP data optimized for analytical processing.

3. C: CQRS. The CQRS pattern can be leveraged to generate projections of the OLAP model out of the transactional model.

4. A: Bounded contexts.

References

Brandolini, A. (n.d.). *Introducing EventStorming*. Leanpub.

Brooks, F. P., Jr. (1974). *The Mythical Man Month and Other Essays on Software Engineering*. Reading, MA: Addison-Wesley.

Eisenhardt, K., & Sull, D. (2016). *Simple Rules: How to Succeed in a Complex World*. London: John Murray.

Esposito, D., & Saltarello, A. (2008). *Architecting Applications for the Enterprise: Microsoft® .NET*. Redmond, WA: Microsoft Press.

Evans, E. (2003). *Domain-Driven Design: Tackling Complexity in the Heart of Software*. Boston: Addison-Wesley.

Feathers, M. C. (2005). *Working Effectively with Legacy Code*. Upper Saddle River, NJ: Prentice Hall PTR.

Fowler, M. (2002). *Patterns of Enterprise Application Architecture*. Boston: Addison-Wesley.

Fowler, M. (2019). *Refactoring: Improving the Design of Existing Code* (2nd ed.). Boston: Addison-Wesley.

Fowler, M. (n.d.). *What do you mean by "Event-Driven"?* Retrieved August 12, 2021, from *https://martinfowler.com/articles/201701-event-driven.html*.

Gamma, E., Helm, R., & Johnson, R. (1994). *Design Patterns: Elements of Reusable Object-Oriented Software*. Reading, MA: Addison-Wesley.

Gigerenzer, G., Todd, P. M., & ABC Research Group (Research Group, Max Planck Institute, Germany). (1999). *Simple Heuristics That Make Us Smart*. New York: Oxford University Press.

Goldratt, E. M. (2005). *Beyond the Goal: Theory of Constraints*. New York: Gildan Audio.

Goldratt, E. M., & Goldratt-Ashlag, E. (2018). *The Choice*. Great Barrington, MA: North River Press Publishing Corporation.

Goldratt-Ashlag, E. (2010). "The Layers of Resistance—The Buy-In Process According to TOC." (Chapter 20 of the *Theory of Constraints* handbook.) Bedford, England: Goldratt Marketing Group.

Garcia-Molina, H., & Salem K. (1987). *Sagas*. Princeton, NJ: Department of Computer Science, Princeton University.

Helland, P. (2020). Data on the outside versus data on the inside. *Communications of the ACM, 63*(11), 111–118.

Hohpe, G., & Woolf, B. (2003). *Enterprise Integration Patterns: Designing, Building, and Deploying Messaging Solutions*. Boston: Addison-Wesley.

Khononov, V. (2022). *Balancing Coupling in Software Design*. Boston: Addison-Wesley.

Khononov, V. (2019). *What Is Domain-Driven Design?* Boston: O'Reilly.

Martraire, C. (2019). *Living Documentation: Continuous Knowledge Sharing by Design*. Boston: Addison-Wesley.

Millett, S., & Tune, N. (2015). *Patterns, Principles, and Practices of Domain-Driven Design* (1st ed.). Nashville: John Wiley & Sons.

Myers, G. J. (1978). *Composite/Structured Design*. New York: Van Nostrand Reinhold.

Ousterhout, J. (2018). *A Philosophy of Software Design*. Palo Alto, CA: Yaknyam Press.

Richardson, C. (2019). *Microservice Patterns: With Examples in Java*. New York: Manning Publications.

Vernon, V. (2013). *Implementing Domain-Driven Design*. Boston: Addison-Wesley.

Vernon, V. (2016). *Domain-Driven Design Distilled*. Boston: Addison-Wesley.

West, G. (2018). *Scale: The Universal Laws of Life and Death in Organisms, Cities and Companies*. Oxford, England: Weidenfeld & Nicolson.

Wright, D., & Meadows, D. H. (2009). *Thinking in Systems: A Primer*. London: Earthscan.

Index

About the Author

Vlad (Vladik) Khononov is a software engineer with over 20 years of industry experience, during which he has worked for companies large and small in roles ranging from webmaster to chief architect. Vlad maintains an active media career as a public speaker, blogger, and author. He travels the world consulting and talking about domain-driven design, microservices, and software architecture in general. Vlad helps companies make sense of their business domains, untangle legacy systems, and tackle complex architectural challenges. He lives in Northern Israel with his wife and an almost-reasonable number of cats.

Colophon

The animal on the cover of *Learning Domain-Driven Design* is a mona monkey (*Cercopithecus mona*), which can be found in the tropical forests of West Africa and the Caribbean islands, where they were introduced during the slave trade. They leap from trees in the mid- to top canopy, using their long tails for balance.

Mona monkeys have brownish fur that's darker around their faces, limbs, and on their tails. Their undersides, including the insides of their legs, are white. Females average 16 inches in length while males average 20 inches—and the tails add another 26 inches or more. Long tufts of fur on the cheeks of Mona monkeys can tint yellow or gray, and their noses have some light pink coloring. The cheeks serve as pouches for food as they forage, holding as much as their stomachs can.

Mona monkeys eat fruit, seeds, insects, and leaves and live for about 30 years in the wild. Each day, they forage multiple times in large groups. Packs larger than 40 have been documented; typically a male dominates the group, mating with multiple females and fighting off competing males. These groups can get very noisy.

Mona monkeys have a conservation status of Near Threatened due to human activities. Many of the animals on O'Reilly covers are endangered; all of them are important to the world.

The cover illustration is by Karen Montgomery, based on a black and white engraving from *Lydekker's Royal Natural History*. The cover fonts are Gilroy Semibold and Guardian Sans. The text font is Adobe Minion Pro; the heading font is Adobe Myriad Condensed; and the code font is Dalton Maag's Ubuntu Mono.

O'REILLY®

There's much more where this came from.

Experience books, videos, live online training courses, and more from O'Reilly and our 200+ partners—all in one place.

Learn more at oreilly.com/online-learning

CPSIA information can be obtained
at www.ICGtesting.com
Printed in the USA
JSHW041054270122
22303JS00003B/67